To Ali,

Blessings + Love,

Cathy Crews

Mom...
It's Cancer

Breast Cancer:
One Family,
Two Women,
Two Battles,
Too Unimaginable!

KATHY CREWS

CROSSBOOKS
PUBLISHING

CrossBooks™
A Division of LifeWay
1663 Liberty Drive
Bloomington, IN 47403
www.crossbooks.com
Phone: 1-866-879-0502

Except where noted as being from a specific version, all Scripture throughout the manuscript is conceptually accurate but paraphrased and quoted from memory by the author.

First published by CrossBooks 11/23/2010

ISBN: 978-1-6150-7600-0 (sc)
ISBN: 978-1-6150-7601-7 (dj)

Library of Congress Control Number: 2010939416

Printed in the United States of America

This book is printed on acid-free paper.

Acknowledgments

With gratitude and thanks to all who contributed their medical knowledge whenever I had questions as I wrote Mom...It's Cancer:
Dr. Nancy Lin
Dr. Stephanie Caterson
Deirdre Fuller-Wiesner, APRN
Abbie Gagnon, PA-C and Assistant to Dr. Stephanie Caterson
Linda Cutone, Administrative Assistant to Dr. Mehra Golshan

My legal advisor: David Wiesner, Esq.

Endless praise and thanks to the amazing and wonderful ladies who labored endless hours READING and critiquing my entire manuscript! They condensed and chopped the text that was on its way to matching the page count of War and Peace, and tried to keep me focused on what was and was not important in this story.
Vicki Therrien
Marion Zanoni
And my #1 critic and best friend who always disagreed with me and she was ALWAYS right: Gayle Troy

Lisa Keene Ridley! Who could have dreamed what was ahead. When you and Tracy were just kids, the two of you were always together playing with your Barbie dolls or writing scripts for Charlie's Angels. Who could have imagined that one day "Tracy's Mom" would write a book and you would have a degree in writing from Sarah Lawrence and become my Editor!

To my mom, who sacrificed spending Sunday afternoons with me so that I could continue working to complete my manuscript for her ninetieth birthday!

To Tracy, who helped with the accuracy of the story and added opinions, insight, and encouragement. You are and always will be a gift from the Lord.

And finally to the one who has made the largest contribution to this book, my husband, Grady. Thank you for your sacrifice. You have tolerated unfinished housework for an additional year beyond cancer and while I have been hidden away in a back bedroom with my computer. You have listened to my endless monologue over sentence structure, editing, and publishing. And again, you have been my support, encourager, and critic. Thank you for loving me through all these years. I love you!

Table of Contents

1. "Mom…It's Cancer" 1
2. The Move from Spain 5
3. Living in "Whoville" 12
4. The Lumpectomy 20
5. "Day Surgery?" 27
6. Cancer 101 37
7. What Are the Odds? 43
8. "Clipped" 48
9. God's Favor 57
10. Thanksgiving 65
11. Radiation 72
12. Back to Normal 84
13. Déjà Vu 90
14. Tests, Appointments, and More Tests 101
15. Deciding on the Protocol 114
16. Setting the Course 121
17. Settling into the Protocol 131

18. "The Moo-o-vie Star…" 142

19. Looking for Answers 152

20. Like Running a Marathon 162

21. The Countdown to Surgery 174

22. I Found *That* "Pony"! 181

23. Giving Thanks in ALL Things 190

24. Count It All Joy 199

25. The Stories 209

26. Home Sweet Home! (Well, for a Little While) 221

27. Our Plans…God's Plans. 230

28. The Endless Infection. 236

29. "Hair" I Am! 251

30. I'm His Child (and Acting the Part) 256

31. I'll Do It! 267

32. Lost in Space 276

33. DIEP Flap: Not for Wimps or Sissies 284

34. "Lord? Say It Ain't So!" 293

35. Living the Lessons 299

36. So…What Is Faith? 307

Chapter 1

"Mom…It's Cancer"

There are moments in time that will forever remain in our memories. No passing of years can erase or fade *that* moment. They remain engraved in our minds as we recall all that was connected to that event and what it represented….

Friday, June 24, 2005, was a beautiful, warm summer's day. Grady and I were out running errands when Tracy made a call to her father's cell phone. In that moment all of time stood still. We were in the car when I answered the phone and heard our daughter's voice. It was quivering as she said, "Mom…it's cancer."

I felt numb and limp. I couldn't be hearing this. *This can't be real. This can't be happening! Thirty-four-year-old, healthy, athletic women don't get breast cancer. Do they?? Oh, dear God…this cannot be!*

Her words were like the teeth of an unseen beast viciously clamping into the back of my neck, and I was suddenly paralyzed with fear. *Lord God…how can this be!*

I tried my best to sound reassuring and composed. "Tracy, are they sure?"

"Mom, the doctor took the biopsy to the lab himself and looked at it under the microscope. It's *cancer*…."

1

I knew Tracy was trembling and close to tears.

"Trace…how can we help? Do you want us there?"

"No, Mom. I need to return to the hospital. Mammograms and other tests have been ordered. Mom, the doctor wants me to have surgery on Monday morning. I need you and Dad here on Monday…. I just can't believe this is happening."

"Well, look, we're only an hour away if you change your mind and you do need us for anything. We're here. I love you, Trace. I'm praying for you."

Tracy's voice was shivering with fear and she was now starting to cry. "I love you too, Mom. Thanks…. Bye."

The cell phone had rung at 1:22 that afternoon. Time came to a screeching halt. In that moment, the course of our lives instantly changed and in ways we could never have imagined, and with more twists and turns and for far longer than we ever could have thought possible.

After the initial shock of Tracy's phone call, I didn't know whether to be mad at ancestors in our family tree who might have had cancer, at the environment, or with myself. Was it because of something I had eaten while I was pregnant? I wanted someone or something to blame; I just didn't know who or what. Poor Trace! *God, how could you let this happen? THIS is our only child! Cancer? Oh, Lord Jesus…NO! NOT Cancer! Not our Tracy!*

Through the hours of that afternoon, we seemed caught in the moment of Tracy's phone call, yet moving forward at the speed of light. I remained *stuck*…trying to both absorb and reject Tracy's diagnosis at the same time.

Tracy and her husband, Antonio, were at a small hospital sixty miles away in Newburyport, Massachusetts. A baseline mammogram and plans for a lumpectomy were being arranged. All I could think to do was to cry out to God.

With each phone call from Tracy, I sent out another email updating a small group of friends with the information that was trickling in and begging them to pray. By 4:30 that afternoon, Tracy was scheduled for surgery on Monday morning.

In times of life-changing trials, I believe we learn more about ourselves, what we are made of, and who our true friends are than at any other time in our lives. Six hours after we received Tracy's call, our friends David and Nancy were at our door. The Scripture says we are to "weep with those who weep; and rejoice with those who rejoice." David and Nance came to "weep" with us.

The four of us alternated between sitting in stunned silence and talking about how impossible it was that Tracy had been diagnosed with breast cancer. How could this be possible? Tracy was a runner. She was so conscientious about a balanced and healthy diet; cancer was an impossible diagnosis! The four of us spent the next few hours trying to make sense out of this unbelievable nightmare.

It's a funny thing when a "family" is diagnosed with cancer. Often, people just don't know what to do. In part, it's a reason for me to write our story.

Friends proved themselves in one way or the other; either they came to love and support us or they headed for the hills, as if cancer was something that they might catch if they came close. And, you know, this was true of family members as well as friends from church. "Cancer." It's a scary word: a disease that very often strikes even the healthiest—and without warning or regard for age.

I remember when I was younger; I mistakenly thought cancer only happened to old people. Misconception number one. I'm far from an expert on the subject, but one of the first things that I learned about cancer when Tracy was diagnosed was this: I didn't know a thing! The upside of that discovery was that I was a blank page and it was time to start learning.

The quick reality was our daughter was truly in a battle for her life. I wanted to know how to support her through this fight, and I knew I needed all of the help I could get. The support and love of friends while going through a crisis is priceless! Even if it's just to lend a shoulder to cry on. The friends who offered support and loved me and Grady through our pain gave us strength, so we could be the Mom and Dad that Tracy needed during this crisis.

Tracy's surgery was scheduled for 10:00 Monday morning. Through the weekend Grady and I began to question everything—the diagnosis, second opinions, better doctors, bigger hospital…just everything. Tracy seemed confident she had a doctor who was well qualified and one she trusted. I must admit, there did seem to be a great patient/doctor relationship, instantaneously. Trace was a grown, married woman; I had to trust her instincts. It was my job as her mother to support her. But I felt completely lost by how little I knew about breast cancer and what we could do to help.

We agonized through the weekend. When Monday morning arrived, as Grady and I drove to the hospital, the shock of believing our "child" had cancer had not diminished. We still felt caught in our disbelief, yet at the same time very thankful that Tracy was living in Newburyport, when just six months earlier she and Antonio were living in Madrid, Spain.

Traveling to the hospital to be with Tracy for her surgery, I began to retrace the events that pushed her to move to Spain and the sudden changes that had brought her back home to the States with her native-born Spanish husband—a second marriage for both of them.

How would I have ever coped with this if she and Antonio were living in Madrid?

Lord Jesus, thank you. You brought her home just in time. Oh, thank You, Lord....

As Grady drove, we were still in shock and we traveled in silence. The series of events of the past several years and the details that had brought us to this day turned over and over in my mind, as I reflected back and searched for clues and questioned "why?"

Chapter 2

The Move from Spain

Tracy had married her college sweetheart as soon as they graduated from college in 1992, but it was less than a match made in heaven. The two struggled between working and graduate school. Tracy was teaching Spanish. As her marriage unraveled during the summer of 1998, Tracy moved to Spain to complete her master's degree in Spanish literature. With her marriage in near ruin, she also needed time to consider how to rebuild the relationship. Her summers had been spent at Middlebury College in Vermont, taking courses for her degree. To complete her studies, she moved to Madrid, Spain, and became a full-time student as the gap in her marriage grew wider.

After living in Europe for five months, Tracy came home for Christmas. She contacted her husband, unsure if there was any hope for their marriage. There was not. The marriage ended rudely and abruptly as boxes of Tracy's personal belongings were dumped in our front hallway on the eve of January 1, 1999.

Earlier that evening, Tracy had requested some time and privacy to talk with her husband when he arrived. Grady and I retired to our bedroom and tried to concentrate on some mindless TV program. Minutes after the boxes were dropped inside our front door, we heard Tracy's footsteps racing up the stairs, followed by the slam of her bedroom door and then sounds more wrenching than I had ever heard from any human being. She could not control her feelings of failure and devastation as the dam of emotion burst. Floods of tears and pain flowed out of her like a river that had been held beyond its limit from too many heavy storms. It was the end to a very strained relationship, and every ounce of grief-filled emotion poured from her.

Even with our bedroom doors closed, we heard how deeply she was wounded. Grady and I just looked at each other, and without a word he rose to his feet. He gently rapped on her door and went to her bedside where she was curled in a ball, sobbing. Grady sat on the edge of her bed and pulled her close, holding and comforting her in his arms. She was still and always will be his "little girl."

The following week, and with no time to recover emotionally, Tracy returned to Madrid to finish her last semester of studies and complete her master's degree. In New Hampshire, uncontested divorces can be finalized very rapidly. By late April 1999, Tracy's marriage was over, allowing the former couple to go forward but in different directions. She was still hurting as she tried to put the pieces of her life back together, when she began to date a charming, energetic, and funny Spaniard.

And so it was that Antonio came into her life as he took center stage and brought happiness to her and made her smile again. Although we were genuinely happy that Tracy had found someone who treated her like a treasure, Grady and I wished she hadn't found that special someone so far from home. Tracy and "Tonx" married on February 3, 2001, and started their life as a married couple in Madrid, Spain.

In August 2004, Tracy phoned with a special prayer request. Trace had celebrated her 34th birthday a month earlier, and more than anything in the world, she wanted the gift of becoming a mother. For many months she and Tonx (pronounced "Ton-ch") had wanted to become pregnant. Yet, they faced repeated disappointment. No baby.

"Mom, I read an article recently in a magazine. It was a study about women who had difficulty becoming pregnant. Half of the women in the study had people who were praying that they would conceive. The women in the study didn't know if they were among those being prayed for or not. The study proved that more of the women who *were* prayed for became pregnant than those who were not. Will you pray for me to conceive?"

When Tracy asked this of me, I had to say one of the hardest things I have ever had to say to anyone (let alone my own daughter). As she was making this request, I had a sense what she asking was not in God's timing. "Tracy...I can't do that right now. I can't tell you why, but I know that the timing is not right."

I wasn't prepared for her response, her hurt, and her anger with me. For the next several months, time after time she made comments, making sure I knew of her displeasure toward me.

And then the reasons "why" began to take shape.

Within a few months after Tracy's request, Antonio took a good, hard look at the financial condition of the small business that he owned and operated. "Disaster" was a kind word for the condition of his business.

Tracy's teaching degree in Spanish left her freelancing. After all, she was living in a land where everyone already spoke the language. She did private tutoring, teaching English to Spanish children, mostly. She also taught English classes to business people; she even translated a book for a Spanish author. But her income was not reliable.

In November, Tracy called unexpectedly. "Mom, Antonio and I are moving back to the States. I'm looking for a teaching position in southern New Hampshire or close to Boston. The financial pressure we are under is more than we can handle. We need to be someplace where at least one of us can be sure of steady income. I know I can do that as a teacher in the States. Mom, we have to move back home."

I was shocked but elated! In the weeks that followed, we busily worked toward the transatlantic move. Antonio had to close his business, while Tracy sent resumes to school districts via the Internet.

I was Tracy's local contact in the U.S. and fielded the calls and arranged workable times for interviews by phone. With careful planning, Tracy coordinated calls to fit the work day in the U.S. with the six-hour time difference in Spain. She hoped to find a teaching job that started at the beginning of the second semester in the new year.

One of our biggest concerns was for the sale of their apartment in Madrid. They needed a cash buyer to show up on their doorstep before January 1, 2005. It seemed like an impossible task for everything to work in such perfect harmony. But with God all things are possible!

Several schools responded to Tracy's very impressive resume, and she was hired by the Newburyport school district just before Thanksgiving. It was a short-term position to replace a Spanish teacher who was leaving in January for maternity leave.

From Spain, Tracy began scouting for apartments on the Internet in Newburyport and within a few days compiled a list of twenty potential places to live. She sent me the list with contact phone numbers, and after talking with the different landlords, I whittled the list to seven good possibilities. I set up appointments based on Tracy's criteria and with the *hope* that I would find the ideal apartment for her and Antonio.

The weeks flew by and now it was December, and the task Kris Kringle had in finding that dream house for Susan in *Miracle on 34*th *Street* was no less daunting than what Tracy put before me with her dream list. The apartment had to be close enough to the school so that Tracy could walk to work. She wanted a second floor unit. It needed to have large, bright windows, a guest room, a place where litter boxes for the cats could be hidden discreetly, and laundry facilities in the building, and it needed to be at least partially furnished. (Good grief!)

Judy, my friend from Maine, was visiting while I was going through this process for Tracy. I had pages of notes about the apartments sitting on the corner of the dining room table. It's a big responsibility finding the right home for someone else. I must have looked concerned and preoccupied with the task.

Without prompting, Judy walked over to the pile of papers and placed her hand on them. With authority and boldness she looked straight at me and said, "In the Name of Jesus, you will know without question which of these apartments will please Tracy and Antonio beyond measure by the Lord's guidance over you!"

I began to laugh. I know God will guide us in (or through) anything we ask, but I really hadn't thought about this! I was caught up with worry about Tracy and Antonio having the perfect apartment. I was acting like it was my job to make that happen. I forgot that it really was the Lord's job to guide me. I overlooked the most basic step: having the faith to trust in the Lord in all things.

Early one Saturday morning, Grady and I pointed the car in the direction of Newburyport with our list of properties in hand. By noon, we were ready for a break. My faith was wavering, and we were feeling a little discouraged. I wondered if we needed to come up with a "plan B" if the Lord somehow had missed Judy's prayer and Tracy's apartment was not among those we had yet to visit.

By 4:30 the winter sky was beginning to grow dim as we scrambled to find the last location on our list. It was a grand old apartment building that was impeccably maintained. When we walked through the doors, we knew instantly it was the perfect home for Tracy and Antonio! Everything on their wish list, and more, was there. The appliances were brand new and even included a washer and dryer in the large, open kitchen. The rooms had high posted ceilings; it was early 1900s classy and had been tastefully modernized.

The rooms were spic-and-span and freshly painted. Even the hardwood floors had just been revarnished. Windows in the front living room were practically floor to ceiling and faced east toward the morning sun. As I stood admiring the apartment, I felt joy and peace. The Lord had done just as Judy had asked of Him! *Tracy and Antonio will love this, Lord. Thank you!*

Fair Street in Newburyport was about to became Tracy's new home. It was perfect!

Over the next few weeks, plans that seemed impossible and sketchy (at best) began to take shape. Tracy's first day at her new teaching job would be Monday, January 10, 2005; she and Antonio were arriving in Boston on Friday, January 7.

Within days of posting a "For Sale" sign in the window of their recently renovated flat in Madrid, two different sets of cash buyers began bidding for the home. The final sale offer was accepted, and in less than two weeks, Tracy and Antonio began packing their belongings to store at Antonio's parents' summer home in La Navata, for retrieval at a later date. A few pictures and clothing were the only things they planned to move. And, oh yes...one more thing...their two cats, with their own story of how, when they were four-week-old feral kittens, Tracy rescued them from a storm drain one rainy night.

Tracy knew she would be landing with both feet running when she arrived in the States. To avoid the hassle of finding new health care professionals in the states (for at least six months), she saw her dentist and gynecologist in Madrid one last time before moving. All tests and exams showed Tracy was in perfect health.

As Tracy and Antonio scrambled to tie up the loose ends in Madrid, the realization of all they would need to set up housekeeping in their new apartment hit home, literally. True, they had new appliances in the apartment, but they had absolutely nothing else. So I did what most moms do. I began scouring department store clearance shelves and the outlet mall. Everything I had that I didn't use or could spare, I set aside for Tracy.

The day after Christmas, we moved all that I had collected into the apartment. Our greatest moment, however, revolved around our prize purchase: the 1950s dinette set. This treasure just made you smile. The chrome was in beautiful condition, and the table top and chairs were red and white. The nostalgic dinette looked incredible as the sun shone through the large windows, bathing the wood floors with warmth, giving the kitchen a homey, "old timey" feel. The 50s dinette, by far, was our proudest moment for establishing a theme and style to the new home.

Long before Tracy had announced their plans to move back home, Grady and I had purchased airline tickets to spend New Year's with Trace, Tonx, and his family in Spain. With moving plans on the horizon, we were a little up in the air about the wisest course to take. There was still a long "to do list" on their end. And I had my own set of loose ends to sort through, having just discovered I had frozen shoulder syndrome and I needed surgery on my right shoulder in early January.

We agreed to shorten our time in Spain, and calculated how to take advantage of our airline status and help in the move. We were allowed three checked bags apiece that were each seventy-five pounds. Grady and I put the few things we needed for our stay in our carry-on bags and checked suitcases nested inside each other, bound for Madrid. Once we arrived, we packed the bags with Tracy's and Antonio's clothes for our return trip.

Every suitcase was maxed out for the return flight—every square inch, every ounce of poundage was used. Our connections in Philadelphia were short, and we recruited the assistance of a porter who, with great expertise, loaded a Smart Cart and helped us recheck our baggage upon clearing customs. Carefully, we watched how he stacked the six suitcases as a future reference for our arrival in Manchester, New Hampshire, when we would need to copy his technique.

It was after midnight when our flight landed in New Hampshire. We were worn ragged after the three-day whirlwind trip to Spain. Gathering up the six suitcases and our carry-on bags, we began stacking the luggage like the porter in Philly. I don't think we copied exactly right. Our tower of suitcases was taller than the porter's constructed masterpiece on the Smart Cart in Philly.

Grady braved the cold to retrieve the car as I stayed with the bags, assuring him that I could manage this ridiculous pile of luggage on my own, despite the limited function of my injured right arm. At last, I saw the headlights of our SUV. As I pushed the Smart Cart as fast as I dared in the direction of the smaller opening of the handicapped entrance, I couldn't see a thing. The rolling Mt. Everest before me totally blocked my view. For a blind shot, my aim was perfect, but I hadn't built up enough speed and the load came to a sudden and full stop against the slightly raised threshold, half in and half out the opening. With virtually no wiggle room to jockey or maneuver the more than four hundred pounds of cargo, I was stuck in the open door! Grady watched helplessly as I pushed then pulled, debating his options and which was worse: letting me fight alone against the mountain of luggage or having our car towed by security if he came to assist and left the vehicle unattended. Suddenly, another traveler came to my rescue as I struggled unsuccessfully, and they moved the "mountain" I could not move alone.

Friday, January 7, 2005, arrived and it was bone-chilling cold. Tracy and Antonio's flight landed in Boston amidst the evening rush hour traffic. While Grady collected the weary travelers at the airport, I shopped for the fresh foods and perishables needed to stock their refrigerator and then drove to their apartment.

When she walked through the door, poor Trace looked terrible! She hadn't finished packing until the wee hours of the morning and had not slept. Antonio had been removing the last of the supplies from his rented office through most of the night. It was nearly dawn by the time they had both finished. To make matters worse, Tracy had caught a cold. The pot of fresh homemade chicken soup simmering on the stove and the crisp, clean sheets on the bed that waited for them was the best "welcome home" they could have had.

We gave them a kiss "hello" and a hug "good-bye" and left them to their soup and a much needed night's rest.

Chapter 3

Living in "Whoville"

In the numerous trips to Newburyport prior to Tracy and Antonio's arrival, Grady and I fell in love with the town. Newburyport is a short distance from the New Hampshire border and where the Merrimack River flows into the Atlantic Ocean. It's an old sea captain's town with lovely homes that were built for the ages by the rugged New Englanders who owned them a lifetime ago.

During the late 1700s and early 1800s the homes were like jewels that glistened and revealed the prosperity of their owners, who earned a living at sea. Most of those homes have been restored to their former glory, and the people of Newburyport take great pride in their town.

Christmas in Newburyport is special. All of these grand old homes are decorated exquisitely for the season. With wreaths and bows, greens and lights everywhere, it's impossible not to feel a heartbeat quickened by the festiveness of the town.

Knowing the circumstances surrounding the move, Tracy and Antonio's new landlord handed us the keys to the apartment weeks before Trace and Tonx arrived and weeks before he began to collect rent. Grady and I doggedly organized and moved carloads of goods (new and slightly used) into the apartment.

The week before Christmas, we were rummaging through one of the local secondhand stores looking for treasures that we could buy for the apartment. As we shopped, a dad accompanied by his little girl came into the store. She was dressed impeccably for the holiday season in a mid-calf-length skirt that had a winter scene on the front of it. She was wearing white stockings, black Mary Jane shoes, and a beautiful dark green wool cape, trimmed with black ribbing. Her auburn hair was in braids and tied with bright red ribbons. A spattering of freckles adorned her turned-up nose, and for a moment I thought I had stepped into a scene from *How the Grinch Stole Christmas*. Here I stood, face to face with Cindy-Lou Who!

From that day to the present, our family has affectionately referred to Newburyport, Massachusetts, as "Whoville"!

Tracy and Tonx had planned to survive short term without the expense of a car. The high school was a mile from their apartment. A few (almost European) bakeries and specialty markets were nearby. Moving from Madrid, where everyone walks or uses public transportation, both Trace and Tonx were accustomed to traveling on foot.

January 2005 was the mother of all snowy winters in Newburyport. It seemed that every winter storm on the east coast stalled, covering the town in ever-deepening drifts of white. One freezing cold morning as Tracy was walking to school, her glasses fogged up and froze solid in the cold, damp coastal air. The snow that was still falling and covered the sidewalk was so deep, there was no option but to walk in the partially cleared road.

When at long last she reached the school, she was so cold she was practically in tears. There were going to be mornings that walking would not be possible, especially if she had to walk in the road and was unable to see through her frozen glasses.

The two new transplants from Europe took a giant step toward becoming Americanized: they secured a loan and purchased a car. The winter storms that settled over Newburyport were relentless, and the snows that seemed never-ending meant priorities needed to be reevaluated. Having warm and reliable transportation went to the top of the list.

It didn't take long before Tracy and Antonio were happy beyond compare, loving their new home and adoring "Whoville." As life settled nicely into place, Antonio filled in as a substitute teacher while seeking employment in Boston and the two set goals for getting back on their financial feet.

Although Tracy had been hired for only one semester, the school system required all new teachers to have a physical. In late February or early March of 2005, Tracy met with her new primary care doctor and had a complete and thorough exam (just as she had in Spain, months earlier in November 2004). She passed with flying colors; no evidence of "lumps" anyplace. This was confirmation; she was in perfect health.

As much as Trace and Tonx adored their new home and felt "Whoville" was the perfect village for them, Tracy knew they were facing another move. She needed to find a teaching position for September, and the new school year. And so the job search started all over again, almost as soon as she began her job in Newburyport.

It had been seven years since Tracy had taught in the public school system, and she saw a marked decline in student attitude and respect. She wondered if the private schools in the area might give her more freedom for creativity in the classroom as well as support (when support was needed). Tracy encourages good study habits and, in general, having respect—not just for teachers, but for other students. She works hard to make learning fun and in years past, she had been a favorite teacher. Jumping into another teacher's classroom mid-term was difficult and sometimes discouraging. The students saw Tracy as a substitute for their teacher who would be returning. (Albeit next fall and after they had finished the year of Spanish!)

During the years that Tracy had been away from the classroom and living in Spain, cheating had evolved to a new, high-tech level. Students were now able to buy or print papers or reports online and pass them off as their own work. Tracy confronted one such student who had done just that!

"Maxine, about this paper you turned in: I'm going to give you a chance to tell me where it came from."

"I wrote it."

"You wrote it?"

"Yes, I did."

"Oh, I see. Maxine, do you speak French?"

"No."

"Maxine, does anyone in your family speak French?"

"No."

"Well…you must have a close friend who is fluent in French?"

"No."

"Then can you please explain to me how you have turned in this paper for your Spanish class and managed to write page four, flawlessly, in French?"

"I don't know…. But I wrote it!"

For Tracy to find fulfillment in her work, she hoped the teaching philosophy in the private sector would match the standard she brought to the classroom. She began the search once more, but this time in private schools. She attended a job fair exclusively for teachers and managed to wow a representative from Phillips Exeter Academy in New Hampshire; she felt that this was an excellent job possibility.

She had arranged an interview with the representative from Milton Academy, in Milton, Massachusetts, also. Having second thoughts about the position because the opening was not permanent, Tracy respectfully went to the appointment simply to thank "Bernard" for his time, but she was not interested in a temporary position.

Bernard, the Head of Modern Languages at the school, began to ask Tracy a few questions. When he learned she was trilingual, he began speaking French and the two conversed. Within minutes, Bernard knew Tracy was right for the job and he was not about to let her decline. Tracy had applied for a job teaching Spanish, but she spoke French so fluently he knew her Spanish had to be even better!

From the job fair, Bernard immediately called the head of the Language Department at the school and told her that he had found the teacher for the opening. The school administrator just needed to convince Tracy to take the job.

Phillips Exeter's offer was more in line with what Trace was looking for: a genuine career move. A date when she could visit the campus was arranged. Preparations were made to observe her teaching one of her lesson plans to the students at Phillips Exeter.

Tracy was torn. Both were excellent schools. For Antonio's sake, she was leaning toward Milton and its location on the outskirts of Boston. He needed to find work. If she took the one-year position that Milton offered, it would mean packing again at the end of the school year and searching for a new job. She agonized with the decisions before her.

Tracy is a woman who needs to talk through the smallest details, and she can nearly talk you to death. When she was a little girl and would see a movie with her best friend, Lisa, I had to be prepared to listen to her reenact the entire movie when she got home. As I preferred not to go through 90 minutes of Tracy's monologue of what she had just seen on film, there were not many movies I missed that she wanted to see. It was more fun to be in the theater and sharing a box of popcorn than to experience the details and the movie script secondhand.

Women can understand this often "female" trait of excruciatingly detailed dialogue; men cannot. And husbands? They make decisions based on the Nike motto: "Just do it!"

In true "Tracy" form, she was examining every option and detail surrounding the job offers from the two schools. I was taken back in time to when she was a little girl, and her way of processing, picking apart, and reassembling everything…lengthy! I knew that Tracy wanted the job at Milton Academy, but the thought of packing and moving again at the end of the one-year contract was unbearable. It was during one of Tracy's endless monologues about her options that she asked for my opinion.

"Well, Trace," I suggested, "if you are leaning toward the position at Milton Academy for its location and the sake of more job possibilities for your husband, your reasons are honorable. Trust the Lord. God can make a way where there is no way."

I continued to express how I would choose if the decision was mine to make. "Your hope was to find a career position that would offer permanence until the day you retired from teaching. Trace, Bernard knows your value as a teacher; he saw that in five minutes and chose you over every other candidate he spent thirty minutes interviewing.

"If you are open and inviting God to work in this situation, He will. Have faith. Pray. Trust—"

Tracy's vision continued to drift toward her fears. "Mom, I'm not sure Bernard liked me—he didn't smile. He was straight business. He was, I don't know, sad or disconnected. What if he really didn't like me?"

A few weeks passed and unexpectedly Tracy received word from Milton Academy that another position in the language department had become available. A permanent position teaching Spanish was offered to her—a position that did not exist at the time Bernard interviewed Tracy at the job fair.

Shortly before the arranged date when Tracy was to demonstrate her skills in the classroom at Phillip Exeter Academy, she was asked for a postponement and future rescheduling. The phone call for rescheduling never came and that door closed.

Although we had no idea what was in Tracy's future, looking back I can see how the Lord was guiding our lives into place for the crisis we were about to face.

During the time that Tracy was seeking employment for the fall school year, our family suffered a heartbreaking and difficult loss. While my mother and father were spending the winter in Florida under the watchful care of my sister, Mim, the unthinkable happened. On March 23, 2005, Dad passed away very unexpectedly.

I am fortunate to have had men in my life who were protective, caring role models. I grew up on a small family-owned farm where Dad and my grandfather were strong father figures in my world. I was not a "girly girl." There was seldom a time that I wasn't with Dad and in the middle of farm chores. I loved working with Dad!

When Grady and I became pregnant with Tracy, we lived in a little house not far from the home where I had lived my entire life. Tracy was my parents' first grandchild, and Dad was the first family member we told. We shared our news on his birthday, January 27, 1970—he was going to be a grandfather in the summer. Dad could not have been happier. He adored Tracy, and he was so proud of the amazing young woman she is.

Dad was a quiet man. He didn't express his feelings very often. He loved all of his grandchildren...but Tracy was his first grandchild. She was special!

Dad died as he lived. No fanfare...he just died. Dad wasn't sick. He had been reading a book and had gotten up for something. As he walked back to his chair and his reading, he fell to the floor. There was no struggle from him as he passed from this life. He just quietly and suddenly died.

My sister called 911, and as Mom watched the paramedics working to revive the man she had loved and been married to for nearly sixty-four years, she, too, crumpled to the floor—overcome by emotion that caused a heart attack. My two parents lay side by side on the carpeted floor as paramedics frantically worked to save their lives. One lived…. One died.

By the time Mom was released from the hospital and was well enough to fly home to New Hampshire, weeks had elapsed. As Mom physically mended, my siblings and I planned Dad's memorial service. That was the beginning of May; and for me, that was when the real grief enveloped my life with heaviness, day in and day out for endless weeks. Quietly, I hid my pain. I cried and grieved alone.

Although Tracy was (thankfully) able to provide steady income for their family, nothing seemed to be opening up for Antonio. Each time it appeared he was about to land his dream job, the door slammed in his face. Against every desire he had to work in the business world, he continued substitute teaching and searched for something permanent.

Antonio is a "Renaissance man," the man for every season, but in some ways a man without a country. He comes from a delightful Spanish family. His dad was an international banker before retiring. During his working years, the family moved several times to different places around the world.

When Antonio was nine years old, the family was relocated to New York City. Although Antonio spoke English perfectly, it was very obvious he was not one of the locals. His accent and European-style clothing were a dead giveaway. When asked where he was from, he would respond that he had moved from Spain, "but now I live in New York City."

The general reply was "Welcome to America." Being a youngster, he embraced the words innocently and as a personal greeting; he thought everyone was *so* friendly! As a child he never quite caught on that the reason everyone asked him where he was from was because he looked different in his short pants, knee-high stockings, and European cap! At any rate, Antonio loved America—"the land of opportunity."

Maybe there was still something there from his childhood and the friendly greetings and warm feelings he had from his days while living in New York, for when it was time for Tonx to select a college, Bentley University, near Boston, was his choice. In some respects, a move back to Massachusetts with Tracy was like coming back home.

Tonx adapts to change easily, but job searching month after month was brutal. I know there were times when he had to have felt completely discouraged and depressed. Perhaps he even felt inadequate because of his business failing, forcing the move to the States where at least they could rely on Tracy's profession for income. Emotionally, the months without work were very hard, and yet he never gave up. He kept looking for leads and networked with everyone he knew or met.

In April, there was an alumni reunion at Bentley University, and Tonx was glad they lived close enough for him to attend. Antonio was looking forward to reconnecting with old classmates, and perhaps even networking to find a job. The reunion didn't provide any leads in the job market, but seeing friends from his college days lifted his spirits immensely. He was especially impressed by the keynote speaker, a former Bentley graduate.

"Lou" spoke that evening about having been through an extremely rare form of cancer. He was alive thanks to cutting-edge medical techniques and an experimental research trial at the Dana-Farber Cancer Institute in Boston. Because he was a Bentley University grad, Lou's story had special appeal as he shared about his unique battle to survive when the odds were not at all in his favor.

Not for a solitary second do I believe that Lou was scheduled as the speaker that night by accident. Nor do I believe it was a coincidence that Tracy and Antonio had just moved into the area, making Antonio's attendance possible. I don't believe that the committee member who remembered Lou's story and how he survived such a rare form of cancer was on the committee by chance.

Everything Lou shared that night became critical information for our family. As the events were unfolding, I was beginning to see God's fingerprints on the pieces that were coming together...including the reason for Antonio's unemployment.

Chapter 4

The Lumpectomy

For the entire month of May, I was consumed with grief following Dad's death.

When Mom moved back from Florida a few weeks before Dad's memorial service, it was to the house that Dad had built for her as a new bride in 1941 and next door to his father's farm and where he had been born in 1914. Without her lifelong mate, the house felt big, empty, and lonely. In retirement, Dad had worked sunup 'til sundown gardening. He loved digging in the dirt, and he was a master at creating gardens with stunning displays of flowers. He loved gardening so much that he changed the direction of our family farm when I was fifteen years old, and built greenhouses. His hobby became our family's livelihood.

Dad never did anything haphazardly. He always had a completed and finalized plan in mind. That was especially true with his flower gardens. With his passing, there wasn't a window in the house that did not look out upon the flower beds that were now void of color, shouting of his absence.

I did my best to support my mom in her loss, as did my five siblings, but it seemed most of the time when Mom called and was in need of cheering up, I was at my lowest point, too. Going from the elation of having Tracy move back to the States and the excitement of helping her resettle to the emotional downward spiral of Dad's passing—there could not have been anything more extreme. Throughout the months of April, May, and half of June, the joy of having Tracy home was overshadowed by encompassing clouds of sadness. My attention was drawn away from Tracy and to my mother and her grief.

Late in May, Tracy called. She had found a spot under her breast that was "hard." Through my sadness, I barely noticed what she was saying to me. Who could have possibly imagined there was any reason for concern? She had been through two complete physicals, in November and again the first of March. This was May. What possible worry could there be? Still, Tracy was uneasy at what she had found and called her doctor.

As Tracy shared with her doctor the details of all that she had recently been through, the emotional stress component was considered into the equation. Her doctor suggested that she would be more concerned if the lump was in a different location. Located beneath the breast, the lump was *less* alarming. Tracy was instructed to call back if the lump did not go away or changed.

School ended on June 23rd; that afternoon she returned to her doctor. Whether it was because of change or lack of change in the lump, suddenly there was concern. Tracy was sent to a surgeon the next morning for a second opinion. Still, we couldn't imagine that there could be any reason to worry. The worst scenario? Maybe a cyst of some sort would have to be removed? To hear the words "Mom...it's cancer" brought me to my knees as I had never been taken to my knees before.

In desperate times, we all react differently. But eventually I think most of us come full circle and line up on one side or the other. We either turn to God...or we turn away from God. Whether we have a church background or not, frequently life's trials can and do bring the strongest protesting atheist back around to decision time. Our beliefs (or lack of beliefs) are reexamined.

As I grieved for my dad, even as a Christian I couldn't pray. When my daughter was diagnosed with cancer, I couldn't stop praying. What's more, I was driven to seek out others to pray for her with me. It was amazing to watch my email list grow with the names of people who asked to be included; Tracy's diagnosis had come as a complete shock. As much as for prayer requests, the emails were sent to share what we were learning about cancer through Tracy's experience.

The support of those who were so faithful in prayer carried us through. The weeks and months that Tracy battled cancer were by far the hardest days I had ever faced in my life.

As Grady and I arrived at the hospital in Newburyport, the rabbit trails my mind had wandered during the drive seemed to hold more presence and reality than the nightmare we were facing inside the hospital where Tracy waited for us.

At the same time, Tracy had visitors from Spain at her home. They were two young boys who were among the first of her English students when she taught in Madrid. Juan was only two years old when she began teaching him English. Luis was a few years older. The boys had adored their teacher, and over the years, Tracy also became very close friends with the boys' mother. Juan and Luis were heartbroken when Tracy decided to move back to the States, until she promised them that they could come and visit America during their summer vacation.

The boys had arrived on Saturday, the day after Tracy's diagnosis. The six-hour time difference with Europe made it impossible to call and reschedule their promised visit to America. Despite the emotional chaos we were all feeling, Tracy loved the boys and was delighted to have the diversion they would create. Emotionally, she needed something other than fears looming over her. Having Juan and Luis meant laughter. It meant day trips to the Museum of Science, Lake Winnipesaukee, fireworks over July 4th…and best of all, a Fisher Cats minor league baseball game! What could be more entertaining than introducing young Spanish boys to baseball and fried dough?

Trace asked for our help, and her father and I were ready. The boys knew us from the years of visiting Tracy in Spain. Having them stay at our house for a couple of nights as Tracy recovered from her surgery would be easy. Grady was such a terrific dad, she knew the boys would love spending time with him (and Antonio). Together, Tracy and I worked out a plan so the boys would never know she was having surgery and not feeling well.

The morning of Tracy's surgery, she told Juan and Luis that she had some things that she needed to do; she would be busy all day. But her father and Antonio were going to have a special "boys' day" just for them. Plans had been made for shooting some hoops, going to the fire station to see the trucks, and lots of other "guy" things. In Spain, so much of the boys' lives revolved around women (their aunts and girl cousins) that this sounded like a terrific vacation plan. We were sure the boys would never suspect a thing, since Tracy would be released from the hospital and I would have her home by late afternoon.

Leaving Antonio and the boys behind, Tracy slipped from their presence to drive to the hospital. Grady and I met her there at 9:00. When we arrived, we hurried to the waiting area for surgery admissions and found Tracy bravely sitting alone. Tracy handed her car keys to her father, and after a few words of encouragement, Grady gave his daughter a hug and a kiss and left quickly before tears began to flow. I stayed with Tracy.

The minutes felt like hours as we sat, waiting for her name to be called. The hands on the clock seemed stuck. Tracy paced and walked and went outside "for air" and finally settled long enough for me to massage her back and neck to loosen the muscle spasms that were forming as tension manifested itself physically.

Finally, sometime after 10:30, the surgical nurse led Tracy into the patient care unit to start the IV for her surgery and to rid her body of the cancerous lump that had so suddenly invaded all of our lives. Once Tracy was prepped and ready, I joined her. As I looked at her, it all felt so strange, like a bad dream that I would wake from at any moment to discover none of the past three days were real. She was a grown and married woman, but as her mother, I was remembering a five-year-old little girl waiting to have her tonsils out as my mind flashed back to the last time I had been with her for surgery.

To break the tension, I told her what I was remembering from thirty years ago. I reminded her how I nearly fainted and I pitched forward, putting my head between my knees, all the while trying to reassure her that she was "fine" and "almost better." Through a window on the interior wall in her room in the children's ward, the nurses saw me keel over and came running. As I recounted the story, we both laughed nervously. But this was so much more serious, and as a mom it seemed surreal that this valuable young woman I had birthed was about to go into surgery for breast cancer.

Slowly the effects of the medication caused Tracy to relax and her eyes closed. I wanted the last thing that she heard from me to be something that would bring peace to her subconscious mind. I read Scripture—some of God's promises. Then I took her hand and prayed with her, kissed her cheek, and watched as she was wheeled away.

The surgery lasted less than two hours. Tracy's surgeon seemed very confident as he shared the details of his findings: the tumor was 2 centimeters and appeared completely contained in a single mass that had not spread to outlying tissue. He removed the sentinel node (the first node in the chain of lymph nodes from under Tracy's arm) and tested it for cancer. The results indicated it was "clear." Had there been evidence of cancer in the sentinel node, he would have removed more nodes to examine for possible abnormal cells. But that was not the case.

I was relieved to hear such good news. Optimistically he explained that four times out of five, the initial testing of the sentinel node was accurate. However, the lab would verify those first findings. Clear margins of healthy tissue beyond the perimeter of the tumor were attainable. He was sure he had "gotten it all," and everything that was removed would be examined carefully.

It sounded like the worst was over. I breathed a sigh of relief. I was *so* glad this was behind her! The next step would be to find an oncologist and learn about the recommended treatment, based on the pathology of the mass.

Tracy bounced back quickly. In a day or two, she was ready for the day trips that had been planned for Juan and Luis. Having them around really did serve as an excellent distraction from the question of "what's the next step?"

The boys' ten-day visit sped by quickly. Their bags were ready to burst at the seams with souvenirs and gifts collected during their excursions. As Tracy finished squashing the last items into the suitcases, she asked if there was anyone they might have forgotten on their gift list. The boys were sure that they had remembered everyone but politely asked if they might have a jar of peanut butter for themselves. The grocery store was a short distance from Tracy's apartment, so Grady drove the boys to the store before accompanying them to the airport. Tracy had an appointment.

Grady later reported to us that once in the store, Juan and Luis grabbed a grocery cart and began to clear the shelves of peanut butter.

"Whoa! Hey! Wait a minute! Your suitcases are completely full. Anything else that you take home will need to be carried in your backpacks."

Juan looked at Grady in all wide-eyed innocence as he grabbed another jar of peanut butter and said, "But when will we ever have peanut butter again?!"

As soon as Juan and Luis were safely on their flight bound for Madrid, Grady called his daughter. Tracy (in turn) called their mother to let her know that the boys had a wonderful time, and to break the news that we had kept secret during their visit.

It was July 6th...Tracy's birthday. And while Grady saw Juan and Luis off for their flight back to Madrid, Tracy and Antonio were with her surgeon to learn what the pathology revealed. Tracy called me. She was sobbing. Further tests on the sentinel node showed trace fragments of cancerous cells. These abnormal fragments had not penetrated the wall of the node, but this news dashed all hopes of an easy treatment plan. The simple presence of something abnormal in the sentinel node changed everything. Tracy would be taken back into surgery in two days to have more nodes removed and an access port installed in her chest for the chemotherapy she would require based upon the pathology. All of this was new and strange information. We were learning words and terms we didn't understand.

It was a difficult birthday. We began searching for information; we all began making calls. Tracy was calling friends who had family members in the medical profession. I was calling friends who were breast cancer survivors for advice. And first and foremost, I was afraid and crying out to the Lord in prayer.

The next day, our panic caused by the recent findings had subsided, and aggressively, I looked for answers...from the Lord. I was constantly at my computer updating family and friends and the hundreds of people who were interceding in prayer for Tracy and our family.

This is an excerpt from the email I sent out on July 7, 2005:

Dear family and friends,

When I spoke with her (Tracy) a couple of hours ago, her spirits were excellent. She is ready to beat this thing! She feels very good about her medical team so apprehension is not an issue.

We are beginning to see her giving "thanks" to God for some of the good things she is starting to see...where she can see His hand. Yesterday as we spoke, she was distressed and reduced to tears. As we prayed on the phone I took authority over the spirit of fear, "for fear is not of God." I reminded her fear is a weapon used by Satan against us.

As we spoke a few hours ago, it was a very different Tracy who was speaking; it was a victorious, secure young woman ready to meet this challenge head on and win!

Thank you all for your love and support...your prayers have made this all so much more "bearable." We are so aware of God's guidance and protection over us!

In His Love,

Kathy, Grady, Tracy and Antonio

Chapter 5

"Day Surgery?"

The morning Tracy was to have her portacath installed and lymph nodes removed, it was her husband who was with her. Patiently, Grady and I waited for Antonio's call to tell us that all was well and the surgery was finished.

We waited the entire day and the call did not come. Antonio did not call.

Grady and I became more and more uneasy. It was 5:00 when the phone finally rang. Antonio was very sketchy with the details, and to this day I'm not sure whether he did not have all of the information concerning what took place in the surgery or whether he was trying to save us from more bad news and further pain. The lymph nodes were removed without incident, but there were complications when her portacath was installed. The veins in Tracy's chest were small and not usable for the device. In order to find a suitable vein, the only option was to go deep into the muscle wall of her chest. During this process, Tracy's lung was "nicked." The surgeon's initial assessment of the injury was that it was so superficial it was unlikely there would be any repercussions. It would be best, however, that she remain in the hospital for observation.

Through the night, Tracy worsened. All day Saturday we waited for the reports from Tonx on Tracy's progress. By Saturday night, Tracy's lung was barely functioning at 70 percent, and it was steadily losing its ability to inflate as air escaped into Tracy's chest cavity.

Tracy's surgeon felt terrible about the accident caused at his hand. In thirty years as a surgeon, he could only remember two other cases that presented so many unexpected complications. Now, Tracy faced another "procedure." A tube was inserted into her chest for her collapsed lung. She was miserable, and had yet to begin her real battle…cancer.

None of us had any idea how painful a collapsed lung is. When we visited Tracy on Sunday, her contorted face revealed her level of misery. She was on the heaviest narcotics and they barely offered any relief. She lay in her hospital bed crying and sweating profusely from the pain that wracked her body. I began to sponge her arms and legs with cold cloths as she moaned, almost delirious with agony. She begged for the pain to go away and for more medication, as every fiber in her body reacted. For hours she cried, and her frustration continued to rise as relief remained elusive.

At that moment, I felt completely helpless as a mom. Her cries pierced to the core of my heart.

Antonio had been at her bedside from early morning until after dark for nearly three days. We suggested that he needed to take a break and do something for himself for a couple of hours. We would stay with Tracy.

Grady was always Tracy's hero and almost "like magic" with his daughter. He was a gifted dad. He knew exactly how to comfort Tracy even when she was a colicky infant. As soon as Antonio left, Grady began to read from a book of funny stories and bloopers. The idea to distract Tracy with humor worked and she began to relax, allowing the pain medication an opportunity to ease her discomfort. Finally, in exhaustion, she dozed off for a few precious moments of sleep.

Grady still had not lost his "magic" as her dad.

Day after day Tracy's hospital stay was extended. (To be completely honest, I was beginning to wonder if that was the safest place for her. At this point, everything medical seemed hazardous to her well-being.) During her hospital stay, we wanted to give Antonio the space he needed to be Tracy's husband and care for her. At the same time, we assured him that any time he wanted a break, we would gladly come. There was packing that needed to be done for their upcoming move to Milton Academy.

On Thursday, Antonio called to take us up on our offer. Upon our arrival, when I looked at our daughter, I had only one word to describe her appearance: "Pathetic!"

Tracy is so fastidious about personal hygiene, and there she was with her hair completely matted to her head and looking like a total grease ball! She looked sad beyond measure. I decided I would approach the subject gingerly.

"Trace, you do know that you can ask the nurses for help with your personal needs and cleaning yourself up?"

"Well, they did help me." She reached to touch the hair that hung in greasy spears from her head. "But they use dry shampoo on the patients who are mostly bedridden."

"Are you able to sit in a chair?"

"Oh, yeah, I can sit. And I'm able to use my bathroom; but because I'm attached to this hose attached to that machine and with this tube that's in my side, I can't do anything else. I'm afraid to move because the tube *thing* inside of me moves and it hurts."

"Okay." I paused briefly. "Would you like me to wash your hair?"

"Mom, you can't! It would hurt my side too much."

I dropped the subject and we talked about other things. And then she brought it up again. "How would you wash my hair?"

"Do you remember when my friend, Gayle, was in the hospital, and as her advocate I spent so much time with her while she was there?"

"Yeah…."

"Well, Gayle wanted a shampoo a few days after her surgery. She was in pretty rough shape. But I wanted to help her to feel better about her appearance. After washing Gayle's hair, I can wash anybody's hair. The room was soaked when we finished, but Gayle's hair was clean. I know exactly how to do this. I promise you, I will not hurt your side."

Hesitantly, Tracy agreed to let me try. Grady helped collect the necessary supplies, and together Grady and I guided Tracy to a chair placed in front of the bathroom sink.

"Okay, Trace, sitting perfectly straight, show me how far you can tip your head back as you look up toward the ceiling…. Perfect! Hold that position. Grady, as I tilt the basin like this, against her neck to catch the water, you pour the pitcher of water from the front of her hairline and back toward the crown of her head…. Great! Trace, this is going to feel so much better. Just relax.

"Grady, hold her face in your hands, giving her support and creating stability for her head while I shampoo."

I gently shampooed and massaged Tracy's scalp, taking care to gain her trust and confidence as lovingly I worked. When we finished, Tracy was delighted. "Good job, troops!"

There was never a time when Tracy appreciated the teamwork of her parents more than for that shampoo. I dried and fluffed her hair and helped her out of her soaked hospital gown and into one that was fresh and dry. We were finishing Tracy's extreme makeover when Antonio walked through the door.

"Tracy, you look great."

"I feel so much better." It was nice to see her smile. She turned to us. "Thanks, guys."

There's nothing like a good shampoo to help you to feel better when you've been bedridden for days on end.

Unexpectedly, Tracy's surgeon walked in. "Well, you are looking much better, young lady."

We all smiled. But unfortunately, the smiles were quickly wiped from our faces as Tracy's lung function was evaluated. We were in horror as we heard the words, "I'm not sure this tube is in the right place. We need to reposition it."

A curtain was immediately drawn, separating us from Tracy; our view was completely blocked. Tracy burst into tears and in rapid machine gun verbiage she pleaded, "Please tell me you don't have to do this. I need more pain medicine. It's almost time for more medicine. Please wait! I have to have something that will help and then it won't hurt so much. Tell me this isn't going to hurt. Tell me you are not going to put *another stick* into my side.... I can't do this.... I can't handle any more pain.... Oh, God, no! No-o-o-o! Ple-ease! Don't do this to me again!"

The momentary joy she had just experienced was shredded by terror. She emotionally disintegrated under the threat of more physical pain.

Grady and I were standing on the other side of the room near the door. As Tracy was crying out to her doctor, he walked to the door and stopped. My heart and ears were with my daughter; my eyes were riveted on her doctor. I watched his face change from that of a very compassionate and caring man to a trained professional who was being emotionally challenged by her cries. Potentially, even more discomfort would be inflicted on a young woman he only wanted to help. I could see how deeply he was torn. And yet, he had to help her—by medically inflicting...more pain.

As the room was prepared with nursing staff and the necessary supplies were carried to Tracy's bed, she was sobbing and shaking uncontrollably. Although I could not see, I heard her shivering cries. Antonio stood by helplessly, unable to console or comfort his wife. Though the curtain was drawn around her bed, nothing that she was experiencing was beyond our awareness as we listened to our daughter's pleas.

One of the nurses asked us to leave the room. With determination I stood my ground as I took Grady's hand and I heard myself say, "We're staying. *We're praying!*" I began to pray from the innermost depths of my soul, crying out to the Lord as I clutched Grady's hands. "Lord Jesus, I beg for Your presence to fall upon Tracy. I beg for Your peace, O Lord, in her and over her...a supernatural peace that surpasses *any* and *all* understanding. Calm Tracy's fears *now!* You are the Great Physician and I call upon You to readjust the placement of that tube in Tracy's side at this very moment to perfection and function for its intended purpose.

"Heal and inflate Tracy's lung, Lord God. Your Word says, 'Whatever you ask in My Name, I will do,' and it is in Your all-powerful and Holy Name I ask You for the sake of my daughter. Jesus, help her."

I continued to pray for each and every person on the other side of the curtain, begging the Lord to bring His calm and peace over Antonio, the nurses, and the doctor. I prayed that His Joy and Mercy be poured out as His Strength and Power were manifested in this crisis.

As I continued to pray, I was completely tuned out and not hearing what was happening on the other side of the curtain. All of a sudden, there were roars of laughter coming from everyone who surrounded Tracy's bed.

One of the nurses coaching Tracy to relax was talking Tracy to "a happy place...a happy time." Calmly and quietly she spoke as she held Tracy's hand. "Tracy, go inside your mind to one of your favorite places. Tell, me, where is that place that is so special to you?"

Tracy answered, "La Navata." In the quaint little village not far from Madrid, Antonio's family has a summer home, and the two would often go to La Navata to escape the oppressive summer heat that stagnates over Madrid.

The nurse continued, "Think of the way you feel when you are there; the sounds of the different birds...the warmth of the sun...the gentle breezes...the earth...the smells...." And at the precise moment the nurse said, "the smells," poor Tracy *expelled gas!* No one could hold back the "waves" of laughter.

Not knowing the cause of the laughter, but having just prayed for "His joy," I began thanking the Lord for answered prayer!

As Tracy's surgeon examined more closely the placement of the tube in her side, he discovered the tube was "in perfect placement"…just as I had prayed. By morning, Tracy's lung was functioning and healed! She was released from the hospital.

As Grady was getting ready for work the next morning, he said to me, "That was the most unbelievable experience I have ever witnessed."

"What are you talking about?"

"At the hospital. Last night as you were praying and calling each person by name and pleading for God's peace to fall upon them…it did. I heard the difference in each person as you called them by name and pleaded for God to touch them. That was the most amazing response to seeing God answer prayer AS it was being prayed that I have ever, ever experienced."

And I was so focused on praying, all I heard were the last laughs!

The entire time that Tracy was in the hospital, Tonx was multitasking on every front. Tracy's day surgery turned into a week-long ordeal that ate valuable time needed for packing. The move to Milton Academy was scheduled for July 27th, less than two weeks away. If there was a praise to be thankful for, it was that they had only been in the apartment on Fair Street for six months and had little time to accumulate extra things. Everything in the apartment was going.

One of the biggest tasks that needed time and attention leading up to the move was finding an oncologist in the vicinity of their new home. Dana-Farber Cancer Institute was suggested to Tracy, but time was of the essence and the waiting list for a first consultation was prohibitive. Suddenly, Tonx remembered the night of his college reunion and Lou, the keynote speaker. Immediately, Tonx began to make some calls. He needed to find the Bentley University graduate, and he succeeded.

Antonio introduced himself over the phone and told Lou he was there the night of the reunion. He told Lou about Tracy and that they desperately needed to see an oncologist at Dana-Farber, immediately. Was there was anything he could do? Antonio told Lou the pathology of the tumor indicated that this was type "3" cancer, which is very aggressive, and Tracy needed to start chemotherapy quickly. Unfortunately, they had been told the waiting list was longer than Tracy could safely delay treatment; but still, Dana-Farber was her first choice as a cancer treatment hospital.

Lou listened to Antonio's plea for help. "Let me see what I can do for you."

When Lou called back, Tonx was given the name and contact information for a brilliant young oncologist, Dr. Nancy Lin, and with Lou's help, an appointment was secured.

The connection between Nancy Lin and Tracy was immediate. They were nearly the same age, and Tracy loved her new doctor from the first meeting. All of Tracy's pathology and lab reports were sent ahead for review, and Nancy agreed it was a certainty that Tracy needed chemotherapy. Dr. Lin ordered the first of eight rounds of chemo to begin the day after the move to Milton.

When I reflect upon Tracy's move to Milton and remember that the very next morning she was scheduled for chemo, I can only imagine the magnitude of Tracy's anxiety level.

Tracy still faced the daunting responsibility of telling her new employer about her diagnosis. There was no time to waste...no time to spare. On the very day she was moving into her new apartment (which was part of her teaching compensation package), she informed her employer that she had just been diagnosed with breast cancer.

The other dreaded task on Tracy's to-do list was breaking the news to her grandmother. As a family, we had held back from letting my grief-stricken mother know about Tracy's diagnosis. Now, there was no choice. Tracy would be losing her hair. Trips to visit her grandmother would become less frequent, and Gram always asked about her first grandchild. Our family could not remain silent indefinitely. And I could no longer pretend life was fine as I carried the grief for my dad, the sorrow for my mom, and the agony I felt for Tracy.

A few days before having her first round of chemotherapy, she visited Gram to tell her about moving to Milton Academy. There is never an easy way to break the news of a diagnosis of cancer, but Tracy found a moment that seemed right and tactfully revealed what had been kept hidden from her grandmother. Skillfully, giving her just enough information to satisfy without an overwhelming amount of detail to cause further grief, she spoke in a positive manner and added in a little humor. As only Tracy can, she talked about how she would be sleeping later in the morning after she lost her hair. She wouldn't need as much time in the shower, and there would be no more "bad hair days" because there wouldn't be any hair to be bad.

She told Gram that since Antonio was already bald, the two of them could buy matching wigs and trick-or-treat as twins! Trace was so funny; her grandmother could not help but laugh. But still, this was horrible news for Gram to cope with. Death was still too recent and real, and her first granddaughter had cancer.

Tracy and Antonio's moving date arrived. Grady and I were there to pitch in with the last-minute details and to transport Tracy and her cats to their new home at Milton Academy...a new home that just happened to be 8 miles from Dana-Farber Cancer Institute and Brigham and Women's Hospital.

On Thursday, July 28, 2005, the morning of Tracy's first round of chemo, I wrote:

Hello Everyone.

Moving yesterday went like clockwork. The movers had everything in the new apartment and were gone by 2:00. We had the bed set up and made and 25 percent of the boxes empty by 3:00!

Later that afternoon, Tracy met with one of her superiors on staff at Milton. She was dreading this appointment; the purpose was to share that she is dealing with treatment for cancer.

God always goes before us!

Once Tracy shared with this man that she had just been diagnosed with breast cancer, he said, "Well, two of your male colleagues will have a great deal of support and understanding for you. Their wives had breast cancer...."

One of these men, Bernard, was the man who first interviewed Tracy and pushed to turn a one-year opening into a permanent position, because he was so impressed with her foreign language skills. During Tracy's interview at the job fair with Bernard, she feared he did not like her...he seemed sad. He had just lost the lady in his life to breast cancer three months earlier.

Tracy slept "like a rock" all night in her new apartment before her first day of chemo.... "Mom" woke up around 3:30 AM and prayed through first light before dozing off for a few needed minutes of sleep before getting up for the day.

Tracy was calm, peaceful, and not anxious facing her first day of chemo. I was the wreck! I most likely would have been fine had I been with her; but *not* being there made my day unbearable... totally and completely unbearable.

Thank you for remembering us in your prayers....

Blessings and Love,

Kathy

I knew Tracy's schedule for her day at the hospital, and the hour when the first drops of chemo would begin to enter into her body. She was in Boston—seventy-five miles away. Grady was at work. I was at home.

In the silence of my aloneness I crumpled to the floor under the weight of emotion that I was carrying, tears of grief streaming down my face. The reality of Tracy's fight against cancer was *now* real. As much as we knew, there were equally as many questions unanswered. How would her body tolerate chemotherapy? Was the disease genetic? Would there be insurance coverage? Were the right choices made in Newburyport and prior to starting with Dr. Lin at Dana-Farber? Would the chemo be effective? How sick would she be from her treatment? Would she be able to carry out her teaching responsibilities? What was her life going to be like for the next many months? Would she defeat this horrible monster? What if "it" defeated her? *Oh, dear Lord!*

I knew she had the support and comfort of her husband at her side, and from our research on Dana-Farber Cancer Institute, we knew that she was in the best cancer facility in all of northern New England and number five in the entire country on the list of best cancer hospitals. But, as her mother, I still had something "protective" pulling at my heart and I wished there was some way I could save her from this pain. Some way...*I could take her place.*

It was the first time I had cried since Tracy's call, when we had learned, "Mom…it's cancer." I was alone, pouring out my feelings and frustrations to a God who claimed to love me, as I let Him know that this certainly did not *feel* like love. I sobbed from the very core of my being. For some crazy and desperate reason, I did not want the comfort of my husband (who was at work). I wanted to talk with my younger brother. *That* was ridiculous! It was 10:30 in the morning, and I knew he would not be at home. He would be working. Just then the phone rang. It was David—my younger brother.

"Kath? It's Dave…. I just felt I needed to call you to see how you're doin'."

Oh, Lord! You DO hear the "smallest" desperate cries of my heart. Thank you for Your way of bringing me comfort and reassurance that You are here, Jesus.

Chapter 6

Cancer 101

Is there anything that brings a person's life into perspective more quickly than the diagnosis of a catastrophic illness? All of sudden you are thrown into the reality of what's important and what's superfluous.

I could relate to what Tracy was going through, to some small degree.

When Tracy was a little girl, I was bitten by a cat that showed every sign of being rabid. The cat had been hanging around our yard, and the morning I was attacked and bitten, the cat literally chased Grady into his car as he was leaving for work. The attack was so bizarre, I never would have recounted the story had there not been a witness. From her window, my neighbor watched in horror as the whole drama unfolded.

One of the ironies leading up to my attack was this: a few weeks before I was bitten, I had read an article about the effectiveness (or lack of effectiveness) of rabies vaccine. This was in 1976; the article stated the injections given to a patient bitten by a rabid animal were only 60 percent effective. The other 40 percent of the time the patient developed hydrophobia and physical decline, and death occurred within a very short time.

For fifty-six hours—from the time I was bitten until the test results on the cat came back from the state lab—I imagined the worst and made plans for my remaining days in light of the possibility that my life might very well end soon. The attack changed the direction of my life. As I prioritized, I wanted to know who God is. That incident broke through the fallow ground of my spiritual life, and Christianity later took root. Being the best wife and mother I could be were also priorities.

As I watched Tracy wrestle with her fear and what could happen, I understood.

Emotional health plays a huge role in fighting disease. It really is true that "laughter is the best medicine." One of the things Tracy was told the very day she was diagnosed was to go home and watch a movie that would make her laugh. The hormones released with laughter serve a good and useful purpose. So laugh when you can!

As a family, we learned about support. There are people who know exactly the right ways to be supportive. There are also people who have a knack of opening up their mouths and inserting their feet clear up to their knees. Some were clueless as they told us about people they knew who were extremely sick while going through chemo. And others rambled on about people they had known who died from cancer. Sensitivity toward a family going through cancer is important, and even I needed to carefully read Tracy's moods and know when to speak and when to listen.

There is no one better qualified to help prepare for a "journey" than one who has taken that journey. There were four women who played a huge role in helping me through Tracy's illness.

As a teenager, Tracy was friends with a boy whose mother had been diagnosed with breast cancer when she was in her thirties. Mary-Kathryn was one of the first women I called for help when Tracy was diagnosed. She knew exactly how to be the right kind of friend, giving me advice, direction, encouragement, and hope for Tracy.

The second woman was the mother of Tracy's best friend and roommate from college. Pat Hart lived close to where our two girls attended college in St. Davids, Pennsylvania. The girls were friendly competitors in college and both graduated Suma Cum Laude, tied in their cumulative four-year grade averages. Pat was like Tracy's second mother.

Pat is a true pioneer "survivor" of breast cancer. She underwent a mastectomy on July 16, 1975. In those days, breast surgery and the chemo treatments were worse than barbaric. I'm amazed that anyone survived the cure. Pat was a constant encourager in the circle of friends who lifted me up when I was down during Tracy's battle.

Claire Fauth: Claire was Grady's assistant at work for several years, before leaving for a position with the American Cancer Society. She was the first younger woman that I knew with a history of breast cancer in her family. Claire encouraged me to familiarize myself with the American Cancer Society's website.

And my fourth resource was Pauline Cote. She was a blessing straight from the Lord! I must share this story.

Within days of learning that Tracy had breast cancer, Carleen (a very close and long-time friend from Maine) contacted me and said, "Kathy, I have a good friend, Pauline, and I'm going to ask her to send an email to you. Her mom has had breast cancer and has been through so-o-o-o-o much. I really think Pauline can help you. Also, her niece, Shantelle, is battling another form of cancer, osteosarcoma. Pauline certainly knows what you are going through."

In the months that followed, Pauline faithfully prayed for Tracy, and I prayed for her mom and for Shantelle. The disease had so weakened Shantelle's seventeen-year-old body, praying for the Lord's mercy and comfort was what she needed most as living became more and more laborious.

Then one day I received word from Pauline that as delighted as the family was that her mom had for the third time gone into remission, Shantelle had peacefully succumbed to the cancer she so valiantly fought for four years. Shantelle passed from this life to one where she was whole and well and dancing before the Lord.

Because I had not met Pauline face to face, I did not know if it would be right for me to attend Shantelle's funeral. I sincerely wanted to go, but was *this* the right time for first meetings? I shared my concerns with our mutual friend, Carleen. The next thing I knew, I was getting a forceful email from Pauline insisting that I come. What's more, she was insisting that I not stay at a hotel but in her home.

We began to bargain back and forth on the phone about my accommodations for the night that I would require lodging; we finally came to an agreement.

"Pauline, I will stay at your house under one condition. I insist that since your family has been through so much, I would like to bring a home-cooked meal. Now, how many am I cooking for, ten? Fifteen? How many?"

"It's a deal! There will be twelve for dinner."

I worked most of Saturday and Sunday morning making a chocolate cake, homemade pies, a special cran/raspberry Jello salad, and our favorite family recipe for chicken over biscuits. I missed church as I continued cooking for Pauline's family.

I'm not in the habit of hearing voices, but as I worked, longingly I said, "Lord, I wish I could be at church worshipping You."

And I heard in my spirit and almost audibly, *"You are."*

As Pauline's family gathered around her table that night enjoying the foods I had prepared, I was nearly taken to tears. This was the first "home-cooked" meal that they had enjoyed as a family in three years. Cancer had completely dominated their schedules. If they had the opportunity to sit down for a meal together, it was fast food someone grabbed as they drove past a restaurant or a casserole from the freezer that someone had thoughtfully made and brought to the house.

There was nothing—*nothing*—I could have done for this family that would have meant more to them. I was the one who received the biggest blessing that night. I fixed a dinner with all of the trimmings. And it was a pleasure to see how much joy it brought. It was an honor to serve this family who had fought cancer for such a long time…by preparing a meal.

Antonio was with Tracy for her first appointment as an extra set of ears. The shock factor of learning about a cancer diagnosis is completely overwhelming. It is critical to have someone who is able to take notes or record the information that is being given. Between the shock of the diagnosis and the need to absorb new information and vocabulary, it's impossible to remember what is said. Tracy began using a recording device at her appointments with her doctors. This made it so much easier to go back and listen again in the safe and relaxed atmosphere of her home.

New skin products, books, prosthetics, and wigs are a part of surviving cancer. There is a wonderful little shop at Dana-Farber on the ninth floor called "The Friends Place." (At the time of Tracy's treatments it was called "The Friends Boutique.") Tracy went into the boutique after one of her first appointments to become acquainted with the different items she would need as her treatments began to change her physically. The staff who work at this particular shop are incredible, sharing advice with those who are facing the challenges of cancer. The information they willingly share is invaluable for the newly diagnosed patient who is still unaware of little facts like even in the summer a sleeping cap is something you might need. All of a sudden, nights are chilly without hair!

Finding a shop specializing in products for cancer patients is a good idea.

Tracy was incredibly fortunate to have the insurance coverage that she had. And as a family we began to look at insurance very differently. Tracy's insurance provided for the best possible care. All of her treatment was covered. In Newburyport, her job and compensation package included coverage through September. Amazingly, when she moved to Milton Academy, her insurance was exactly the same coverage plan.

When she signed her contract with Milton Academy in March/April, she was healthy with no sign of cancer. It's hard to comprehend how life can change so radically almost overnight.

As we learned about cancer and surviving the disease, we began to understand that cancer hospital ratings really do mean everything. Cancer *research* hospitals are unique. These are the hospitals with cutting-edge treatment and technology. Doctors working in specialized research hospitals are singularly focused in their specific expertise. Clinical trials and new technological equipment are often used in applicable situations, offering the best of best results.

We learned there is no diagnosis of cancer that can be taken lightly. Our experience taught us if there is a research hospital caring for cancer patients and offering new treatment studies, that's where to go. Even when a commute borders on ridiculous but is possible, it's worth having the opinion of a *reputable* cancer research facility when such a diagnosis is suspected, and before *any* treatment begins. Successful eradication of the disease without an accurate diagnosis is impossible. The diagnosis must be accurate!

Annually, ratings are published for the country's "Best Cancer Hospitals;" that information is easily found online. In Tracy's case, considering her unusual complications, she needed to be in the hands of the most skilled oncologists. Dr. Nancy Lin at Dana-Farber Cancer Institute will always stand head and shoulders above the rest.

God's hand was upon us. I see it as no accident or chance occurrence that Trace moved back to the United States from Spain six months before her diagnosis. I don't see it as coincidence that she was hired from an interview she was canceling for a position that did not yet exist. The location of that job placed her eight miles from the fifth best cancer treatment hospital in the country, and at a time when she was completely healthy, only to have need of Dana-Farber Cancer Institute and some of the country's best oncologists the day after she moved there.

Explain that if you can!

No two people respond to chemotherapy and anti-nausea medication exactly the same way. In spite of the numerous cases that doctors and nurses see at a cancer facility, for the patient, that first round of chemo is a first experience.

Dr. Lin knew the expected response to treatment, the statistics, and the odds. But Tracy rewrote the book on new experiences. She was a "case study" unto herself. The hospital where she was treated *mattered*.

Chapter 7

What Are the Odds?

Tracy's first round of chemo was administered slowly, and it took most of the day. We learned that just as all hospitals are not created equal, all breast cancers are not created equal. There are different types, stages, and treatment plans, and Dr. Lin consulted with other experts in the field on Tracy's behalf as Tracy surprised her with unusual side effects and problems.

Tracy was diagnosed with "stage II type 3 triple-negative breast cancer." We also learned that of the different types of breast cancer, this was one of the most aggressive, least understood breast cancers and accounted for fewer incidences of the disease.

Tracy would be treated with conventional chemotherapy: A/C (Adriamycin and Cytoxan). The proven track record of using these drugs seemed to indicate that older women had fewer side effects than women under forty. Once more, there was Tracy—under age forty and in the minority as a breast cancer patient.

On Thursday, August 4, one week after Tracy's first round of chemo, it seemed her body accepted her treatment fairly well, except for mild nausea and fatigue. We felt apprehensive but hopeful. Then, out of no place, Tracy spiked a fever and Antonio rushed her to the hospital.

Twenty-four hours after her chemo, Tracy had received an injection of Neulasta, which is a standard practice after treatment with many different types of chemotherapy. Neulasta stimulates the growth of neutrophils, a type of white blood cell. And at the time those white blood cells *should* have been showing up in a blood test, her counts were continuing to plummet. The Neulasta shot seemingly was ineffective with Tracy.

I sent out another email for prayer:

Date: Thursday, August 4, 2005

Subject: White Cell Count

Dear Family in Christ:

Well...once more Tracy is in the minority. She is in the 2% who doesn't respond as expected to the shot she was given to increase her white blood cells after chemo. She developed a fever and her white blood cell count continues to drop. I don't understand what these numbers mean, but Tracy told me the "count" needs to be at least "500." She was "300-something." She is back in the hospital and on antibiotics. And her new garb includes a surgical mask.

Please pray that her white blood cell level would return to a normal range.

She is feeling very weary of hospital visits. And this is only the beginning. She is hoping her levels will allow her to be released on Saturday. All I want for my birthday this year is for Tracy to be well. I am hoping she will be well enough for us to visit sometime over the weekend.

Thanks.... Blessings and Love,

Kathy

Tracy's white blood count plummeted to 48, and she was kept in the hospital through the weekend. Early on Monday morning, she called and she was in tears.

"Mom, you've got to pray! My white blood counts are not increasing, and my second chemo infusion is on Thursday. I "must" stay on schedule to finish the worst of my chemo treatments before I begin teaching my classes on September 12th. The white count has to increase *now!* My blood cells are not maturing fast enough. Mom, you have to ask everyone to pray."

And that was exactly what I did. I sent a prayer request very specific in nature. Hundreds of people in different prayer circles were asked to pray for Tracy.

Later that day, Tracy was released from the hospital but still wearing a surgical mask.

Caretakers are the forgotten victims of cancer, and Antonio had no one except us to support him, until his parents arrived from Spain. He still did not have a job, which was both a blessing and a curse. There was no escape for him from the 24/7 care he provided for Tracy. For the second time in six months, he had been uprooted and moved. He didn't know anyone, and there was no opportunity to make friends. He didn't even have coworkers to talk to about what he was going through with his wife.

The responsibilities of setting up their new apartment, cooking, cleaning, laundry, and shopping as well as all of the trips to the hospital in the middle of the night were his and his alone. Tracy's care became his sole existence, with nothing and no one to give him a break. We lived eighty miles away—close, but not close enough to always be there if and when he needed our help.

One night, after her first round of chemo, Tracy called. She began to cry, but not for herself. She was crying out of gratitude for Antonio. This vibrant, energetic, athletic woman he had married had turned into a woman who was sick, helpless, and in and out of the hospital.

"For better or for worse...in sickness and in health." Antonio was walking this out; some men might have left. Some men do leave under the stress. What are the odds for failed relationships under such emotional strain?

Antonio proved his love for our daughter, day in and day out. He loved her "in sickness" month after month, before Tracy once more enjoyed good health, proving what love is...a choice.

Sent: Wednesday, August 10, 2005 2:28 PM
Subject: Round 2 of Chemo

Hello Everyone,

Yesterday after Grady finished work for the day, we went to visit Tracy, Antonio, and his parents (from Spain), who have come to look after Trace and Antonio. They do love Tracy.

This was the first time we have seen Tracy since her first chemo treatment two weeks ago. Despite what she has endured, she looks good. And she has not lost her hair, although it is much drier and the texture is brittle. She will most likely lose her hair after her second chemo treatment.

That brings me to the purpose of this update on Tracy's progress. As much as she dreads the treatment, she wants to move on and get this behind her. There is some question as to whether they will be able to give her the next dose of chemo tomorrow. Her white blood count went so low, we will not know until tomorrow if it is high enough for her to receive treatment.

Tracy asked for prayer.

Pray that the Lord would increase her white blood count; that His perfect timing for her treatments would be done. Our desire is that it be now. In my spirit however, I ask for His will in this. He is all knowing and loving.... I trust for "that which is perfect."

When she was tested last Friday, 10 percent of her white blood cell count was immature "baby" cells that needed to "grow up"!

Tracy is already stressing over this. Last night as we were visiting, all of a sudden Tracy blurted out, "Mom, I can't stand this any longer. Will you give me a massage?" Her back was just one mass of rock-hard stressed muscles. This poor child! She is trying so hard to face this bravely, but there is a point when what we deal with emotionally settles and moves upon our physical bodies. I know that! My body couldn't take any more and even I ended up in our local Emergency Unit Saturday night. I'm fine...my body is just rebelling and saying, "NO MORE!"

Tracy's mother-in-law, Pilar, brought many beautiful scarves from Spain for Tracy to use to cover her head when the time comes. We tried many of them, tying them in different styles. I bought Tracy some new long, gold dangle earrings that were very feminine and pretty. Tracy will be beautiful...even without her hair. She has ordered a wig to wear when a hat or scarf is not appropriate.

Thank you for your continued prayers for our family.

In Jesus' Love,
Kathy, Grady,
Tracy and Antonio

Thursday morning Tracy returned to the hospital hoping her white blood count would be within the normal range and allow her to continue on her scheduled chemo. Tracy's white blood count had risen over 3000! Dr. Lin was astonished. Tracy was beaming. "My mom and half of America are praying!"

To the best of my knowledge, there was no medical explanation for the drastic and sudden increase in Tracy's counts.

August 13, 2005, as I kept everyone updated, I wrote:

Subject: And the next concern...

...Tracy said her doctor was mighty surprised to find that in less than one week, Tracy's white blood count went from "48" to over "3000"! She had the opportunity to tell her doctor that she could not take the credit. Trace knew there were people praying for her that she does not even know.

Again, thank you ALL!

On a sadder note, last night I had two dreams and I told Grady about them when I woke up. In both of the dreams, I was crying. One of the dreams was about Tracy.

I dreamed that Grady and I were walking into Tracy's new home and Tracy was sitting on a stool and crying. Antonio had clippers and was shaving her head in the dream because her hair had begun to fall out. I stood beside her holding her hand and crying with her.

This morning as Grady was out running errands he called Tracy. She was crying. This morning her hair was falling out. Antonio was preparing to get the clippers to shave her head. How does one truly emotionally prepare for this day?

Kathy

Chapter 8

"Clipped"

My little episode that placed me in our local emergency room required me to see my primary care physician because of an allergic reaction to antibiotics I was prescribed. It had been several months since I had last seen "Dr. John."

"So, let's see. You had right shoulder surgery in January…. Everything went well…. You were released from (doctor) Mark's care. What happened that caused a trip to the ER?"

"Well," I began as I tried to put all of the pieces into some sort of order in my mind. "I've sort of had an abnormal amount of stress over the past several months. I think my body just couldn't take the overload."

John looked at me, unprepared for my answer. "What has happened?"

I began my dissertation. "In March, my dad died without warning. Mom had a heart attack when he died and was hospitalized for close to a week. We weren't sure she would survive the shock of Dad's death.

"My sister, who was caring for our parents in Florida, was following Mom's ambulance with all of her medical information and was in an accident en route. That delayed her arrival at the hospital and decisions that were needed for Mom."

I took a breath and continued. "In June, Tracy was diagnosed with breast cancer. While installing her IV port, the surgeon accidentally punctured her lung. That kept her in the hospital for a week. Almost as soon as she was released, she moved to Milton Academy. She had signed a teaching contract with them a few months ago. God only knows how she is going to survive fighting cancer *and* starting a new job."

John was looking slightly shocked as I continued.

"The poor girl had complications with her first round of A/C. Her body has not tolerated the chemo combination, and her blood counts dropped so low, she was admitted into the hospital for several days. Yesterday, she received her second round of the A/C. I'm concerned that, again, she will have difficulty.

"My mom is not handling anything very well since Dad's passing, least of all Tracy having cancer. She calls me frequently for reassurance. If this hasn't been enough, a very close friendship ended abruptly and on an unpleasant note. It was another huge and significant loss. I'm internalizing a lot; it hasn't been easy.

"Recently, I began attending a different church. It's larger than my old church and I don't know anyone, yet.... Grady didn't make the church move with me because of committee obligations and that has been difficult. But other than being in an emotional washing machine on the spin cycle for about six months, everything's just fine, John."

John looked at me, blinking in disbelief. "Ya know, if all this was written into a script for a soap opera, people would say, 'That could never happen in real life.' How's your blood pressure? ...100 over 66??? You are a rock."

What John didn't know was that on my own, I couldn't make it through a single day. Jesus was my "Rock," and on His word and promises I was firmly anchored. I *refused* to lose my faith and become consumed by the storms around me.

Date: Sunday, August 14, 2005
Subject: "Clipped"

Dear Family in Christ:

In 1998, I personally went through an extremely extended period of time of one trial after another. One of the biggest lessons God taught me that finally broke the bondage of despair, oppression, and depression that I was under was the importance of praise when I felt like God had gone on an extended vacation and not left a forwarding address.

I believe the Scriptures. They are my example to live by. In Acts16:25, Paul and Silas prayed and sang "praises" to the Lord. And you know what? God "moved" the Earth! There was an earthquake. It isn't such a big deal to sing praise to the Lord when everything is going along just fine. But Paul and Silas had a different story. All of this happened after Paul and Silas had been beaten with rods and put into stocks in the dungeon of the prison. Yet there they were singing praises to the Lord...a sacrificial offering of praise. Now isn't that just interesting! I think there is a lesson here, something the Lord wants us to remember and to do when things in our lives are tough. *There is power in praise and worship!*

Grady and I went to see Tracy yesterday. It was a pretty terrible day for her. Physically she felt sick from the chemo. To lose her hair magnified the reality of the disease she is battling. Kathy K. thanks for the conversation last night. You are such a blessing. You helped walk me through some of Tracy's reality.

Before yesterday, every time Tracy looked in the mirror she still looked like "Tracy" and there was still an element of denial that her body is fighting a very real disease. Losing her hair means there is no more denial. She is in a battle for her life! And now every time she looks in a mirror, she sees that truth.

Tracy and I spent several hours together yesterday. We retreated to her bedroom and the two of us lounged on her bed talking... crying...reading books about breast cancer. We talked about the fears, hopes, and "what ifs." I spent a lot of the time just listening to her trying to work through all that she was feeling. And offering what comfort I could as her mom.

These are the prayers that need to be brought before the Lord:

Again, the white blood cell count to increase and mature quickly enough for Tracy to receive her chemo on August 25. It is assumed that Tracy will have a drastic drop in her count. We ask that the Lord would turn her blood count around quickly so that she can stay on this brutal regimen of chemo; for her, it is more effective at destroying lingering cancer cells than having three weeks between treatments.

That her red blood cell count would not drop off. The chemo lowered her red cells, also. The doctor did express a concern.

Clean genes! Tracy has been approved for the gene profiling. We can't even think about the horror of what Tracy will have to endure "**IF**"...

We are claiming and believing Jesus for His mercy...clean genes!

Deep restful rest when she is sleeping. Her body is fighting so hard through all she is physically going through; her body needs to rejuvenate when at rest.

Spiritual peace. She gets so far out ahead of the next day or two, she continually overwhelms herself. Doesn't the Scripture say that each day has enough to "give thought to" that we are not supposed to worry about tomorrow? Somehow that is Scripture that never took root in Tracy's little worrying heart! She plans things out years in advance and always tries to meet expectations way beyond superior! Since she was a child, she has made me nuts with this personality trait.

When Tracy was a little girl, she had a Fisher Price village, a farm, and a castle. In the 1970s her bedroom had shag carpeting. She would become very upset when the little men in these villages would not stand upright and where she put them. I named this problem "shag carpet syndrome." I have reminded Tracy through this ordeal as she labors and mourns over the plans that she had made—plans for a fun summer, and enjoying her return to the States after being away for so many years: "The world is full of 'shag carpeting.'"

The Scripture says, "For I know the plans I have for you, declares the Lord, for wholeness and not for evil, to give you a **future** and a **hope**. Then you will call upon me and come and pray to me, and I will hear you. You will seek me and find me, when you seek me with your whole heart." Jeremiah 29:11-13 (English Standard Version)

We all continue to value your interceding for us. As a family we are emotionally tired, physically we are weary.... This family needs Jesus to love us as only He can!

Blessings and Love,

Kathy

When Grady learned that Tracy's hair was falling out and Antonio was shaving her head, the reality of the disease shook his world. The circle of women I had in my life helping me to cope and preparing me emotionally along the way eliminated some of the shock that we were walking through. My conversation with Pat Hart's daughter, Kathy (and Tracy's best friend from college), was so insightful. Kathy had been there and through this with her mom on more than one occasion. She poured such light and understanding on this step Tracy was going through. Kathy told me that Tracy's shaved head was a visible reminder. Now, every time we looked at Tracy, her fight for life was a reality. It was in front of us in her appearance.

Tracy was napping when we arrived at her apartment. When she emerged from her bedroom, I will never forget how ill she looked. Chemotherapy drugs are cumulative in the body. If this was only her second dose of A/C, I could not imagine what to expect in the treatments that were yet to come.

Trace, who ordinarily loves her mother-in-law Pilar's cooking, managed just a few bites of food and retreated back to her room. I followed to try to comfort her. I allowed her to pour her heart out, including the fears. Tracy was learning more about triple-negative breast cancer, and she was frightened by the number of unknowns about this cancer.

In the Friends Boutique, Tracy had purchased an excellent book written by Carolyn M. Kaelin, M.D., M.P.H., a breast cancer surgeon at Brigham and Women's Hospital. Dr. Kaelin is a breast cancer survivor, also. Her book *Living Through Breast Cancer* is an incredible resource. As a patient and a doctor, she has walked the walk. Her book is a survivor's story, and an essential source of medical information about treatment. She explains in understandable terms the different types of breast cancer and types of surgeries. The book answers all sorts of questions that a newly diagnosed patient faces.

Tracy and I thumbed through the pages, reading aloud and learning as we read. This was all so new and foreign to us. Emotionally, Tracy was still overwhelmed by her diagnosis. Physically, she felt ill from her treatment.

We remained cocooned in Tracy's room for hours, until Tracy was finished pouring out all that was on her heart and we had attacked her fears in prayer. I left her to sleep.

Pilar was still working in the kitchen when I emerged from Tracy's room. As I fought back tears, all I could do was repeatedly thank Pilar.

Her understanding heart and love for our daughter was so evident. Her willingness to cook and serve us allowed me to be the mother Tracy needed that afternoon as we spent time together. Pilar's presence was both a blessing and a gift.

Tonx called Grady the following Thursday. It was exactly a week after Tracy's second chemo treatment. She had constant nausea and was unable to eat or drink. Diarrhea can be associated with so many different chemo drugs, and there is constantly the risk of dehydration. Trace was dehydrated. Her white blood count had dropped to 78 and she was in the hospital, sick and feeling like she was about to die from the cure if not the disease. Dr. Lin knew changes needed to be made in Tracy's chemo script, but it was a balancing act of killing the disease but not the poor patient!

As Tracy lay in her hospital bed that night, she made a vow to herself. She promised to use the information and her experience to help someone else *IF* she lived through this!

When Tracy phoned us from the hospital, she was depressed and weepy from the anti-nausea meds that seemed to be doing almost no good at all. She was despondent over the fact that she seemed to be considerably worse after her second treatment, and she was feeling sick and tired of being shanghaied by a stomach that had signed up for a six-day rollercoaster marathon without her consent.

I tried to encourage my daughter and give her hope. "Tracy, Dr. Lin is not going to let you go through this a third time. She's going to figure this out. You have the best doctors and you're in the best hospital. And you are halfway through your A/C treatments. 'Give thanks!' Bring in your long-range plans, Trace. If you have to take this an hour at a time, 'give thanks' that the hour is behind you and not ahead of you. You are one hour closer to being well. If you can only handle fifteen-minute blocks of time, give thanks for the fifteen minutes that have passed and you are closer to your goal and being well."

Together we were both learning what it means to have a thankful heart and look beyond feelings. I was just beginning to understand what a "sacrifice of praise" *is* while in a battle and being crushed under the weight of emotional heaviness. The Bible teaches that Paul and Silas "were praying and singing hymns of praise as the other prisoners looked on." I was going to do my BEST to copy their model. If the Lord (Again) brought me back to this Scripture, there was something I had not learned.

That evening I requested prayer for Tracy's blood counts. Overnight, Tracy's white counts rose to 1,000 and she was released from the hospital.

Dr. Lin consulted her colleagues, who are among some of the most renowned breast specialists in the world. Tracy's lag time for responding to the Neulasta shots to boost the growth of new white blood cells was unexplainable. Neither her white cell count nor her red blood cells were in a normal range and increasing when they should have been. Ultimately, it was agreed Tracy could not tolerate her chemo schedule and she would not be able to receive infusions of Adriamycin and Cytoxan in one scheduled treatment. This would extend Tracy's weeks on chemo, but it was hoped that she would feel better and be able to function when given the drugs separately.

Dr. Lin was right. Tracy's third round of chemo, on August 25, was tolerated with fewer side effects. She received a round of Adriamycin alone. The "queasies" still lasted for several days, but at least her white cells did not drop so dramatically that she was hospitalized.

Date: Wednesday, September 4, 2005
Subject: Chemo "4" Next Time!

Hi Everyone!

We had an incredible weekend with Tracy. The nausea from her third chemo treatment subsided just in time for her cousin Amanda's wedding on Saturday, September 3. Trace did have eight days of nonstop "queasiness," but on Saturday, she was feeling great!

When she arrived here at the house, I had a big lunch ready for her since she goes from being unable to eat to eating everything that isn't tied down.

Grady and I had to leave early for the wedding. He was singing and we had last-minute setup and sound checks to do with our sound techs, Dan and Gayle.

When Tracy arrived at the church, I couldn't help but "be thankful".... She looked terrific! If you didn't know what she had been going through, you never would have guessed. She looked beautiful!

This was a huge blessing for my mom. It was the first time she had seen Tracy since the beginning of July. Until now, Tracy had simply been too sick to come for a visit.

It was such a delight to be with Tracy at the reception. Watching her scarf down her prime rib dinner the way she did, I expected mine to mysteriously vanish if I turned my head....no nausea to report at the reception!

She and Antonio danced...and danced...and danced.

Grady and I caved in around 10:30 PM to head home. Tracy and Antonio were among the last guests to leave...enjoying family and friends while feeling well enough to enjoy the party. They came home shortly after midnight.

Seeing her having such fun gave me one of the first night's sleep I've had in a month! Maybe we just needed to be together to share a really wonderful time...and to be able to laugh together. I finally had some peace...and I believe she IS on her way to wellness.

In the morning, after Grady left for church, she crawled in bed beside me and we laughed, talked, and reflected on the highlights of the wedding. What a blessing it was that she was feeling so good and had a great evening with her cousins, aunts, and uncles. There was a feeling of "hope" that there really will be an end to the bad days.

Blessings and Love,

Kathy

Tonx was still sleeping when Tracy slipped out of their room and knocked on our bedroom door to visit with her father and me the morning after the wedding. As soon as Grady got up to start the coffee, Tracy slipped under the covers and into the spot he had vacated.

As beautiful as Tracy looked at the wedding, it was Tracy the cancer patient snuggled in the blankets and in my bed that next morning. Although Tracy's head had been shaved in July, some of her hair continued to grow. It was sparse...sort of like a badly seeded lawn. But it was trying against the odds to grow!

Her eyelashes and eyebrows were courageously trying to hang on. Many had fallen out, unable to stand against the chemotherapy that does not distinguish types of fast-growing cells, thus killing the cells that promote hair growth. She was in a battle, and the wounds of that war were showing.

Despite her tattered appearance, as we talked and laughed that morning, I saw a young woman who refused to be knocked down for the count. She would rise to her feet again, as friends cheered her on and lifted her in prayer.

Chapter 9

God's Favor

Sent: Sunday, September 25, 2005 7:13 PM

Subject: Clean Genes!!!!!!

Hi Everyone.... I have good news concerning Tracy!

On September 16, last Friday, Tracy drove herself home to New Hampshire for Mom's 85th birthday. Trace was feeling that well! It seems important to be together for special occasions (or any occasion) given the events of this past year.

Tracy shared stories about her students, how happy she is at Milton Academy, and how she told her students that she is presently going through chemo (and she made the announcement funny as only Tracy can do!). She told them she had "lost" her hair. She said, "To some of you that may sound like a very careless thing to do but...(for her) it meant being halfway through chemotherapy for cancer and that was a successful milestone!"

Her students clapped and cheered at her enthusiasm, honesty, and openness about what she is going through. She has left it open-ended and invited students to ask her questions about her treatment for cancer. And they are asking questions.

We all had a wonderful evening celebrating Mom's birthday. But when we got home, the depth of Tracy's fears and honesty poured forth in a sea of tears. I'm so glad my relationship with Tracy has matured to the point that it has and she can "unload" on me. She knows that through this whole ordeal, my relationship with the Lord has become even stronger and a source of "Living Water" for her to draw from.

Her concerns and fears were for the results she expected on the genetic tests that she thought would be back the first week in October. She sobbed as she told me she could not handle the thought of more surgery, including the removal of ovaries.

She said, "Mom, I'm trying so hard to accept why God would allow this to happen to me, but I wanted so much to be a mother. I keep hoping that when the chemo and radiation is over I still might. But if the tests indicate the cancer is genetic...I just can't face that."

I could only listen to her heart, hold her...and try to encourage her. She cannot look that far ahead. Again, I told her to pull in her sights to the next hour and to trust that God knows her heart, has heard our cries and our prayers for "clean genes," and He is a God of mercy.

Tracy was surprised on Thursday when she went for her first infusion of Taxol, the next chemo drug in her treatment. The doctor who did her genetic profiling had Tracy's reports and walked into Dr. Lin's office. Tracy just looked at the doctor and reached for the tissue box on Dr. Lin's desk. The tests were back.... **"CLEAN GENES!!!!!!!!"**

God IS a God of mercy! Tracy was filled with such relief and hope.

Tracy's first Taxol treatment produced normal reactions.... No nausea! Praise the Lord! The side effects are extremely intense flu-like symptoms for two to three days with body aches and even painful skin; but Tracy is so relieved not to have the "queasies"! She was even able to teach on Friday before the side effects became too severe.

Trace is hoping that tomorrow she will feel less achy and able to teach on Monday morning.

Antonio is the new assistant coach for the soccer team at Milton Academy. And he is getting a pay check for having fun! As he is meeting more of the staff, he has found staffers who are from Spain and other countries in Europe. For him, there is a connection.

We are all able to see, now, that Antonio's unemployment was a blessing. Their needs were completely met by God as He provided this teaching position at Milton Academy for Tracy. We are so thankful and we do rejoice in God's goodness!

Again, I want to thank those of you who have stood beside "this" little family in prayer, support, encouragement, and love from the first email I sent out early in the summer announcing that Tracy had "a lump...please pray." I can tell you in all honesty, I don't believe I could have made it through and been a real mom to my child without you upholding me in prayer. God has been SO CLOSE! I have all but been able to physically touch Him. His presence has carried me and allowed me to be strength for Tracy.... Through the pain, the disappointments, the fears, we have been lifted by your prayers. As our lives are being "broken," we are being made "perfect" in Him.

Jesus never promised to keep us from trials and pain.... He **did promise** He would "never leave us nor forsake us." He did not keep Shadrach, Meshach, and Abednego **from** the fiery furnace, but was **with** them and protected them **in** the fiery furnace. God is good...especially in bad times when we surrender into His goodness and grace.

Thank you, again. God does hear our cries.... "Clean Genes"... Thank you, Jesus!

Blessings and Love,

Kathy

With the changes that Dr. Lin made in Tracy's treatment plan in late August, life became tolerable, but this extended her weeks of chemotherapy into December. Under the new plan, once Tracy finished the "A" (Adriamycin), she started a third chemo drug, Taxol. The last two doses of the Cytoxan (that her body could not tolerate in combination with the Adriamycin) were reintroduced into her script after the Taxol.

With concerns about Tracy's teaching schedule as the weeks of chemo extended deeper into the school year, I cried out to the Lord for His favor to be upon her. I prayed that she would not become overwhelmed with her school responsibilities or teaching duties.

All of Tracy's chemo infusions were on Thursdays, a day that her class load was light, making it easy for her to arrange her appointments at Dana-Farber. She usually felt okay the day after her infusion, but still, Friday's class activities were built around student creativity projects, as her energy began to dwindle through the day. She rested as much as possible over the weekend and organized her lesson plans for the upcoming week.

The effects of Thursday's infusions lingered into Monday. She was still exhausted. But after teaching her morning classes, she had a three-hour break around lunchtime, providing an opportunity for her to return to her apartment and rest. With an opportunity to nap, she had the energy to teach her final class of the day.

Tuesdays were the longest and hardest. She managed to teach all of her classes, but it was difficult. There were times when she did not have the strength to sit through the required weekly evening staff meetings, but everyone understood.

On Wednesdays, her last class of the day finished late morning. Tracy's responsibilities for dorm duty began at 3:00. Her apartment connected to the dorm, making it convenient to rest before her duty time started. She managed her assigned duty until 9:00 p.m., but then the effects of chemo kicked in and fatigue made it impossible for her to supervise the forty girls in her charge all evening long. Antonio stepped in to complete whatever Tracy was physically unable to do. He oversaw room check and "lights out" at 11:00 p.m., wrote the evening dorm report, and walked the corridors of the dorm for the final room check at 1:00 a.m. before settling in for the night.

Tracy's Taxol infusions took most of the day, as the chemotherapy dripped into her body over a six-hour period. To prevent allergic reactions, she was given Benadryl, and for Tracy that meant sleeping through most of the treatment.

Taxol and the derivatives of this drug often cause neuropathy—nerve damage that can result in numbness and tingling in the hands and feet—

and muscle pain. After Tracy's first dose of Taxol, she experienced minor numbness and extreme muscle pain. Dr. Lin was practically confounded. With each infusion of Taxol, Tracy spent the entire weekend in bed with body aches that matched the physical pain associated with a severe case of flu. She was very happy to have a calm stomach, but she wondered if it was worth the "swap" to be in bed for almost three days after the infusion with body pain this intense.

As a teacher, it was also necessary to hold a pencil to correct papers. The numbness in her fingers became an obstacle. There were times when it was essential for her to become creative, planning lessons that worked within her limitations.

Although normalcy often returns once Taxol is finished, some people never fully regain feeling in their fingers and feet. It's a "wait and see"; waiting over a period of years in some cases. For Tracy, it became a career concern. She worried how long or permanent the effects of the drug would be as feeling and sensitivity worsened with each treatment. She dreaded the weekends after her treatments and being incapacitated by the muscle pain associated with the Taxol.

When he was hired as the assistant soccer coach, Tonx loved having a job on campus, and who was better qualified than a European! He was still free to help Tracy and support her with all of the things she was unable to accomplish on her own.

Coaching on the weekends kept Tonx from going stir crazy while Tracy rested. It felt good to work. Considering his devotion and the endless hours he spent caring for Tracy, the social aspects of having a job were as important as the paycheck.

There is no way to put a dollar value on a caretaker's worth. It's tough duty. Cancer is a demanding illness. But still, I'm sure that for Tonx, being unemployed and not producing an income was difficult, even though we saw his devotion and contribution as *priceless!*

Tracy amazed us with the energy she continued to invest in her students. Lots of people receiving chemo need time off from work. Granted, Tracy got off to a tough start, and side effects consumed her weekends. But overall she functioned well through the week. She missed very little time from work thanks to the way her teaching schedule *fell into place*. I can see

God's hand was on her scheduling and His grace and favor made it possible for her to fulfill her responsibilities to her employer and her students. Her schedule could not have worked better if God himself had made Tracy's daily planner and sent it Special Delivery to the department head to be commissioned and followed.

On November 9, 2005, I sent this email as Tracy battled her emotions.

Subject: Update on Tracy

Hi Everyone…

Please Pray for Tracy to be at peace, believing that she is HEALED!

Tracy is often a little ahead of herself. A few weeks ago she had an emotional meltdown. Fears of EVER having to go through this again overwhelmed her.

Sometimes being "Tracy's Mom" is not easy. I feel I need the faith of Moses as he stood believing God to part the Red Sea!

…I pour my faith into Tracy, believing God to calm her heart…to bring her peace and calm the churning of her fears. I have had the dauntless task of encouraging her to trust that the cancer that was in her body is no longer *her* cancer. It's gone! It's sitting in some research lab frozen for science.

We have learned some facts about the cancer that she had, and they are worth sharing.

This type of cancer is among the least common forms of breast cancer. Tracy is "triple-negative." That means the cancer was not fed by hormones or proteins. It's a wildcard. Research scientists don't know what feeds it.

Only 15 percent* of breast cancers are of this variety, and they are usually found in younger women. (*Interjected updated percentage. This is the figure from 2008 studies. In 2005, the percentage of *diagnosed* triple-negative was slightly lower.)

It is one of the most aggressive forms of breast cancer. Research has only begun to understand this type and the most effective means of treatment in the last five years.

And last and most important: **For us to be able to truly breathe easy, Tracy must remain cancer free for five years! Please pray that our God, the Great Physician, would heal, clean, and protect every healthy cell.... Pray cancer would never again invade any cell in Tracy's entire body!**

Tracy still needs to make up the two doses of chemo she could not tolerate in the beginning. This is the chemo that she feared had caused her white blood count to drop and put her in the hospital. It also made her nauseous for up to nine days!

The timing of her infusion has put Thanksgiving in jeopardy. My family has a big gathering for Thanksgiving, and my mom will leave for Florida with my sister shortly after the holiday. Tracy wants very much to be home and with the family, but she has already asked if Grady and I would spend the holiday with her if she is admitted into the hospital again. My heart hurts for her....

Pray that her white blood cell count would not drop to the point of putting her in the hospital and ruining Thanksgiving for her. We would indeed have much (again) to give thanks for...to all enjoy the holiday table together!

Tracy finishes chemo on December 1. She and Antonio will fly to Madrid for Christmas. (I am not convinced such a long trip is wise so soon after completing chemo...but....) When Trace returns, she will begin radiation.

Antonio has recently begun teaching full time at a (public) high school. As delighted and happy as Tracy is with her students, Antonio is at the opposite extreme. Many of his students are tough, angry kids who feel they have nothing to lose and do not see school offers anything to gain.

Pray for these kids.... Pray that somehow God would touch Antonio and he might impact their lives. This is more of a challenge than Antonio was expecting.

Love,

Kathy

As much as Tracy wanted to believe the cancer was gone, she was oppressed and plagued by fear that it was not.

I found myself feeling the only way I could help her (and myself) was to spend time each day walking for my physical well-being, and praying the entire time to bolster my spiritual well-being. For years I had been a "prayer walker," but more than ever there was greater commitment to the "exercise in faith" as I walked and prayed three miles each day.

Antonio was having difficulty as a new teacher, and Tracy was doing all she could to help him in this new venture. In the public school where Tonx was hired, there seemed to be a revolving door for teachers in the foreign language department. There had been such a turnover, the position was opened to college graduates with a comprehensive background in Spanish to broaden the number of candidates who might apply for the position. Obviously, Tonx spoke the language flawlessly, but teaching the language to high school students was a challenge. If there is one thing that can be said about Antonio, he's tenacious. He's no quitter. He'll hang in there no matter what, and by golly, that was his approach to teaching.

Tracy had saved all of her lesson plans through her many years as a teacher. She worked with Tonx, modifying the lessons as necessary, to help him as a novice teacher. But if there was ever a first year of teaching that was tested by fire, Tonx was in it.

I remembered these kids in prayer, and Tonx. I petitioned others to join me in lifting them all in prayer. At the time, I had no idea how great the Father's heart was for these teens.

Time and time again the Lord repeatedly brought Antonio's students to my remembrance in prayer.... And I prayed.

Chapter 10

Thanksgiving

In the weeks leading up to Thanksgiving, as I walked and prayed, there were several things the Lord seemed to be speaking to my heart. I worked harder at being sensitive and listening for God's voice. I also spent more time praying for others even though my own prayer boat was overloaded and about to capsize.

One morning, I received an email from Pauline. Our friend Carleen needed prayer. Pauline had noticed Carleen distancing herself from friends and suspected she was depressed. As I walked and prayed, I asked the Lord how we could reach out to Carleen in some special way. Suddenly, in my spirit I sensed, "Calgon, take me away!" That was a line from an old TV commercial for a powdered bath product. Carleen used to dramatically use that line from the commercial whenever life became overwhelming.

"Lord, you're kidding, right??? Well, okay…if you say so."

I sent an email to Pauline. "Pauline, can you buy a candle and some bubble bath and bring it to Carleen this weekend?"

"Yes, I think so. If not, Carleen's husband works nearby and I'll make sure I get it to him the first of the week."

On Friday, I heard from Pauline. "I bought Carleen bubble bath and a *card*."

As I read the email, I began to talk out loud to the Lord. "Lord? I thought I sensed that Carleen needed to receive bubble bath and a *candle*. Did I hear wrong? Should I tell Pauline I really think a candle needs to be in this care package from us? I don't know Pauline's financial condition. Is a candle too much for her to buy at this time? I don't know what to do. I'm so sure in my spirit I heard bubble bath and *candle*.... I'm troubled that Pauline got bubble bath and a *card*.

"I'm going to trust you, Lord. You need to make this right for Carleen, and if she needs a candle, **Pauline will get a candle!**"

On Monday morning I received an email from Pauline.

"YOU ARE JUST NOT GOING TO BELIEVE THIS! On Friday night, a friend of mine, and Carleen's, came to my house looking very confused as she stood at my door. She said, 'I was leaving work and I had this candle, and I had the strongest feeling that I needed to bring it to you. Do you need a *candle????*'"

I burst out laughing when I read Pauline's email.

Carleen began to cry when she opened her care package and card from Pauline, me and Sue. "You guys.... I was having myself a private pity party, and feeling forgotten by my friends. You are all so busy with the problems you are facing. I knew I was just being silly; I know that you love me. I just couldn't seem to snap out of it. I was telling the Lord how lonely I felt. This is such a gift from the Lord. I love you guys so much!"

God indeed cares about the smallest details when our hearts hurt. He is a comforting and loving Father who has all of the time in the world to listen to our pain and He sends friends to rally around us when we are hurting.

Exactly one week before Thanksgiving, Tracy had the first of the two chemo rounds she needed to make up. Breaking up the A/C and giving them separately seemed to be the right thing to do. She had done well with the Adriamycin alone. Dr. Lin felt certain she would manage her last two rounds of the Cytoxan without another hospital stay. Tracy wanted to trust Dr. Lin's expertise, but she found it difficult to hope for the best when so many times her reactions surprised even the experts. Tracy was gripped with fear.... Thanksgiving hung in the balance.

Emotionally, I was running back and forth between my mom and Tracy and their needs. Mom was in the hospital with congestive heart failure and very ill. I was constantly on the phone with family and nurses and then sending out email "updates" requesting prayer as I received new information. I walked...and I prayed for Mom and for Tracy.

As well as Tracy did through the weekend after receiving her chemotherapy, Mom was doing poorly at our local hospital. On Monday, it was the other way around. Tracy was doing poorly as her blood counts began to decline, and Mom began to stabilize.

Tuesday night, Tracy was reduced to tears as we talked. She was feeling worse as her blood counts dwindled. The dreaded temperature that would send her to the hospital for the umpteenth time was 100.5, and she was hovering close to it. We were sure if her body would respond to the Neulasta shot, she would begin to feel better.

This was Tracy's first Thanksgiving at home in years and a holiday she had sincerely missed while living in Spain. She bemoaned the possibility of being without family and in the hospital. My heart broke for her. She cried as fear and frustration gripped her emotions. Together we prayed over the phone. We prayed that God would give us the holiday together as a family...all of us.

When we are weakest, God is our strength.

Subject: Re: Tracy...Wed. A.M., November 23, 2005

Miracle of miracles! I spoke with Tracy last night. During the night after praying with her on the phone, Tracy had a **complete turnaround!!!!!** This is amazing and SO incredible! **Tracy woke up in the morning feeling energetic, well, no pain...completely great!**

This really blows our minds. Logic says this has happened because her new blood cells that were developing to replace the ones that died after the chemo have grown with supernatural speed. WOW! She and Antonio will be coming this afternoon, and we will all be at the Thanksgiving table together. Mom is being released from the hospital this morning. We are so thankful and excited!

Thank you, Lord, for meeting the desires of our hearts and hearing our prayers. This will be a true day of "Thanksgiving"! Thank you all for praying!

Blessings and Love,

Kathy

Gathering together at the Thanksgiving tables, there were twenty-three; it was a joyous occasion. Tracy was with us. Mom was still very weak from the seven days she had spent in the hospital…but she was able to come.

There was no way to escape Dad's absence at the table. In remembrance of him, a candle flickered. Despite our hearts missing Dad, we had so many reasons to give thanks. Before enjoying the feast my sister, Barb, had graciously prepared, Grady reminded us of God's blessings as he led us in prayer…a prayer of thanks.

The afternoon turned to evening, and then into night. Trace and Antonio slept at our house rather than drive back to Milton after such a long day.

There are some things I don't believe Trace will ever outgrow. She always loved coming into our bedroom when she first woke up, even as a teen. She always had lots to talk about after a night's sleep! Just as she did after her cousin's wedding in September, as soon as her father vacated his place in our bed to go downstairs for coffee, Trace made a beeline under the warm covers.

Tracy talks to me on so many levels. Sometimes woman to woman, sometimes as a daughter, and then there are the times she is like a best friend. That morning, she was especially happy as she talked about having one final round of chemotherapy to finish.

She talked about starting radiation. On she chattered about how happy she was to have the weeks off from teaching at Christmastime, and how she looked forward to going to Spain to celebrate Christmas with Antonio's family. Then the conversation bounced back to the fun of Thanksgiving with our family. On and on and on she went. It was wonderful to see her happy and laughing.

After the long months of chemotherapy accumulating in her system, even when Tracy was wearing makeup, it was evident that she was a cancer patient. It was easy to tell. Just to add to her side effects, her hormones were as wacky as they could be. If her exuberant chatter and mood swings (at times) didn't personify the fact that her hormones were affected, hot flashes would. She would be freezing one minute and then red-faced and perspiring the next. Without warning, in mid-sentence, a burst of heat overtook her body. She ripped the sleep cap from her head and threw back the down comforter.

There is "bald" as a result of going through chemotherapy, and then there is *bald!* Beneath her light blue sleep cap, Tracy didn't so much as have downy baby chicken fuzz. In the *glow* of her bald head, the effects of the chemo were more pronounced.

As I looked into her face in this vulnerable condition, I saw that all but three of her eyelashes had succumbed to chemotherapy. Her eyebrows were barely distinguishable.

She looked so plain...like the face of a blank "Muppet" waiting to have the added character of features to give her face "personality." Tracy looked battered and worn from the war she had been through. But there was a sparkle in her eyes, and as I looked into them, I saw *hope.* "Hope" that the finish line was just ahead.

Five months of the battle was behind her. Five months of the race was in the past. There was one final round of chemotherapy ahead and then a break from treatment for one month. (What a Christmas gift: freedom from chemotherapy and the hospital!) With the arrival of the New Year, January 1, 2006, the home stretch and the finish line would be in sight as she began the weeks of radiation.

Chemotherapy was nearly finished! The final seven weeks and three days of radiation would begin with the new year; and then...and then...it would all be over and our family would return to *normal.*

There was hope that all of this would end. Tracy would be healthy and well...and HOPE was beautiful in the face of one who had been through so much!

From the very beginning of Tracy's many trips to the hospital, Grady and I assured Tracy that if there was ever a time that she needed us, we would come.

For Tracy's meeting with her radiation oncologist, she called us. Grady and I were more than glad to support Trace and add an extra set of ears as she met with Dr. Jennifer Bellon. We were also pleased to learn firsthand what radiation was all about.

Days before Christmas I sent an email.

Date: Wednesday, December 21, 2005
Subject: Tracy—One Month Closer

Merry Christmas Everyone!

On November 28, Grady and I took Tracy to her first meeting with her radiation oncologist. It was a great opportunity to fully come to an understanding about the course of Tracy's treatment.

Chemo kills cancer cells that may have been in her body systemically. The radiation is to treat any abnormal cells that may be trying to grow around the original lumpectomy site. The radiation is directed to just the breast area and where the lymph nodes were removed. Statistics prove there is a definite difference in the number of recurrences of breast cancer in women who have had radiation and chemotherapy, as opposed to those women who went through only chemotherapy (depending upon the type and stage of the cancer and doctors' recommendations). In Tracy's case, radiation is not an option but a *necessity.*

Please pray that the Lord would continue to strengthen and heal her as only He can...physically and spiritually.

Tracy had her final chemo on December 1.... That is behind her. Hooray!!!!! It made her pretty sick, but despite feeling poorly, she continued working.

"Mom" was a little upset that "daughter" would not take the time her body needed to recover and rebuild itself! Not even twenty-four hours!

We celebrate the evidences of Tracy's steps toward all of this being behind her and her wellness! This past week we celebrated "HAIR"!!! Yup! On December 11, Tracy had the first signs that she will once more grow lovely locks. On December 17, her hair had grown to the great length of at least a quarter inch! You can almost watch it grow!

And the celebration of eye lashes. And eyebrows! They are all showing signs that once again they will appear and Tracy with be transformed from her "plain Muppet" look into the glorious woman she is!

Tracy has handled the changes in her appearance so well. This is a story she shared with me:

She had a male student who appeared in class wearing a baseball hat. When Tracy asked him to remove his cap, he gave her the excuse that he really didn't want to take his hat off because he had terrible "hat hair." Tracy said to him, "Well, John, just be thankful that you have hair.... Now please remove the hat."

Tracy and Antonio are leaving on Saturday to celebrate Christmas with Antonio's family. When they return, Tracy will begin radiation.

She has already received four freckle tattoos used for the radiation beams that are directed into her body. She will have thirty-three treatments starting on January 3. She will report to the hospital five days a week until the treatments are finished. Her doctor told us that she expects Tracy to do fine energy-wise through this process.

The hard part will be that the treatments will be taking a minimum two-hour bite out of every day, including her travel. That is two hours that Tracy will not have to prepare for classes, less time for devoting to the demands of life. Imagine YOUR week being shorter by ten or twelve hours for the next seven weeks!

Pray for Tracy to have organizational skills, extraordinary. Tracy is excellent in this area...but I think she will need all the help she can get.

Continued prayer for Antonio. Pray his students would catch the "vision"...the importance of education.

All of YOU remain in my prayers.... Merry Christmas!

Kathy

Chapter 11

Radiation

From Tracy's home at Milton Academy, the shortest route into Boston was through Mattapan: a township with an extremely rough reputation. Some of the teens living in Mattapan were Antonio's students.

Each time we drove through the town, Jubilee Church drew my attention. There were plenty of churches, but Jubilee stood out for some reason. There wasn't anything about the building itself that captured me…but there was something about that church. I began to pray for their ministry within the community.

Shortly before Christmas, I was watching the Boston evening news. The pastor from Jubilee Church, in Mattapan, was being interviewed. Recent gang violence caused this pastor to make a plea for help. He was appealing for mentors for these kids. He wanted the young people in Mattapan to find a better life than one filled with violence, gangs, and drugs.

Wow. That was confirmation from the Lord that God really cared for these kids. To Him they were worth saving. It was on the news. I had, indeed, been hearing correctly. The Lord had put it on my heart to pray for them. In turn, I had asked others through my emails to pray with me for them, and God had created a prayer chain for these teens.

As I prayed for Tracy and our family, the Lord reminded me to have compassion for others. Even those I did not know.

My mom had recovered well enough from her bout with congestive heart failure to return to the warmer weather in Florida and left with my sister Mim shortly before Christmas.

Tracy was in Spain.

As a family, we were so grateful and indebted to the wonderful care which Tracy had received at Dana-Farber that we made our gifts to each other gifts to the hospital to further research and finding a cure for cancer.

Christmas was a quiet day in our neighborhood. It was unusually warm, and Grady and I took a long walk. The snow that had fallen in early December had melted. We walked past homes with families who were inside, enjoying their Christmas morning. Our Christmas was quiet, in part by choice, in part by circumstance. I couldn't help but think about people who were alone because they had no choice. I thought about families coping with a new diagnosis of cancer. ...I remembered those feelings.

Our daughter was finally on her way to wellness, and she was celebrating *life* with her husband. She had choices. She was strong enough to enjoy those choices. We were happy that she could celebrate Christmas in Spain without being tied to hospitals.

We returned to our home and put an inviting fire in the fireplace and reflected on the true meaning of Christmas. We remembered the birth of the Christ child to a virgin more than 2000 years ago. Because of His birth, our lives were different. He was the gift who brought promise and gave purpose and meaning to our very existence.

Grady and I were alone for the holiday, but there was no reason for sadness…only joy!

Trace and Tonx flew home from Madrid on New Year's Day. When Tracy arrived, she was ill and running a temperature. She was admitted into the hospital. The fact that she had a raging headache for three weeks gave Dr. Lin concern, and she promptly ordered a CT scan. She had to be certain that a stray cancer cell had not spread the disease to Tracy's brain.

I was so sure that Tracy was cancer free and healed that for once, I was not concerned. I was, however, not happy that Tracy had traveled without wearing a surgical mask to help protect her weakened immune system from airborne viruses. I was positive she had a virus, and I felt miffed that she was sick enough to be back in the hospital, and only days before beginning radiation!

Other than being dehydrated and having a minor bacterial infection, tests showed nothing abnormal. The timing to start radiation after chemo is precise. Tracy's trial run for radiation was scheduled on Tuesday afternoon. She was released from her hospital bed just in time for her trial run appointment and in time for her first radiation treatment on Wednesday, January 4, 2006.

One of the most important things I learned at Tracy's appointment with Radiation Oncologist Dr. Jennifer Bellon is how critical it is not to miss any appointments. Come sleet, snow, tornado, or hurricane, the radiation had to be done! In early December, I was worried about how severe the winter might be. What about the road conditions, and what if Tracy had to travel alone in a blizzard? Trace scheduled her appointments late in the day for most days. However, it takes a few weeks before a permanent appointment block is established. A few of her first appointments were during normal school hours, while Tonx was working.

I became hyper-focused on Tracy's safety as she traveled to her appointments. I prayed for clear roads...no snow, ice, traffic...anything that might be a hindrance to her radiation appointments. I was asking the Lord to "clear the way." I became so focused on the winter weather, it was practically an obsession. I prayed for Tracy's safety and angels to encamp about her and to protect her as she traveled.

Some of my close friends and family teased and laughed about my "prayer march for clear roads." I walked and prayed and prayed and walked, pleading with the Lord as I begged for Him to keep the roads free of snow and ice...praying Tracy would not miss any of her appointments and her life would not be in jeopardy as she traveled.

On Friday, February 10, 2006, as Tracy was nearing the end of her radiation treatments, I shared this testimony of God's goodness and answer to prayer.

Subject: Tracy—A testimony

Hi Everyone,

It's been a long, up and down, emotionally draining road since that phone call from Tracy on June 24, 2005. And now, here we are just a few more radiation treatments left to go! Tracy will finish radiation next Friday, February 17, 2006.

Overall, Tracy is doing pretty well with the radiation. She is tired. She has second-degree radiation burns that don't feel like burns but a constant ache that encompasses most of her ribcage and the site where the cancer was removed. But she is doing pretty well!

Her entire head is now covered with hair; it is still a mite short, but I think it has come back thicker than ever. The color seems to be the same. I think it looks like it is going to have more body than it did before. Chemo often changes straight hair to curly. Tracy looks really good!

I have a neat story to share:

The week of January 15 was a miserable week for Tracy. (No, that's not the neat part.) Trace had run another high temp and ended up back in Brigham and Women's Emergency Department. Fortunately, this was not serious. She had a temp and a terrible cold.

I was spending hours in prayer and seeking God for her; one of the things that I felt impressed to pray about was for Tracy to begin to confess her healing...in front of Antonio. And that she begin giving the Lord the glory and honor He is due. It seemed VERY important to me to begin to hear these praises from her lips! This is what happened....

Sunday, January 22, was Grady's birthday, and of course all he really wanted for his birthday was a few hours with his daughter. It was Tracy's hope that she would be able to come to visit, but as the week was unfolding, she told us she couldn't come; she was behind in her lesson planning. My heart was heavy.

All week I had been praying for "a grain of evidence" of Tracy's heart honoring God for her healing.

I attended the 8:30 morning service at church and felt I "received my 'grain' of hope" in the message, "God is working behind the scenes." Sometimes we just can't see what He is doing...but He is 'DOING'!!!

When I got home at 10:30 AM, there was a message from Tracy. She and Antonio wanted to know if they could come for dinner and surprise her father.

I called her back. "OF COURSE YOU CAN COME!!!!!!!!"... Silly!

I whipped up a birthday cake, put a fire in the fireplace, fixed dinner, and was finished and waiting for them when they arrived at 1:15.

Grady would be late getting home from church. He was helping to install a new sound system and wouldn't arrive home until 1:30.

The first conversation Tracy and I had went something like this:

"Ya know, Mom, as Antonio and I were driving up here, I was looking around and I said to Antonio, 'Look.... There's no snow.... It's January.... It's nearly fifty degrees.... I KNOW MY MOTHER'S PRAYERS ARE ANSWERED!! ... I know I AM healed! My mother's biggest concern over my radiation treatment was that I needed to receive my treatment **every day. Snow, ice, sleet...it didn't matter. I needed to GO! My mother's prayers ARE answered.... There has been no snow! I'm HEALED!'"**

I was smiling SO-O-O hard I thought my face would break! (As my heart rejoiced in thanksgiving) I said to Tracy, "And as you are speaking 'these words' at this moment, again *I have* answered prayer. I have been praying for this evidence of healing from you (your lips) all week! ... YOU ARE HEALED!"

We had an incredible birthday. Grady was so surprised to find that Tracy and Antonio had come for dinner. What a day of blessings.

In the afterglow of the day, and once Tracy and Tonx had gone home, my heart was filled with joy and thanks for such a special day. That night my time with the Lord was so precious.

Sometimes I find myself feeling like a child who has just had a favorite story read, and loved it so much they wanted to hear it again, when receiving God's blessings. "Gee...was that real? Tell me *'that'* again, Lord!"

February 3 (the next weekend) was Tracy and Antonio's fifth wedding anniversary. They spent the weekend in Tamworth, New Hampshire (ninety minutes north of where we live). Tamworth is a quaint little New England village where they were married. On their way home to Milton, they came for dinner.

Once more, Tracy spoke confirmation of her trust and acceptance of her healing. "Mom, the next time that you are concerned about snow...and me traveling, do you think you could ask God to be a little more 'centrally located' with *where* He answers your prayers? There is no snow anyplace! You prayed **BIG**!!! I **know** I'm healed!!!"

We had to laugh. There is nothing *halfway* in how I plead with my Lord in prayer.... And there is **nothing** 'halfway' in how my Lord answers!

So what is the most valuable lesson that has been learned?

Tracy is already saying that she knows that it's still a little soon... but she wants to help others when they 'are' where she 'was,' as they make their way through and in their *healing from cancer.* No trial that the Lord **allows** in our lives is wasted.

The Scripture says, "God's word will go out and accomplish the purpose for which it was intended." Either God's Word is accepted and enlightens our lives or it is rejected and we remain blinded to the love and purpose we were created for. Trials draw us toward a relationship with our Creator...or we grit our teeth and sing, "I Did it My Way" One thing is for certain, cancer changes your life and how you view what is really important...life, death, and what is in between.

Tracy **knows** what is important now. She has been the recipient of hours of prayer, and she has seen its evidence and felt the power of that prayer on her. She **KNOWS**. Now it is up to her how she will allow the experience and God to change her.

The first time I went to Spain to visit her, in 1999, Tracy and I had an argument. I was confronting her about her relationship with the Lord...or more the LACK of her relationship with the Lord. We were arguing about (strangely) "what is important in this life."

Tracy blasted at me, "Mom, I don't believe God cares about the little things!"

I paused a moment and said, "Tracy, the Scripture says **God has every HAIR on your head counted**...and He sees every sparrow that falls.... I think He cares about the little things."

Chemo cost Tracy "every hair on her head.".... To God, the little things *ARE* important...every *little* thing!

Was that the Lord speaking through me in a prophetic manner to my daughter? I would not be so bold or arrogant to say. But how she sees things, how she views life and God, has to be reevaluated by her experience with cancer and losing "every hair on her head."

What is the most important thing I have learned? In a word, "PRAISE"!!! PRAISE!!! PRAISE!!!!

Psalm 34 has become my prayer, my battle cry, and my comfort. *The Message*, a paraphrased version of the Bible, says it this way:

"I bless God every chance I get; my lungs expand his praise. I live and breathe God; if things aren't going well, hear this and be happy: Join me in spreading the news; together let's get the word out. God met me more than halfway, he freed me from my anxious fears. Look at him; give him your warmest smile. Never hide your feelings from him. When I was desperate, I called out, and God got me out of a tight spot. God's angel sets up a circle of protection around us while we pray. Open your mouth and taste, open your eyes and see—how good God is. Blessed are you who run to him. Worship God if you want the best; worship opens doors to all his goodness...."

Praise....

Thank you all.... Tracy will be watched very closely for the next five years.

It's been a tough road to walk. We could not have made it though without your constant love, support, and prayers. We give all praise and honor and glory to Jesus! Praise Him! **He is Lord!**

With His Blessings and Love,

Kathy, Grady,

TRACY & Antonio

Kathy and Tracy on Tracy's first birthday. July 6, 1971

Tracy enjoying a ride on her "Grandpa's shoulders." September 1973

Tracy with Grady in Spain. March 1999

Tracy with Tara's kitten, "Baby Tigger."
October 1985

Tracy, Grady, and Kathy in Cordoba, Spain.
January 2002

Tracy had made a surprise visit home from Spain for her grandmother's birthday. This was our last family photo with Dad before his unexpected passing the following spring. Early October 2004

Tracy and Antonio "asleep on their feet" on New Year's Eve and only days before their move to the States. January 2005

"Our prize purchase for Tracy's Fair St. apartment was a 50s dinette set."

Tracy as she neared the end of chemotherapy, posing with Dr. Nancy
Lin at Dana-Farber. November 2005

Tracy and "Gram" at Cousin Amanda's wedding, looking just like
"a movie star!" September 2005

Chapter 12

Back to Normal

The more time that passed after Tracy's last chemo treatment in December 2005, the more her side effects associated with Taxol lessened. The feeling in her fingers began to improve. Pain in her feet lessened. Although, to this day, all of the effects from the Taxol have not gone away completely, she is better than she was. Mornings are the hardest. Those first steps on the floor after a night's sleep and inactivity are painful; stretching helps some, but this is all part of the process and the residual effects from the cancer-killing drugs.

Tracy remained physically fit, exercising the entire time she was not well. She had been an athlete and a cross country runner in high school and college and never quit. Her father was the one who encouraged her to be a runner, and for the two of them, it was part of their special bond and father/daughter time. Even when Tracy did not feel well, she always walked or would bike with Antonio to maintain fitness. She amazed me and so many others by her will to push herself to exercise and to be as strong as she could be, even when it was hard for her.

After radiation was finished on February 17, 2006, Dr. Lin and Tracy's radiation oncologist, Dr. Jennifer Bellon, each continued regular exams every six months. The four annual exams gave Tracy assurance that she was not simply being set free from their care and that she was still closely watched as a patient that they wanted to keep well!

While under such intense care as a cancer patient, it is not uncommon to have feelings of separation anxiety from the doctors who have become such a part of your life. There is a sense of security in seeing them so often. It sounds a little crazy, but it is not easy to make the transition back to "L.B.C."...life before cancer.

More than a year after finishing chemotherapy, one winter's day Trace and Tonx decided to come for a visit. The roads were covered with a heavy slush, and although most of the main roads coming from Massachusetts were clear, the back roads of New Hampshire were not!

As Tonx came down the untreated hill the turn for our road is on, he lost control of their SUV. The road was so slushy and slick, there was no way the turn could have been made successfully. The car slid across the entrance to our road and crashed over a four-foot embankment. It came to rest on its side and against a tree. Trapped inside, Tonx called us for help on his cell phone. I could hear Tracy's screams when I answered the phone. She was hanging in midair, her full weight supported by the seatbelt. The restraint pushed deep into her still painful, radiated ribcage. She had removed her coat during the drive, leaving little to protect her (in the way of extra padding) from the bite of the strap against her ribs.

Grady and I sped to their rescue. Before we got to them, Antonio had managed to open the sunroof as an escape hatch, and they had climbed up the banking and onto the road. Although Tracy was badly shaken, the only visible injury was a small cut where her eyeglasses jammed into the bridge of her nose during the impact.

After the accident, rib pain lingered as if to taunt her mind. Maybe the cancer wasn't really gone. The tumor that was removed in June 2005 had been resting on her rib; she continued to fret. In the weeks after the accident, fear overpowered Tracy's faith. What if one stray cancer cell survived and was growing?

Dr. Lin ordered a bone scan...just to be safe.

When Tracy called me with the results of the scan, her voice was filled with relief and excitement. "Mom, the bone scan was clear. No sign of cancer!"

"I told'ja you were healed. You've got to quit doubting and start trusting. Believe God, Tracy. You *are* healed! Move on with your life. Cancer is in your history, not in your future. It is finished!"

I had my own set of issues of what normal was to be. At the beginning of Tracy's illness, I had felt the Lord leading me to a new church: Grace Capital Church in Pembroke, New Hampshire. I didn't know at the time if I was permanently leaving our old church or if I would be returning. Grady had not made the change with me.

As I began to pray and seek the Lord concerning where we were to worship together, it became more and more clear we needed to be at "GCC." The Lord spoke to my heart through a series of odd and interesting events.

Pastor Peter Bonanno, the senior pastor, was preaching a series of messages entitled "Change is Good!" In a nutshell, Pastor Peter shared that God always nudges us forward and out of our comfort zone. Change does not always "feel" good. But God is good as He leads us forward. Following after those things of the Lord, initially we might not do so with a willing heart. There's always something "better" He is calling us toward. We only need to be willing to move. He leads us forward…not backward.

There was so much that I sincerely loved about Grace Capital Church, but there were a few obstacles I wasn't sure that I could continue to ignore. As wonderful as the music and the praise and worship were at Grace Capital, the sound was not good. As a pretty good recreational musician, the less than perfect sound quality would be more than Grady could simply overlook.

For the first seven months that I attended, I deliberately remained anonymous among the many hundreds of worshipers who flocked to the Sunday morning services. One of the few people I was connected with, however, was my niece Carla, and she was on the worship team.

One Sunday, I called her to ask a few questions about the sound system. Carla explained that those running sound and the pastors were aware of the problems but didn't know how to make corrections. They were frustrated. The church was a new, modern facility with a sound system that should have offered better quality than what was being produced. Carla suggested that I send an email to Mark, the Pastor of Worship and the Arts.

Some talents just evolve over time. I don't think I realized how much of an ear for sound I had developed. For more than twenty years, I had been a sound tech for Grady and with different music ministries.

I followed my niece Carla's suggestion and emailed Pastor Mark. "In all humility I'm writing to you concerning the sound ministry at church. I'm more than glad to try to help your sound techs with what I am hearing in the room, but I am equally glad to simply go to my prayer closet and pray for the worship teams and the sound ministry."

Pastor Mark emailed back: "We have been praying for someone to help us with this problem; can you be at worship practice on Friday night at 6:30?"

Before I even had time to think about it, the Lord had nudged me from my comfort zone to become the sound team leader at Grace Capital. Several times I questioned the Lord, "Lord, are You sure there isn't anyone among the eight hundred plus people who attend this church more qualified than I am for this job???"

God does not always call the most qualified; He does, however, call those willing to serve. **And sometimes that serving is in the most unexpected ways.**

It was a very special season of time. Becoming the sound team leader sealed the decision about which of the two churches Grady and I would attend. It was yet to be revealed why this was such an important church move for us. At that moment, we could not see what God was about to allow into our lives and why it was important for us to be connected to this church, its leaders, and a much larger community of believers. It was not an easy adjustment; the church was so much larger than what we were accustomed to. For Grady, it might even be fair to say he was angry about being in a larger church, where first impressions were that it would be more difficult to connect and make new friends. However, the Lord has an answer for everything (even if it might require willingness on our part to find those answers by putting one foot in front of the other and moving out from our comfort zone!).

As the sound team leader, I was responsible for assigning sound techs for our Sunday services, special events, and weddings. There was also a satellite church location for Grace Capital. With only a month's notice, Chris, the sound tech at the satellite church accepted a transfer with his job and moved away. Young and dedicated to the ministry, Chris knew much more than I, and I relied on him heavily for his technical skills. I was left trying to convince sound techs from the larger church to drive to the second location, set up the sound system each week, mix sound for the service, and break down the set, only to do it again the next week. It was not an easy job or ministry to sell.

Grady had the skills needed and agreed to take on the task. Through the winter months, he joined forces with a small group of hardy souls who set up a "portable church" out of the back of a truck at a rented movie theater on Sunday mornings. He developed close friendships with the people he worked with on those bitter cold mornings, and that became a starting point for him to feel he was a part of the Grace Capital Church community and ministry.

Our second point of connection was joining a small group meeting: cell groups (as cells make up the whole body) that met weekly. Within our cell group, close church family ties grew. "Cell" is a structured yet informal time for questions and discussion based on the Sunday morning message. It's a time to share, laugh, and pray together about personal concerns. I had no idea how important these strangers were about to become. There was a train wreck just ahead.

With the exception of the accident at the end of our street, Tracy was feeling incredibly well the winter of 2006–2007. She was not totally out of the woods as far as her doctors were concerned. But "Mom" was certain she was healed.

Antonio had survived the public school system and made changes for the 2006–2007 school year. Tonx became the real life lead character in *Mr. Holland's Opus*. He experienced a complete turnaround and instead of dreading each day, he couldn't wait for the school day to begin. He was hired at a private school and it was a match made in heaven. It was evident to everyone that Tonx had found an oasis and truly discovered his life's career and calling as a Spanish teacher. Life was good!

Shortly before Christmas, and a few weeks before the crash that totaled Tracy and Antonio's car, we were all shopping together. When we returned to our car and I positioned my left arm to buckle my seatbelt, I yelped with pain.

"Gee, Mom, you better see the doctor who did your last shoulder surgery and get that looked at."

It hadn't even crossed my mind; but Trace was right. Once more I had the beginning symptoms of frozen shoulder syndrome! *Oh, Lord!...*

Give me a break! As much as I loved being outside in the wintertime and running the snow blower, the years of clearing snow and chipping ice from the driveway had taken a toll on my shoulders. Both shoulders had been damaged. *Oh, man...not again!* I had hoped when I had the surgery on my right shoulder just after Tracy had moved to "Whoville," that would be my first and last surgery in this century.

During the weeks that followed, the symptoms became more prevalent. The pain and restriction in movement was undeniable. I was losing mobility with my left arm, rapidly. Much to my chagrin, I knew that Dr. "Mark" and I would soon be having another date in the operating room. This was not on the list of fun events for my social calendar. I procrastinated as long as possible. Finally, I could not stand the lack of function and I made an appointment for surgery on Wednesday afternoon, March 7, 2007.

Chapter 13

Déjà Vu

I began to wake from the anesthesia after the surgery to my left shoulder, and as soon as he was allowed, Grady came to sit with me while I fought my way out of the grogginess. Grady never knew what to do when I was sick; it rarely happened. It was awkward and unnatural for him to be the caregiver.

Dr. Mark came to check on my progress about the same time the fog clouding my mind began to clear. "I have some pictures of what we did inside your shoulder. There is no question; there's no way you could have regained a normal range of motion without surgery. It's done. And you'll be as good as new in a couple of months. You've been through this before, so you know the routine. I will order the same type of program as you had in 2005, after your right shoulder surgery. You will begin physical therapy on Friday."

"Friday??? You're kidding, right? Today's Wednesday, Mark."

"Yup. Friday. We can't let this go all weekend. You can start some mild therapy. It will freeze up if we don't keep it loose, and the surgery would be for nothing. I assume you want P.T. at the same facility as last time? I'll see you in about a week. Hang in there."

When my attending nurse coaxed me to my feet and fixed my arm in a sling, she handed Grady a bag with the clothes I had been wearing earlier. He looked a little surprised that my care was in his hands while there was a nurse present.

"Grade, I'm ready to go home. I need you to guide me to the bathroom and I need help getting dressed. I've only got one arm that works."

Never in the thirty-nine years that we had been husband and wife had I asked Grady to dress me! "I'm so embarrassed," Grady said as he pawed and fumbled with my clothes trying to figure out where to begin. I was still woozy and unsteady. In my frustration and helplessness as I struggled to assist, I only had three little words to lovingly encourage my husband. "GET OVER IT!"

By 4:30 that afternoon, we were home and I was miserable but settled in the recliner that would serve as my bed for the next many weeks. I still remember the bizarre dreams I had (from the pain medication, I'm sure). I dreamed my arm did not regain feeling or functionality and it remained a limp, dead, useless limb as it hung from my shoulder...a dream that was nearly prophetic.

The surgery to my left shoulder became a bitter source of frustration and aggravation. I worked diligently to regain mobility and range of motion, but the arm remained stuck and very limited in its use as weeks passed. Retrieving anything above eye level was practically impossible. Having had shoulder surgery before, I felt I knew what to expect. My right arm responded very well and I had almost complete range of motion in four weeks. But this time.... This was awful! I was a few days shy of my four-week check-up after the surgery and the two shoulders compared as equally as apples and a bucket full of rutabagas! There was no commonality.

Dr. Mark tried to encourage me. "Kathy, give it time. Your accomplishments after your surgery in 2005 were exceptional. This time you are below average in recovering, but there were some differences in the two shoulders. Your left shoulder had an abnormal amount of inflammation in the joint even before the surgery. Short term, that is causing added swelling and even greater restriction and additional pain. It will improve."

"Terrific. I need mobility now. I'm due next week for my annual mammogram, and I can't imagine how I'm going to raise my arm into position for the imaging."

While my shoulder healed, I took a hiatus from emailing. But there was one woman to whom I did continue to send notes of encouragement. That woman was Kelley Tuthill.

Kelley is a lovely young mother and news woman with Channel 5 News in Boston. Just before Christmas, she was diagnosed with HER2/neu breast cancer. Rather than remain silent about her diagnosis, Kelley shared her story publicly with her Channel 5 coworkers and her viewing audience.

Throughout her journey—start to finish—Channel 5 News followed as she shared what it is like to go through treatment for breast cancer. The news team followed her to the hospital, and each week they shared a segment during the evening news of "Kelley's Story…a battle against breast cancer."

When Kelley announced to her viewing audience that she had been diagnosed, my heart immediately went out to her. Kelley was Tracy's age, a professional woman, the mother of two pre-school little girls, and she was diagnosed with stage III breast cancer. (Later it was determined that she was stage II.) How frightening and devastating for this beautiful young woman. I emailed to encourage her by sharing my own daughter's story of beating cancer at the very same hospital where Kelley was being treated: Dana-Farber.

Kelley and I began to correspond. Before she received her first treatment of A/C, I encouraged her; if Tracy could make it through, she would make it through. Dana-Farber was the best. I had every confidence she could do this.

After each of her treatments, I encouraged her. "Kelley, the first round is behind you…three more infusions of A/C to go!" And then, "Kelley, you're half way there. You go, girl!"

With every five-minute segment updating "Kelley's Story" that Channel 5 News would broadcast, I wrote and cheered her on for being so unselfish and bringing attention to women's health. All women are at risk for breast cancer, not just women over age forty. Within our television viewing area, Kelley gave younger women who are diagnosed with breast cancer a face and a voice.

After our experience and our daughter's fight against the disease, I became one of Kelley's cheerleaders and was grateful to her for being so open about her battle. Knowledge is a key component for winning the fight against breast cancer.

After Tracy's diagnosis, my doctor and I agreed to change my annual routine. I would have my annual exam in the fall and schedule my mammogram six months later. That way, I would have a breast exam twice a year. Even though I knew the cancer Tracy had been diagnosed with was not genetic, I was not going to take any chances. Making such a simple change in my health care gave me the peace of mind that I was in the hands of professionals twice a year and nothing would be overlooked.

I had seen Dr. Richard for my annual physical and breast exam in October, and six months later, on Monday, April 9, 2007, I had my mammogram...painful left shoulder and all! If mammograms are not miserable enough, the recent surgery to my left shoulder was the match to the dynamite that made the exam *completely* intolerable.

As soon as I was released after the mammography, I drove to my mom's to prepare the house for her arrival after her winter in Florida. For years as a gift, I opened up her house and did her spring cleaning. When she arrived home, I had everything sparkling clean, and the refrigerator was stocked.

After finishing the cleaning at Mom's, I returned home to find a message on my answering machine. "This message is for Kathy Crews; Kathy, we have you scheduled tomorrow morning at 10:00 for a retake of your mammogram. Thank you."

"Well, maybe I have plans for 10:00! Wait a minute.... This doesn't sound right. Something's wrong. They're not giving me a callback number for a different retake date...**or a choice!** Oh, Lord God, no! NO! **NO!!!!!**"

I didn't tell Grady about the message. I knew that the largest percentile of callbacks for mammograms were false alarms. There was no reason to go off half crazy with worry; our family had just gone through breast cancer with Tracy. God wouldn't allow our family to go through this again. I chose to firmly grab any runaway fears. In all of my years of having mammograms, this was not the first time I had been called for a retake of films. This had to be a precaution...or a mistake. In 2001, I even had a biopsy on my left breast, and that came back negative. ...I was fine.

The following morning as I sat waiting for my name to be called for my retake films, I knew this had to be a false alarm.

After the films were retaken, I waited for the technician to return and tell me I could dress. When she returned, she said, "The radiologist would like another set of films on the left side."

I chalked up the request to the possibility that my injured shoulder had prevented me from proper alignment in the imaging machine. Back to the machine we went.

Again, I sat waiting to be released.

Once more the technician returned. "The radiologist would like another set of x-rays on your left side."

Lady, can we get it right next time? My shoulder can't do much more of this!

"Okay…I'll do the best I can. I know it's hard for you to position me with my injured shoulder…but I'll do my best to work with you."

Again, I waited. The technician returned. "The radiologist would like one more set…."

"Wait a minute. Obviously, the radiologist thinks he's seeing something. I think it's time for me to talk with him. We're not doing any more films."

I dressed and was led to a room where the radiologist had my films on the screen in front of him. I sat down beside the young doctor who had ordered the battery of films. And he began. "Do you see this area right here? This is an abnormal cluster of calcifications. There are about forty in this small area. And over here, about 3 centimeters from the larger circle, there is another, smaller cluster of eight or so."

He held a magnifying glass in front of the films and in the air circled over the clusters with his pen as he talked. He continued, "This is extremely 'worrisome.' I want you to see one of the specialists upstairs. I will ask our patient care advisor to come in and escort you to our cancer center."

There was an immediate disconnect between me and the doctor. I think he was expecting the woman before him to crumple into a heap, flooding the room with tears. He didn't know that I had already been through the worst news I ever could have heard when Tracy called to say to me, "Mom…it's cancer."

What this doctor did not know was that I knew better than he what I needed to do in seeking medical help. I didn't need to meet doctors at our local "Pretty Good Hospital"; through my daughter's experience, I knew who I needed to see.

I asked questions about the films before me. "I understand. I'll schedule an appointment with a surgeon I know in Newburyport, Massachusetts, for an opinion."

"Mrs. Crews, I don't think you do understand. You need to schedule with one of our doctors upstairs before leaving here today."

"Thank you for your concern. I'll make an appointment right away with a surgeon in Massachusetts. I really have some things I need to take care of today, and I will take care of this tomorrow."

The young doctor excused himself for a moment and returned with a patient care advisor. "Mrs. Crews, before you leave here today you must make an appointment upstairs."

I was beginning to feel equally as perturbed with this doctor as I was with the possible diagnosis! "I assure you, I will make that call tomorrow. I have shopping I must do for my eighty-six-year-old mother, who is arriving home after wintering in Florida. I will make the call for an appointment to see a surgeon tomorrow. I promise you, this will be taken care of. I have plans for today. I am *busy*."

As I was leaving, I was followed to the door while pamphlets were stuffed in my hands about the new cancer care unit at our local hospital.

I tried to be polite. "I'm sure the new facility is beautiful. But I really don't think it makes any sense for me to come here. My daughter just successfully completed her treatment for breast cancer at Dana-Farber in Boston. Because they are a cancer research hospital, and now with this unique oddity, *if* I do have breast cancer, that's where I think I need to begin...with their counsel first. And that's only *if* there is any possibility for concern. Don't you agree that is a reasonable plan to follow since we just finished treatment for breast cancer with her?"

"Well, I suppose so. But if you change your mind and we can—"

"Thank you so much. I am sure I will be fine but will call if I need your help."

That evening I told Grady about my morning with the young radiologist and that I would most likely need a biopsy. However, I would not jump to any conclusions until after consulting Tracy's surgeon in Newburyport.

The next week, I received a phone call from my gynecologist of seventeen years. "Kathy, I received your radiology report and a letter. The letter says you refused, after being asked three times, to see a doctor in the cancer unit?"

"Well, that's part of the truth. What else does the letter say, Dr. Richard?"

"The calcification clusters were concerning and of a 'worrisome' pattern. There were two clusters...left breast. Shadowing in right breast... inconclusive. Retake in six months on right breast."

"Does it say anything about my appointment with Tracy's surgeon in the letter?"

"No. There is no mention of your plans to see anyone. Kathy, I'm sorry. After what you have been through with your daughter, I should have known this would not be anything you would ignore. I wish you the best. Please have your new doctors send me their findings. Call if there is anything I can do."

"Thank you, Richard. I appreciate that. Hopefully, I'll see you in October."

After I had signed to take possession of all of my mammography films taken over the last five years and read the radiologist's report, I understood Dr. Richard's concern. From the young radiologist's impression during our meeting, he thought I was in total denial and unwilling to seek treatment. The truth was that cancer was just all too recent and familiar. Tracy was only fourteen months from having finished chemotherapy and radiation. We had been through nearly two years where breast cancer dominated our conversations. For me, there was no shock value to the disease...any longer.

Days after my conversation with Dr. Richard, I saw Tracy's surgeon in Newburyport. He agreed. The clusters didn't look good. He also read a very interesting line to me from one of the papers I had initialed before having my mammogram.

"Well, that's the first time I've seen that. You initialed this form that states that you understand that there is a 30 percent margin of error in the mammograms you are about to have." He peered over the tops of his glasses at me. "I guess they don't want to take any chances with lawsuits."

"You're kidding me! Unbelievable. That's like agreeing to play Russian roulette with a gun that has ten chambers and three of those chambers have bullets. That's crazy. Are mammograms *that* unreliable? What's the point if that is true?"

"No. I don't think they are that unreliable, but things are missed on occasion. And you do remember that the tumor Tracy had was not visible in her baseline mammogram. We knew it was there and it was 2 centimeters. But the mass could not be seen in any of the films that were taken before surgery. This facility is just being overly cautious."

He continued. "I do agree with the radiologist. The clusters are 'worrisome.'" (There was that word again.) "It might be nothing...but I've only seen a handful of cases where something that looked like this on a mammogram was not cancer. Let's palpate the area. In a cluster this size it's very likely we should be able to feel the mass if there is one there."

Pressing systematically where the calcifications were and where he expected to find a mass, the doctor scowled. "I would have thought in an area this large that the chances were good that I would palpate some sort of mass. I don't find anything. I would, however, recommend a biopsy and an MRI. You might be in the handful I've seen where this is nothing. But you need further tests before we can say that for certain."

After my appointment I felt relieved that no lump could be palpated. I still had a grain of hope that the biopsy would come back clear.

Tracy was stressed and stretched beyond her limits with year-end activities at school. I did not want to add to her overload with my "worrisome" mammogram. I was beginning to dislike that word immensely. "Worrisome." Each time I heard it, I envisioned ominous black billowing clouds on the horizon. I had to keep my emotions in check and not allow myself to become fearful. I had to believe there was not any reason for worry. God wasn't going to allow our family to go through the horror of cancer again. He is my loving Heavenly Father. He wouldn't do that.

I would go through the biopsy and MRI with Tracy's surgeon in Newburyport, and we would all live happily ever after when tests came back negative.

Coincidentally, Tracy called later in the day and after I had returned from Newburyport. Much to my dismay, Grady told Tracy that I had seen her surgeon, and why.

"Trace, it's nothing. I'm fine. I'm going to have these tests and I'm sure there is nothing to find. Dr. Richard didn't find anything with his exam in October, your surgeon didn't find anything today.... I'm sure it's nothing."

"Mom…what are you thinking! *I* didn't have a lump in November. And *I* didn't have a lump in March. But I had cancer in June! You get yourself to Boston and set up with doctors here for these tests! I'm emailing Dr. Lin right now and you will do *EXACTLY* as she recommends."

Tracy called in the reinforcements as she barked orders. "Dad, do you hear me? You make Mom come to Boston. I'm not going to let Mom have tests anyplace that Dr. Lin does not approve. You are going to listen to her recommendations!"

Trace had such confidence in her Boston doctors, no other place would do. This was late Friday afternoon. By 10:00 that night, Tracy had contacted Dr. Lin and forwarded Dr. Lin's response to me.

Dear Tracy,

I'm sorry to hear about your mom, but hopefully everything will work out. I would recommend this list of doctors. *[And she provided a list of names from which to choose.]* Though to be honest, just about any of the breast surgeons in our group are excellent. I'm cc'ing the new patient coordinator. If you could forward your mom's contact info, I will ask that your mom be given a call to schedule. The first step is to see a surgeon; once a diagnosis has been made, the surgeon could then refer on to a medical oncologist. I would, of course, be happy to see your mom, but think about whether you and your mom want the same oncologist or different oncologists, and if the latter, I can definitely refer her to my wonderful colleagues.

Nancy

I couldn't believe a doctor would respond in a non-emergency so quickly and with such concern! As Dr. Lin had promised, the new patient coordinator called on Monday morning. I had a strange feeling that the first surgeon on Dr. Lin's list should be my choice. I asked if Dr. Mehra Golshan had availability. He was available, and I was scheduled for the first of May.

Over the next few days, shock began to set in. I had a heaviness in my spirit and a million questions swirling inside my head. There was no doubt; Dr. Nancy Lin would be my oncologist if the tests proved I needed one.

Tracy immediately became my wilderness guide and took command as she made sure I stayed on the right path. She emailed Dr. Lin and asked her to call me to answer some of my questions. When Dr. Lin called, I explained what we knew (to this point). There were "worrisome" clusters of calcifications, but no mass presented in any of the many films that were taken. Nothing was palpable in October or by the surgeon in Newburyport a week ago. I faithfully had mammograms and annual checkups. I was better than average about physical exercise and walked three miles four times a week, and I consumed a pretty healthy diet...no tobacco ever, and rarely a glass of wine. What more could I possibly do?

Nancy listened and offered encouragement. "You have done everything you possibly could. It sounds like if there is cancer, and *if* it is not visible in a mammogram and cannot be detected while palpating, this has been found early and treatment will be less invasive than in Tracy's case. It is possible that only radiation will be required if it is at the initial stage of development and *if* we have caught this soon enough. Let's wait and see what Dr. Golshan finds and what a biopsy reveals."

Although Nancy's words were encouraging, cancer is an unnerving word, especially when it is directly attached to *your* health, personally.

On Sunday morning, when I reported to church for our 7:00 a.m. sound check, Pastor Peter sensed that something was bothering me. He asked, "Is everything alright?"

I tried to smile and told him I was "wading through some issues that were not so easy to wade through," but hopefully I'd have better news in a week or so.

Pastor looked squarely at me and said, "Listen closely to today's message. I think it will bring you a new perspective and hope for whatever it is that you are facing."

As Pastor Peter began to share the message the Lord had put on his heart, I nearly fell over backward and out of my post at the sound booth. The Scripture was from Acts 16:23–26...the story of Paul and Silas... beaten, in the dungeon of the prison, in stocks AND SINGING HYMNS AND PRAISES TO THE LORD...as others looked on...the exact same Scripture that the Lord had me bumping into every which way that I turned when Tracy was sick. The very same Scripture that led me to Grace Capital Church. The identical Scripture the Lord impressed upon my heart in 1998 during another difficult time.

Lord, what am I missing that You want me to learn? What did I NOT see in this Scripture when Tracy was fighting breast cancer? What didn't I learn the first time You stuck this Bible passage under my nose? Tell me!

Later that night, I emailed Pastor Peter and told him it appeared I had early stage breast cancer but it had not been confirmed. His response was gentle and compassionate, and he ended his note with a challenge for me to bring before the Lord. "Whatever the outcome, remember God's grace is always sufficient, Kathy."

My thoughts and emotions began to swing from one extreme to the other, as though they were riding a pendulum. "Hope" on one side... "anxiety" on the other. Back and forth I swung between the two extremes, trying all the while to grab "faith" as I passed the center point of the wild ride my emotions were dangling from. Knowing that "faith" would create stability in the here and now, faith remained just beyond my reach. In frustration, anger, and fear I cried out, *"Lord, you need to show me how to do this! I'm having a little trouble seeing how your grace is sufficient if I do have cancer. How could YOU allow our family to go through this horrible experience TWICE in less than two years? Show me HOW your grace is sufficient to face this...."*

It all felt like a nightmare...again. Shoulder surgery and Tracy's diagnosis of cancer. Shoulder surgery and now my diagnosis? It felt like déjà vu...a horrible, horrible case of *déjà vu*.

Chapter 14

Tests, Appointments, and More Tests

In March, Grady was scheduled to attend an upcoming business meeting in Hawaii. There was absolutely no way I would be left at home for that trip! All of the arrangements were in place; we were leaving on May 5 and would return home in exactly seven days. I was sure Dr. Golshan would make us cancel our plans and replace them with appointments for the tests I was facing in Boston.

Dr. Golshan wasn't at all like I thought he might be. I was apprehensive at our first appointment, and I wanted to distance myself from this new doctor. I should have seen the depth of his compassion during our first meeting, but I was blinded and swallowed up by the uncertainty of my fate.

He palpated the site where the tumor should have been found and agreed with everything Tracy's surgeon had told me two weeks earlier. He explained all of the possible scenarios and what the courses of treatment would be.

"First impressions are you have ductal carcinoma in situ: DCIS. If the cells have broken through the wall of the milk duct, it is an invasive form of cancer. We need to schedule a diagnostic stereotactic core biopsy, and that will tell us if this is a form of cancer or not. If it is cancer, you will need surgery: a lumpectomy or a mastectomy."

When Dr. Golshan said "or a mastectomy," I remember thinking, *Well, that's out of the question! Why is he even mentioning such a thing? There is nothing on the mammogram except a bunch of little white specks. No way!*

We told Dr. Golshan about our trip to Hawaii, and his kindness was evident. "Don't change your plans. A week is not going to make any difference one way or the other. If anything, you need a break from the anxiety this has caused. Go. Don't worry about this and enjoy your time. As soon as you get back we'll do the biopsies; just be sure to schedule the appointment with Linda before you leave."

I made the necessary appointments, and the next morning we boarded our flight for Kona, Hawaii.

I was still battling for all I was worth to gain back the function of my left arm. Physical therapy was still a part of my appointment calendar, and I was looking forward to physical therapy—my way! In Hawaii, I would have the opportunity to swim every day, snorkel, and sea kayak; all were physical activities that would strengthen the shoulder as well as encourage greater range of motion. Dr. Mark loved my P.T. plan.

Dr. Golshan was absolutely right about our need for a change of scenery and taking a break for mental health. I had not recognized what a churning stew I had been simmering in for nearly a month as I steadily became more and more anxious about the "worrisome" calcifications and still did not have any concrete answers. When we arrived in Hawaii, the anxiety dissipated in the soft and gentle "lomilomi breezes."

For a week, cancer did not exist. For a week, the world was beautiful beyond compare. For a week, my life revolved around the sea, the sun, and the aloha island spirit. Beyond the meetings Grady attended, we laughed, we played, and we gave thanks for such a wonderful respite from everything we had been going through and everything that was ahead and waiting for us back home. I didn't realize how laden down emotionally I had become until we were in a truly relaxing environment.

Shortly after our return, the endless battery of appointments began. Tracy and I had coordinated our appointments the day of my biopsy. She was due for a checkup with Dr. Lin at Dana-Farber. I was across the street at Brigham and Women's Hospital for the biopsies. (The two hospitals work together. Dana-Farber is a research and cancer hospital, and it is truly a "day" hospital. Brigham and Women's Hospital provides care where Dana-Farber leaves off. Dana-Farber patients have surgeries at Brigham and Women's and the Faulkner Hospital. The hospitals work harmoniously together.)

It wasn't until months later that I learned that while Tracy was in Nancy Lin's office, she completely broke down. Her own battle against breast cancer was much too fresh in her mind. And now I was next door and about to find out if the two "worrisome" calcification clusters in my left breast were, without question, cancer. She finally composed herself, and minutes before I was led into the procedure area, Tracy arrived to sit and wait with her father.

The biopsy I had in 2001 was not a pleasant ordeal. The nurses had a difficult time controlling the bleeding. It was my understanding that excessive bleeding was uncommon. I was optimistic that this would be a better experience.

I sent an email and shared about my Friday at the hospital on Monday, May 21, 2007.

Subject: Re: Biopsy

...All I can say is this: I certainly am glad that for these biopsies I was under the care of the best of the best doctors in Boston! Apparently, the platelets in my blood are still on vacation and a two-hour procedure took more than four hours because of excessive bleeding.... In fact, both wound sites continued to weep blood through yesterday morning. (Would someone please explain to me how it is that when the doctor instructs you to ice until all bleeding stops, it's NEVER 90 degrees outside but abnormally cold...like 40!?!?!)

Yesterday morning when I was finally able to shower, I was trying to find reasons to "give thanks." Emotionally, this is tough and I'm having a little bit of trouble. And you know what? I found my biggest reason to give thanks is YOU! As bad as this procedure was, I can't imagine how bad things would have been without prayer!

My medical support was incredible; everyone was so kind and patient. They did all they could possibly do to keep me comfortable during a very uncomfortable ordeal. The actual biopsies only took about fifteen to twenty minutes for each site. And most of the discomfort I had was because my *still* healing shoulder was compromised during the biopsies. I had to extend my arms in a range the shoulder does not have as yet.

I was so cold from being "iced" my teeth were chattering, as my nurse attempted to stop the bleeding. Not only were the wound sites being iced...but so was the shoulder! I was amazed how calm I remained despite my circumstances. I was worked on for four hours. Yet the time passed quickly, even though I was half frozen when we finished. God is good!

While Grady waited, Tracy stayed with him. I am thankful that she lives so close to the hospital. We went back to her house to allow the Friday night traffic leaving Boston to clear. I was emotionally and physically exhausted.

I guess I am most thankful for that "peace that surpasses all understanding."

I know how I am reacting in this; what I am feeling emotionally is beyond what is natural. Thank you for interceding for me. I have been at peace.

We should have the results from the biopsies by Wednesday. I'm still asking God for a miracle and that the tests would prove I AM CANCER FREE!!!!!!!!! Please continue to beg God for mercy for me.... My flesh is tired. I'm tired of being in perpetual recovery from one injury or another. I need a break. I just need a rest for a few years and some time on the mountaintops instead of trudging valleys of recovery. I need mercy.

Thank you for your prayers and support.

"And the peace of God, which transcends all understanding, will guard your hearts and your minds in Christ Jesus." Phil 4:7... Amen!!!!!!!

Blessings and Love,

Kathy

A few hours after I sent this email, Dr. Golshan called me with the biopsy results. Considering that the tissue samples were taken late Friday afternoon, I was in shock and disbelief when Dr. Golshan had the results on Monday afternoon and was calling.

At 6:30 p.m., I sent a second email as a follow-up to the one sent just a few hours earlier.

Subject: Re: Biopsy

Well... A phone call I expected in two or three days came this afternoon. My surgeon in Boston called at 3:00 p.m.... Both locations are cancerous.

I am dreading sharing this news with my mom. Please pray for her. I will try to find the courage and the time to see her sometime over the next few days.

Right off the cuff I can't think of a thing in the world I **really** need to learn by going through cancer. All I can say is if I ever needed your support in prayer...I need it now! Grady is a **terrible** nurse and he can't cook worth beans! Lord, help us!

Okay...reality.

This week I will be going back to Boston for an MRI and to meet with my surgeon. It appears we are safe to stall on the surgery for up to six weeks, and I really need at least three or four weeks to continue in P.T. for my shoulder. I'm sure you're all thinking, "What is she thinking? Cancer? And she's worried about her shoulder????" Trust me. Leading up to this I've been asking all of my medical support what is reasonable, and timely, and what can be done to work in coordination so that I'm not making any wrong choices in my treatment (jeopardizing my health or losing the benefit of the surgery on my shoulder that is improving so slowly). I feel confident I am being advised wisely.

Guys...I'm doing okay. It's the old saying, "How do you eat an elephant?" Answer: "One bite at a time."

I'm sure before I'm finished I will have covered the whole spectrum of emotion.... But in my first hours of knowing, I *believe and* "I **will be victorious** over cancer." I praise God that YOU are in my life!

Blessings and Love,
Kathy

I didn't cry. I did feel a bit like a "water balloon" as my life seemingly splattered before me. Breast cancer was found in not just one but both locations where calcifications had been extracted during the biopsy. I had cancer!

There was a strange relief in knowing there was finally something definite that we needed to be concerned about and we weren't just hanging in limbo. We could begin to move in the direction of finding the cure. This certainly was not the news I was looking for, but now we knew the abnormal cells had broken outside of the duct and it was an invasive cancer.

I thought of the advice I gave to Tracy so many times as she battled cancer. "Count your blessings, Tracy. What do you have to be thankful for?" And I thought to myself, *Well, at least I don't feel alone in this. I have Tracy and her experience and guidance; she is a wealth of information and support.*

I have a husband who will be at my side through this. And I have the best bunch of intercessory prayer warriors I could have. I had known most of the people who were praying for me for ten or more years.

Now that the diagnosis was confirmed, the first thing I immediately began to dread was how I would be able to find the words to tell my own mother, *"Mom...it's cancer."* How could I tell her *I* had been diagnosed with breast cancer too? How???

The first emails I sent out requesting prayer for myself went to a select few. Within twenty-four hours those prayer warriors began to send back emails of what they were sensing as they prayed. I was *totally* blown away at what the Lord was telling each person. The message was the same: "This is not about you, but about God's glory." Those who responded with this identical message lived in Maine, Wisconsin, New Hampshire, and New Jersey. None of them knew each other; each person was sensing in their spirit the same exact thing from the Lord as they prayed.

On Wednesday, the final confirmation of what the Lord was repeating came from Cherie at our church cell group meeting. I had not shared with our group about my appointments in Boston nor about the biopsies. I was still getting to know our cell family. Attending cell group was still a new experience. And at this point, I had shared prayer requests with only my very closest friends.

Somehow, Cherie transitioned from the subject we were discussing to something entirely different as she said, "I think Christians can be hard on each other during difficult times—almost judgmental. When I was ill a year ago, a close family friend challenged me by saying, 'There must be unrepentant sin in your life because you are ill.'"

Cherie explained her Biblical position. "Look at the book of Job (in the Bible). What sin was he unrepentant of? None. His livestock died, he lost support of his friends, his family, and he was sick with sores and boils. Awful things happened. God allowed all of that to happen in Job's life for HIS glory. It really had nothing to do with Job. All the while he continued to trust and believe in God's grace, mercy, and love through it all."

If Cherie's statement wasn't absolute confirmation and God's voice, I didn't know what was. This was about His glory.

As we finished our discussion and were voicing our prayer requests, Grady looked at me and said, "Kath, would you like to share what has happened?"

I looked at the faces all looking in my direction. I began to speak. "Monday I received a call from one of my new doctors in Boston. I have been diagnosed with breast cancer."

Eight mouths simultaneously fell open in shock. I had shared with our group about Tracy's battle against the disease, and now here I was, also facing breast cancer. Wendy broke the silence. "I knew it! As soon as you walked in here this evening, I saw something was different; you had such a presence of peace around you, I could see it!"

Denise found herself drawing back and thinking, *I could never do that! I could never go through breast cancer.* A few weeks later, Denise was diagnosed also. With her diagnosis, our cell group grew closer than most families, with a bond of love and concern for each other that is indescribable. In the months that followed, Denise and I relied heavily on the encouragement, support, and prayer from our cell group.

The next morning was Thursday, May 24, just before Memorial Day weekend. Grady and I had an appointment in Boston for the MRI that Dr. Golshan had ordered. I expected my reports to be delayed because of the holiday. There was no delay. On May 30, Dr. Golshan called. I noticed a difference in the tone of his voice immediately. "Kathy, this is Dr. Golshan. I have the test results. The MRI reveals a mass that is 7.5 centimeters by...."

I stood...completely numb. As the voltage jolt tore through my every fiber, I couldn't hear. Instantaneously I felt joy and sadness meshed together. "Joy" as I was swept to thoughts of heaven and then "sadness" as earthbound ties pulled me toward thoughts of my family. For the first time since "my" whole terrible nightmare began, I was nauseous and faint as disbelief paralyzed my senses the same way it did when Tracy called me with her diagnosis.

"I need you here to have bone scans and CT scans right away. Can you be here tomorrow at 9:00?"

I choked out an almost inaudible "yes."

Dr. Golshan reassured me, "We're going to get you through this. We will get you through this. If you have any questions, I'm here for you, and if I'm unavailable, leave a message with Linda and I will get back to you as soon as possible…. We will get you through."

Somehow the tone in Dr. Golshan's voice seemed to speak louder than the repetitious phrases he was using as he tried to sound reassuring. To me (in my spirit), I was sure this was not the news he was expecting. To me, it sounded like even my surgeon was feeling challenged, worried, or maybe surprised by the MRI and what it revealed.

With each step I had taken until this point, it had never crossed my mind that what I might be facing could be this serious; I'd go through some tests, and we would move on with life. Now, for the first time and with Dr. Golshan's call ordering scans, there was a reality that this *thing* might be in my vital organs and bones.

I sat silently, dumbfounded by the words that had me in a stranglehold and were choking the air out of my lungs. I began to wilt under the heaviness as I asked God, *"What if?"* I pondered the only two possibilities, and what that meant.

Two facts challenged my intellect and my faith as I turned the findings of the MRI over and over in my mind.

1. One of two things would happen: I would live…or I would die. If I lived, I won! If I died…if I died… What if I *died?* What choice did I have about this? *Hey, God… I'm a little busy down here. Check in with me in about another thirty or forty years.* No. It doesn't work that way. My heart and my soul belonged to the Lord. I had trusted my life to Him years ago. My faith was secure in Jesus as my Lord and Savior. If I died…if I died…I *still* won!

2. God was and is sovereign. I knew I had no control over the outcome and what was ahead of me. There was nothing I could do to change whatever it was God was allowing to happen in my life. I had no say in the matter. There was only one choice: trust in God's infinite wisdom and His providential will for me. Somehow, I had to totally surrender and be at peace.

I was certain my Heavenly Father did not just wake up one morning and say, "Oh my goodness! Kathy, one of my beloved children, has cancer! How on earth did that happen?"

I needed to learn God's purpose and what there was for me in this "suffering." But in the meantime, I also needed to fully trust that whatever happened, it was not because God had forgotten me. Somehow this trial... this journey of fighting cancer would be beneficial.

As I thought this through, Pastor Peter's words echoed in my mind: "Remember, God's grace is sufficient, Kathy." God was beginning to show me exactly how that is true. Already I was beginning to surrender myself into His hands and accept there was a path ahead of me I would not have chosen. It was not going to be easy. But as my loving Heavenly Father, He would be there with me every step of the way. His grace WOULD somehow be sufficient. He promises that in His Word, and His Word is truth! God had reasons for this that in my finite mind, I could not understand. This seemed so unreasonable! In my own wisdom, it was an impossible journey stretching ahead of me. But there was virtually nothing I could do to change what was. Life as I knew it was about to become *different*.

By cognitive choice, I began the process of melting into a new level of surrender and a turning point in my faith.

A few months before this entire ordeal of shoulder surgery and breast cancer diagnosis, I read one of Corrie ten Boom's books, *Tramp for the Lord*. It's a story about how Corrie traveled by faith to various places and shared her testimony wherever God led. What an amazing woman to model!

Corrie had survived captivity in Nazi Germany. She never doubted God's presence or his love even in the vilest of circumstances. Through a clerical error in the Nazis' paperwork, Corrie was released from that concentration camp. Within days of her release, all of the prisoners at that camp were executed.

Somehow, I would try to find the same courage and faith Corrie had found. Cancer wasn't exactly like being in a concentration camp, but there did seem to be some remote similarities of uncertainty about what might happen from one day to the next.

What else was there for me—except cling to my faith and trust Jesus with my life.

My physical therapists continued to work my shoulder beyond its limits. I was gaining mobility, but I was still unable to raise my arm over my head while lying flat and have the arm rest on the floor. That may sound like an insignificant problem, but there would hardly be a single exam in the upcoming weeks and months for which the simple action of raising my arm over my head would not be a necessity.

As miserable as my shoulder recovery was, I was glad I had the operation. In its preoperative limitation, I was unable to move my arm higher than eye level when raising the arm in an upward motion. Little did I realize at the time how great a part my injured shoulder would play in the decisions that I needed to make in the upcoming weeks. I had every reason to "give thanks" for the injury (although I did not know it at the time).

The MRI revealed that the mass in my breast was more than three inches long. I was in shock. Now each and every test was processed in double time. The bone scans and CT scans that were ordered on Thursday kept me at the hospital for the entire day. I was scheduled to meet with a plastic surgeon to begin gathering information for my reconstructive surgery. A unilateral mastectomy was imminent. The mastectomy that Dr. Golshan had spoken of during our first appointment, and which my mind immediately rejected, was now a welcome alternative to possibly having cancer in my vital organs and bones. A breast I could live without. I needed my liver and pancreas. I needed my bones. I needed my brain….

After an excruciatingly long day, Grady and I stopped for something to eat in the hospital cafeteria before starting home shortly before 8:00. Subtle colors were forming in the evening sky. We traveled in silence, individually consumed by our thoughts. I was still contemplating the "what ifs" and the worst case scenarios and then "taking every thought captive" and remembering how deeply my Heavenly Father loved me as I watched Him painting the sky as if the beauty of His masterpiece was just for me that night. As I was chasing and being chased by fears, the Lord brought to mind one of my most favorite experiences:

I love hummingbirds! For years I have put out feeders and enjoyed watching them as they feed. They are such delicate yet feisty little birds. I have read that their metabolism is so rapid they require nourishment every few hours or they will starve.

The summer prior to my diagnosis, I volunteered to transport my neighbor's daughter, Melissa, to her field hockey practices. She needed to arrive at 7:30 a.m.

Grady had thoughtfully opened my garage door before he left for work. As I was getting into my car one morning, I heard a funny thumping sound against the wall in the garage attic. I wasn't sure what it was, and I didn't have time to investigate before taking Melissa to her practice.

When I returned, the thumping was still "thumping"…but it was weaker. *Oh my goodness! I'll bet that's a disorientated hummingbird! How can I save him?*

With nothing to lose and everything to gain, I retrieved the hummingbird feeder from its hook and climbed the ladder to the attic. The little "hummy" was perched on an electrical wire that ran along the open sides of the attic floor and close to the rafters. He was weak from his lack of food and kept tipping backward like he was about to fall from the wire and onto the car below. Then he would flutter his wings and upright himself, perch for a few moments, and tip backward again.

I leaned out over the rafters holding the feeder inches from the tiny bird. He barely had the strength to fly and perch on the feeder and consume the sugar-water he desperately needed. My position was precarious; my extended arm dangling the feeder was awkward.

Within a short time, my arm began to wobble and the hummingbird became alarmed as the feeder swayed. The food he had consumed was just enough to revive him. He flew from his perch full steam ahead, but in the wrong direction! Instead of flying down and out the open garage door, he flew straight up and into the attic wall again. *Thump, thump, thump…*and then silence as he fell to the floor.

In the shadowy dimness of the attic I could barely make out where the poor little thing had fallen in amongst the clutter of boxes. When I found him, I gently scooped him up. For a brief second, he squawked in protest as he struggled and attempted to escape from my cupped hands. Then in his weakness, he rested. He became still and quiet as he surrendered into my tender and protective grasp.

I'll never forget the thrill of how that tiny bird felt in my hands. He was so small, he was barely there! My motivation was to "rescue" and to set him free because of my love for hummingbirds; my focus was on this single bird and my desire for him to survive. I wanted to save his life, and yet as small and weak as he was, he struggled against the hands that gave him back his freedom and for him meant *life*.

As I gazed out the windshield and across the evening sky at the patterns from God's palette of colors, I thought to myself how much I was like that hummingbird. I was imprisoned by a life-threatening illness; but I knew I had to choose to be still and find safety in the hands of the Lord, even though my heart was struggling with fear. For me, the answer was to rest in what I knew was His truth. "Be still and know that I am God." (Psalm 46:10)

Dr. Golshan thought he might have the results for my scans as soon as Monday morning. I asked Grady to stay with me until the call had come. I didn't want to be alone when I learned what the reports said.

As each hour passed, I became more and more anxious and more and more unsettled. By 11:00, Dr. Golshan still had not called.

Grady had an appointment and it was impossible for him to spend the entire day waiting for a call that may not come. As he was leaving, he promised to return home as quickly as possible.

At 11:30, and just after Grady had left, the phone rang. That cold, numb feeling of fear took over my body instantly. I did not want to answer the phone, knowing the call was most likely from Dr. Golshan's office. I was terrified. *Oh, Lord God, please....*

Shaking, I slowly reached toward the phone. "Hello?"

"Hello, Kathy? It's Dr. Golshan. We have good news! All of your scans were clear. It looks like there is some lymph node involvement, and we will schedule a biopsy on the nodes to verify our initial findings.

"There are some tiny spots on your liver that are not alarming and too small to even biopsy. We will watch for abnormalities in liver function just to be certain, but this has not spread to any of your organs or bones. They are clear!

"I will be turning you over to Nancy Lin and she will work with you on a plan for your treatment. I will continue to consult with her and will meet with you again prior to your surgery. You're going to get through this just fine. We have a better idea of what we are dealing with now. Nancy will take over from here."

I didn't know whether I should laugh or cry. *Thank you, Lord. The cancer has not spread. Reassure me with your peace and knowing that Your loving hands are, indeed, wrapped around me and holding me firmly in Your grasp.*

With each email, more and more people were requesting to be added to the list. The words of encouragement that I received played a huge part in how I viewed the battle ahead. One of the most valued notes of encouragement came from our pastor and was sent to Denise and me shortly after we were both diagnosed with breast cancer.

Subject: Fwd: Be encouraged

Hello Kathy and Denise—

1 Timothy 1:12 says, "I thank Christ Jesus our Lord, who has given me strength, that He has considered me trustworthy, appointing me to His service."

When I read this scripture recently I thought of each of you. You are not alone in this battle against cancer. In fact, you are being given a kind of strength that must be supernatural. The calling and the service you have been given is to be victorious and to be used by helping to bring faith and hope to others who are/will be in similar situations. Here's the key—you are trustworthy according to the Lord's consideration. He thinks you are able to cling onto Him, be strengthened in your inner person, and carry out the service of worship and testimony!

I am praying for you both today that the Lord's presence will be more than enough and that faith will grow stronger within you!

In Christ---

Peter Bonanno

Grace Capital Church

http://www.gccnh.com

Chapter 15

Deciding on the Protocol

Tracy was nearly frantic as we were learning what, exactly, my diagnosis was and what the course of treatment would be. The day before Dr. Golshan's call with the results from my scans, she had flown to Spain with a group of students from Milton Academy. The student exchange program was a four-week commitment. Tracy and Tonx had made plans to spend time with his family in La Navata for an additional four weeks. All of their plans had been made months earlier and long before my diagnosis.

During the first two weeks of the exchange, between the six-hour time difference and her travel plans with the students, communication was nearly impossible. We relied on email and Tracy's chances of finding an Internet café to log into her email account.

As soon as I knew that the bone scans and CT scans were clear, I not only notified Tracy but also contacted Kelley Tuthill. Kelley was nearly in shock and disbelief that while I was cheering her on in her battle against cancer, I was diagnosed. One of the first things I told her was, "Kelley, I can handle this in one of two ways: I can be bitter or I can be better. I choose to be better!" Kelley decided to be "better" too.

Late in the spring, as Channel 5 News followed Kelley through her treatments at Dana-Farber, a half-hour program for "Chronicle" sharing

Kelley's story was produced. "Chronicle" is a local favorite in the Boston viewing area. It is a news magazine program devoted to worthy matters or special interest stories. Sometimes it's about travel or vacations spots, or about people or crafts that are unique in some way. But it's always interesting and usually has special ties to New England or the Boston area.

Some of the breast cancer survivors who had contacted Kelley after she announced her diagnosis were interviewed for "Chronicle." That telecast created so much interest that the production staff decided to film and broadcast a second program in October, for Breast Cancer Awareness Month. Kelley asked us, as a family dealing with breast cancer for a second time in less than two years, if we would share our story with "Chronicle." I was a little taken aback by the idea at first, but then felt if just one woman might be encouraged and helped by our experience, it would be worth it. The producer, Kathy Bickimer, called and we had a long talk about what it was like going through breast cancer for a second time as a family in less than two years.

On Sunday, June 10, 2007, I continued with my updates.

Subject: Course of Treatment

....Hello Everyone.

Last Thursday, Grady and I were back to Boston and were given some clearer information about what lies ahead. Despite the original report of this tumor being 3 inches long, I was given clarification. The tumor is 1.5 inches long, and there is an "abnormal" border surrounding the tumor that is indefinable and a question. (I prayed that God would "encapsulate" this tumor and prevent it from spreading. Could it be???)

I was presented with three different means of treatment. We have ruled out having surgery at this time but will take a different route. I need to make my final treatment choice by Tuesday. Here is what we are leaning toward:

I have the option of being part of a research trial. The drugs being used are all tried and true and in use for the type of cancer that I have. The difference is these drugs have not been studied in earlier staged cancer (stages 0 through early stage 3) in the combinations that I will be given. I will receive twelve weeks of chemo, have a break for four weeks, then surgery and recovery. After the pathology reports are examined, my continued chemo treatments will be tailored to me individually rather than being a standard follow-up treatment program. Start to finish, this will be a fourteen- to sixteen-month commitment as best I can figure, plus three years of follow-up for research.

The downside to all of this is that I will have to endure two additional biopsies! That does not thrill my little heart. Also, there will be at least one extra MRI.

I will be assigned to one of two different treatment "arms" (groups of women) for the research project. This study is to compare the results between two different chemo programs. Forty women will be in each of the "arms" of the study. I will not be allowed to choose which arm of research I would like to have as my treatment.

Please pray that God would place me in the program that is best for me.

The upside is: having chemo before going through surgery will allow the extra time I need for more physical therapy for my shoulder and more time for me to regain range of motion. I still have a long way to go before my shoulder is as good as new! Another huge plus is I will be watched super close for the next three years! I'll have the best doctors you could ask for and cutting-edge treatment. My regimen after surgery could be shortened...there's a good reason!

And finally, the information gathered from my experience will be used to save the lives of others. I don't want to sound benevolent here.... My first interest was selfish. *"Give me a short cut out of this l-o-n-g sentence of treatment!"* But then I thought...if the Bible is true (and I believe it is) and the origin of disease and tribulation was founded all the way back in Genesis 3, what a great way to give the devil a black eye—being used for research to save lives and **defeat** breast cancer.

On Thursday, it's back to Dana-Farber for another biopsy from the tumor for the research project, blood work, and to see Dr Lin, my oncologist.

Please pray that the timing is orchestrated by the Lord. We need to begin chemo the week of June 18; I need to have a port put into my chest for the chemo infusions. Much needs to be done for me to take part in this research; I will need a biopsy of the sentinel node, also.

Please pray for my strength to be found in the Lord. I really cannot do this alone. The length of this treatment is overwhelming. I need His strength to see me through. Physically, I'm going to be stuck, cut, and dissected—you name it....

Continue to pray for my repeated healing with every procedure I'm put through. I'd still like a miracle healing...maybe with the way I am going to be watched so closely by my doctors, the Lord will shock them and heal me in front of their eyes by the power of prayer!

Blessings and Love,

Kathy

In my own mind, I was trying to put together the puzzle pieces of what seemed to be two similar but different puzzles. The tumor in my breast was invisible on a mammogram? The tumor Tracy had was invisible on a mammogram? Why??? These were two different types of breast cancer. I began asking questions.

I was diagnosed with stage III HER2/neu positive breast cancer. It was hormone receptor negative. When I asked Dr. Lin about this cancer, I learned HER2/neu breast cancer is accountable for about 15 to 20 percent of the cases of breast cancer. The tumor (even though it was of significant size) was neither palpable nor detectable in a mammogram. "Occult" breast tumors are detectable only by an MRI. Approximately 15 percent of breast cancer tumors *do not* show up in a mammogram.

From Dr. Lin, I learned that triple-negative (Tracy's diagnosis) is more likely to be the type of cancer found in younger women and has a higher incidence of being missed on a mammogram.

In 2005, when Tracy had a baseline mammogram the mass DID NOT present on the films. Her surgeon had examined her biopsy slides and knew she had cancer. He knew where the mass was located. But the mass DID NOT present itself in the films. The radiologist looked at the films with Tracy's surgeon and admitted he would have missed this tumor, even as the doctor pinpointed and circled its location on the films.

Mammograms are not perfect; they do not have 100 percent accuracy. Both for Tracy and for me, that fact was proven. We were in the minority of women where a tumor existed and did not present in mammography. We were in an even greater minority as daughter (first) and mother with two different and less common types of breast cancer.

I have come to realize how truly unprepared we are as women to know what questions to ask our doctors concerning breast cancer. When something questionable is detected, it can be a horrifying event and fear can override any chance of absorbing what we are told. New terminology can be like hearing a foreign language for the first time.

As women, it is critical to have the courage to understand some basics about cancer and about breast health. What does a lump feel like? How often should I do a self exam, and how? How much does family history matter? Does lifestyle play a role? What are calcifications? How often do breast biopsies detect cancer? What are the numbers?

The largest percentile of retakes and biopsies come back negative for cancer. Of the millions of women who will have mammograms, the statistics I have heard from my doctors are that there will be around 189,000 newly diagnosed cases of breast cancer annually. Having been one of those women diagnosed in 2007, I was glad that I understood as much as I did about the disease. I learned from my daughter.

As I began to understand more about breast cancer (after Tracy's diagnosis and then my own), I found a platform concerning women's health from which to challenge other women. Knowledge is your best friend in detecting and fighting breast cancer. Learn! After a diagnosis of breast cancer (or any cancer), good choices cannot be made while in a state of shock. A little bit of general knowledge prior to a diagnosis, and most importantly, knowing which hospital to go to, can be a lifesaver. Chances are that someone you know has, or will be fighting against, this disease. Fear is an enemy against the ability to make sound and reasonable decisions under pressure. And the first emotion experienced after a diagnosis of cancer is *fear!*

I began to learn about the HER2/neu cancer that was an unwelcome invader in my breast. For reasons still not understood, a protein called HER2/neu is excessive in its presence on the surface of some of the cells, causing them to divide abnormally in this type of cancer. From what I read, before the approved use of Herceptin as a means to combat this type of cancer, remission and/or cure of HER2/neu cancer was almost nonexistent.

I remember watching the evening news and hearing the announcement when the FDA approved the use of Herceptin. It was shortly after Tracy's diagnosis and before she began chemotherapy during the summer of 2005. Herceptin was not a viable drug to combat the cancer Tracy was fighting. It was, however, the primary drug used in saving my life! And it was a drug that was still being researched. Data was being compiled in studies using Herceptin in combination with other chemotherapy drugs.

On the Internet, I found documented research using Herceptin dating back to 1998. The studies I read about were for late-stage cancer that had metastasized in other parts of the body. Even in those patients, Herceptin used in conjunction with other chemo drugs was proven beneficial.

Dr. Lin asked if I would be interested in speaking with a research studies nurse about taking part in a clinical trial at Dana-Farber. At first I wasn't sure about this idea. (Wasn't it safer to use conventional chemo drugs to fight this?)

Grady asked Dr. Lin an interesting question. "Nancy, if this was your diagnosis, your choice, what course of treatment would you choose?"

Without hesitation, Nancy answered, "I'd choose the protocol." And she began to give us all of the reasons why. Not the least of which was, if for any reason I started into the research project and decided I did not wish to continue, I could stop the clinical trial and select a different avenue...a very important point.

Nancy explained the differences in being a part of the protocol, as opposed to conventional treatment (which at that time was the same combination of chemo drugs Tracy had taken, plus many months of Herceptin). One of the facts that especially caught my attention was how my treatment would differ after having chemo and beyond surgery. Nancy explained that after my surgery (which would be sometime in October), I would have further chemo treatments, but those infusions would be based on my pathology report. She told us that after I had completed the protocol, I would receive an abbreviated conventional treatment plan. Unfortunately, that would include Adriamycin/Cytoxan, the combination that wiped poor Tracy off her feet.

Knowing Tracy's experience on A/C, I did not want to have that combination of drugs if I had a choice. It appeared that there was not going to be a complete escape from having A/C (along with Herceptin), but I might have fewer doses of the combination if I had good results from the chemo drugs in the trial.

Nancy invited Peg to talk with us. She was the nurse responsible for collecting data and monitoring the patients who entered into the study.

Yes, it did require more of me for science. In fact "part of me" will remain frozen in time, in test tubes and/or slides reserved for future study for up to ten years. But, hey, what a great opportunity to be a pioneer in the science for women's health!

Peg gave me a seventeen-page protocol description and contract to review. The study was sponsored by two pharmaceutical companies and overseen by some of the most renowned breast cancer specialists, not just in this country, but in the world.

I called my friend Deirdre, who is a medical professional and had received some of her training, years ago, on the oncology ward at one of the top cancer hospitals in New York. I asked for her opinion. After some serious thought, prayer, and counsel from people I trusted, I agreed to take part in the study.

On June 14, 2007, I returned my signed contract to Peg, and the flurry and fury of scheduling the extra appointments for the study began.

Chapter 16

Setting the Course

The research study was small. Only eighty women would be selected to participate. Forty women would receive a slightly "kinder and gentler" chemo program...and then there were the rest of us! I had requested prayer and asked the Lord to place me in the arm (group) of the study that was right for me. I asked the Lord to "set my course of treatment" and that He would "assign to me the chemo drugs that would kill this cancer."

When my information was entered into the computer, the chemo drugs I was assigned, in addition to the Herceptin, were Taxotere and Carboplatin. These were the drugs that more women had difficulty tolerating. In my heart of hearts, I was hoping for the milder arm of the study. But I had asked the Lord to "direct"...and I trusted that this was His direction for my best outcome.

Carboplatin causes nausea and vomiting in 65–75 percent of cases and decreased blood counts (both red and white) as well as platelets.

Hair loss was almost guaranteed from the Taxotere. Taxotere is in the same family of drugs as Taxol, one of the chemo drugs Tracy had been on and the one that causes neuropathy as one of its most common side effects.

Dana-Farber has an organized system of scheduling each doctor's patients. Dr. Lin's patients were assigned chemo on Mondays and Thursdays, and Mondays worked best for my appointments. I needed to successfully complete: a biopsy for the research, a MUGA scan to know the efficiency of my heart, another mammogram, blood work, and surgery to install my port before my loading dose of Herceptin. It seemed there was no way to do everything by June 18. It was an impossible situation! My frustration peaked after a conversation with Peg that had a resemblance to a "shell game" as her focus seemed to center on the research and the date for my first round of Herceptin kept moving. Suddenly I was feeling that somehow the importance of the research was overshadowing the patient!

"Dr. Lin, when are we going to begin to kill the cancer? I don't know how all of my appointments can fit into the schedule, but it's time to start focusing on why we're here. Isn't there some way to move this along and get the preliminary things finished and not delay the chemo date? When will I have my first infusion of Herceptin? Are we stalled because of the added tests?

"I'm also finding it hard to follow some of Peg's instructions. I'm confused. The date for my loading dose of Herceptin keeps changing as more requirements are added. Let's move forward and kill this *'thing'!*"

I was practically frustrated to tears and my exasperation rolled forth. "It's been more than two months since this cancer was first suspected. How much longer is my life safe without treatment? How much am I risking for the sake of science? Won't this spread? Isn't the cancer in my lymph nodes?"

Dr. Lin gently responded, "Kathy, I will make you a promise. You will have your first chemotherapy on Thursday, June 21. If the pretests are incomplete, we will move you out of the protocol and into a standard chemo program so that we can begin fighting cancer."

I discovered that when Dr. Lin gave the order to "move," things happened! Dr. Lin understood my frustration. The appointments I needed were almost miraculously scheduled. Not every patient who came through the doors of Dana-Farber would be a good candidate for this protocol; not every patient would be emotionally able to face cancer and willing to be a part of a research trial.

Two days were booked chock-a-block full from morning through early evening with appointments when the hospital called with my schedule.

Thursday, June 21, was especially jam-packed, including my loading dose of Herceptin. All that was left that did not get squeezed into the schedule of to-dos was to have my port installed, and we all agreed that I could survive my first infusion of Herceptin through an IV in my arm.

Based on past experiences, I obviously had some concerns about more biopsies. However, despite how draining and long the experience of the diagnostic stereotactic core biopsy on May 18 was, more than a few good things came to the surface. I don't understand how or why, but after that biopsy the tumor that was invisible showed up! It was easily palpated once the bruising began to subside. I still don't understand the physiological reasons for its sudden appearance.

I didn't want a repeat experience like I had in May. Respectfully I presented an idea to the nurse who would be assisting during the biopsy as tissue samples were taken. This was an ultrasound-guided biopsy, and a completely different procedure from the one I had previously, but I still thought that those working on me should be forewarned. "Um, I had a little problem with my biopsy in May; I seem to bleed a little more than what might be normal."

"Well, what do you mean you bleed a little more than normal?"

"Um, well...the two hours allotted for the stereotactic core biopsy took four hours because of bleeding."

Just then, one of the nurses who had been with me that day and iced my shoulder and the wounds that refused to stop bleeding walked into the room. "She isn't kidding! I was there!"

I started to laugh. "Hey! How are you? The kids? The dog? The car repairs? What other trivial things did we discuss during those hours? What are you doing at Dana-Farber? Are you just visiting, or do nurses float between the two hospitals, too?" Having a nurse who had been there for my last biopsy was like having an old friend arrive to hold my hand (or at least a bag of ice for me).

I offered my suggestion and found that sometimes even the most brilliant doctors are willing to consider good old common sense when it is suggested! "I have an idea. If icing restricts blood flow to an area, is there a reason we don't ice first?"

The two nurses looked at me curiously and then broke into smiles. One of them said, "That's a great idea! Let me check with Dr. (Jack) Meyer for his 'okay.'"

She returned carrying an ice pack.

Most of the doctors I had met at Dana-Farber and Brigham and Women's were quite young. Dr. Meyer was stately and more mature in years. He was gentle and quiet, and I liked him immediately.

As I rested on my right side, facing the wall with my obstinate, restricted, impossible left arm supported in midair by one of the nurses, I decided to interview my new doctor. "So…Dr. Meyer, how long have you been here at Dana-Farber?"

As he answered, his eyes were riveted on the screen before him as the needle moved through a tiny opening in my skin and penetrated the tumor to extract tissue samples. "Twenty-five years."

"Wow…I can't begin to imagine the changes you have seen through the years and the advancement of diagnostic testing and treating breast cancer. What has that been like?"

With that question, I found this man's heart and his passion to save lives as he began to talk about the technology that has made his job easier and more precise. He spoke of how things have changed through research and how treatment has become more successful and easier to tolerate. Twenty-five years and the improvements were almost unimaginable.

He finished the procedure, and there was practically no bleeding. "Oh my goodness! Dr. Meyer, I can't believe this! I'll need another biopsy within two weeks. You have to do the next biopsy for the research study. Will you *please* do that one, also?"

He looked a little embarrassed as I praised his expert work. He had a slight grin forming at the corners of his mouth as he quietly answered, "We'll see."

It wasn't until my next appointment with Dr. Lin that I learned "who" Dr. Jack Meyer was. He was the Director of Breast Imaging at Dana-Farber!

Dr. Meyer was on vacation the week of July 4th, when I was due for my next research biopsy. But Dr. Meyer informed Dr. Lin that he would come in…just for me!

I was so grateful for this man's kindness; I could not believe his willingness to oblige my request. A little embarrassed, I wanted to do something to let him know how much I appreciated the sacrifice he was making by coming in on one of his vacation days.

The Lord seemed to be impressing upon me that a gift bag filled with homemade chocolate chip cookies would be exactly "what the doctor would order." While I was still well enough and able to bake, I was glad to do something as old fashioned as bake cookies for someone so special and so kind. To me, it seemed important to express my gratitude…especially in this case.

I began to understand how critical the whole timing issue was for each stage in the study. Everything had to be exact, on schedule, and done in a specific way. Peg instructed me to stop all over-the-counter vitamins and supplements. I could not have anything that didn't meet with her approval and that might interfere with blood chemistry, or might interact on any level with the chemotherapy and skew research findings.

I kept notes about reactions after chemo and the effectiveness of my anti-nausea medications. Before actually starting, it seemed like a bit of a rigmarole. But other than jotting down a few notes and recording my temperature a few times a day, it was no big deal. It was the time investment for the added appointments in the beginning that wore me out. It was a demanding and tumultuous pace!

Overall, Grady's time is flexible. He was able to remain connected to the office via computer and cell phone during my hours at the hospital. If not for the flexibility he had, it would have been difficult for me to take part in the study. As I went from appointment to appointment and was totally occupied by the science project I was now a part of, Grady worked from our location. I was grateful for his willingness and his desire to be with me at the hospital for each of my appointments, and to be a part of each step in my battle against breast cancer.

There is a price that goes with being sick, even with the best insurance coverage. As a part of research, all of the extra testing was paid for by the sponsoring pharmaceutical companies. Because of expenses associated with cancer, sometimes agreeing to a research protocol is a wise consideration—for a myriad of reasons.

Upon finishing all that needed doing leading up to my loading dose of Herceptin, I sat and waited to see Dr. Lin, knowing that once I left her office it would be for the real reason we were at Dana-Farber. For comfort, I opened a devotional book I had with me. Although the date was June 21, I felt led by the Holy Spirit to go back and read the Scripture and the devotion I had missed the previous day. The Scripture reading for June 20 only confirmed all the Lord seemed to be saying. This was not about me, but about God's glory. I was not to be INWARD focused as I fought this cancer but OUTWARD focused…trusting God and praying for those who were praying for ME and praying for those I met on this journey.

The devotional Scripture was from the Book of Job. "The Lord restored Job's losses when he prayed for his friends." (Job 42:10)

Dr. Lin and Peg measured the tumor one final time and gave me instructions about calling when I developed a fever after the Herceptin infusion. (It was almost a certainty that I would.) This dose was larger than what would normally be given. It would be dispensed at a slower rate, and my oncology nurse would watch for adverse reactions during the ninety-minute infusion.

The day filled with tests and preparations came to an end. It was time for my first trip to the tenth floor at Dana-Farber; the reality of what was about to happen hit. We were here to kill cancer. That cancer was in *me*. My heart began to pound. Fear…faith…fear…*faith!*

On Dana 10, Grady and I sat in the waiting room outside the double doors that hid from view the mysterious world of chemotherapy. As I waited, I wished I had accompanied Tracy during one of her infusions so that I would know what to expect.

There were several people waiting to be taken into the ward. I looked at the faces. There was a young woman wearing a scarf to cover her head. She looked pale and sickly, the way Tracy did toward the end of her treatments. She had a small baby.

I saw a young man who looked to be in his twenties with his parents. It was the younger man wearing the hospital identification bracelet.

Men and women of every age, race, ethnic background, and economic level were patiently waiting. There was no way to stereotype the mix of people. We were there, *all* waiting for chemotherapy to be infused into our bodies. We were all…the *same*. Most seemed somber. I wondered about their lives. I wondered about their families. I wondered about the types of cancers they were fighting. I hoped I didn't look as worried as some of them appeared to be.

Shannon, one of the attendants, called my name and led me through the doors and into the infusion ward. My weight, height, blood pressure, and racing pulse were recorded. Then Shannon led me to a "pod" of infusion chairs for the Herceptin that would begin killing the abnormal cells that now seemed to be in charge of my entire life.

The ward was extremely large and designed with little nooks where there were small pods (groups) of reclining chairs. Some of the nooks had many chairs, but others had two or four recliners and a few chairs for visitors. Beside each recliner, there was a pole that held the fluid bags used during the chemo process. For each patient there was a small television suspended by a metal arm. I saw private rooms with beds.

A canteen area was stocked with coffee, tea, bottled water, fruit, yogurt, sandwiches, and snacks. The ward was airy, bright, with huge windows—"friendly" and downright pleasant. Already I felt better!

I was nervous as the nurse checked my hospital wrist band against the bag of chemotherapy in her hands and she asked me to state my name and date of birth to double and triple check against the possibility of medication errors.

I watched the first drops of Herceptin enter and slide down the tube that ended with an IV needle inserted into my left arm. Grady remained close by. The reality of being hitched to a small IV bag bearing my name, hospital I.D. number, and in bold print the word CHEMOTHERAPY made this something other than bad casting in a dress rehearsal for a ghoulish play. It was real...and I had the leading role. I couldn't believe that this was "me" sitting and watching the bag of fluid that was hanging and dipping.

The oncology nurse checked frequently as she looked for evidence of possible side effects. I asked for a blanket as I felt a chill and tried to shake off the feelings associated with the experience. My nurse zeroed in on the request and watched me closely. In particular she was monitoring for "rigors"—uncontrollable shivering and shaking.

As the ninety-minute infusion finished, I was fine. I felt completely fine! I was kept waiting and was observed for an additional thirty minutes to be sure I was tolerating the drug.

I seemed to be okay, but as we traveled on the interstate, about fifteen miles from home I thought I was going to die! By the time we pulled into our driveway, I was shivering and shaking so hard that I couldn't even talk. The muscles in my neck stiffened rock-solid, and I thought my head might snap off as I jolted and jerked uncontrollably. My temperature began to soar.

During the night I did exactly as Dr. Lin had instructed. (Well, almost...and with the exception of the most important thing.) My temperature climbed to more than 101 degrees. I had been instructed to call the hospital when my temp rose above 100.5. I was simply too exhausted and did not want to wake Grady during the middle of the night for another trip down to Boston. I took Tylenol (one of the few pain relief medicines I was allowed) in an attempt to lower my temperature. I stayed awake and prayed.

Once my temperature dropped under 101, the tired and heavy feeling I was experiencing took over and the only thing I cared about was rest. I returned to my bed and fell into a deep slumber and never stirred until I heard Grady's voice quietly calling me. The morning sun was shining softly into our bedroom, and he stood beside the bed with water and more Tylenol, along with a nice, hot cup of tea.

By noon, the side effects had subsided and once more I was back to normal. I felt a little tired, but other than that, I was fine. I had a sense of relief. I was going to be all right.

Every third week my treatment day for the H/T/C was long. My blood was drawn through the port that was in my chest and analyzed before more chemo could be administered. Measurements of the tumor were taken and documented. It was a six-hour commitment at the hospital every third Monday. But the two Mondays in between, when I received just Herceptin, the infusion time lasted just thirty minutes.

Before I could begin my consecutive twelve Mondays of treatment and establish a routine, there were extra appointments required by the study to understand the effectiveness of the loading dose of the Herceptin. It was during that time, and before starting into that schedule, that insanity reigned! Those who were arranging my appointments were pulling their hair out as they tried to find openings to accommodate the protocol. Time was of the essence!

In order to complete all of the protocol tests after the loading dose (which was done on a Thursday), time was squeezed from two weeks down to eleven days so that my normal infusion schedule would begin on a Monday. In itself losing three days for scheduling protocol appointments doesn't sound like much of a problem. However, a certain number of days were needed to allow the loading dose of Herceptin adequate time to attack the cancer. Three lost days made a crazy, gigantic difference!

Peg was close to coming apart at the seams under the pressure of the compressed timing. I found myself trying to reassure her that I would believe God for a miracle and everything would get done for the study, and somehow I would have the surgery for my port installation by July 2. Peg saw this as impossible. I had to "hang tough" and look at this as "all things are possible with God," including smoothing Peg's very ruffled feathers! It was actually funny how the Lord met the deadlines for the tests. The Lord is never early and He is never late. He's always exactly on time—right to the second!

On Thursday afternoon, June 28, I was down to the wire and waiting for appointments for my next MRI and a surgery time for my port. At 4:20, the phone rang.

"Hello, this is Brigham and Women's Hospital calling...Kathy Crews?"

"Yes. Thank you.... I've been waiting for your call. What appointments have you scheduled?"

"Well, we have you booked for a port installation tomorrow, Friday morning, at 7:30, and an MRI at 4:30 p.m., here at Brigham and Women's."

I groaned. "Ugh! Here's the deal: it's been really hard to get all of my appointments to fit together. Ideally, I would have the MRI, and then have the port installed. I just can't imagine having surgery on my chest and then laying face down on that fresh surgery incision for forty minutes and not moving during the MRI."

"Oo-o-o...you're right. Can you be here at 6:15 a.m. on Monday morning for the port? There is an opening at 5:30 p.m. at Dana-Farber tomorrow for the MRI. Would that schedule work? I will call over there and reserve that opening if it does."

"Oh yes! God bless you! That is absolutely perfect! I'll take it. Thank you."

Friday morning my mom called to say my niece, Amanda, was on her way to Brigham and Women's Hospital to deliver triplets!

"That's great, Mom. I'll be in Boston late in the day, so I will definitely check in to see how she is doing. I will give you a call when I get home."

After my blood drawing for Monday's surgery, I raced to my appointment across the street at Dana-Farber. Grady stayed at Brigham and Women's Hospital with my brother, David, and his fiancée, Lori. Patiently, they waited for news about the birth of the babies.

Hours later, a slightly dazed new dad came to where we were all gathered and waiting. He proudly announced, "Everyone is doing okay." He rambled off the height and weight of each baby…two boys and a little girl.

This was a first for "Grandpa" David; he was beamin' so big he was practically bustin' his buttons!

The joy of the triplets' birth was the buzz of conversation through the weekend. Someone else and something pleasant was in the spotlight. My mother needed something to occupy her thoughts other than breast cancer—something happy to think about, and for her, no thought is "happier" than babies.

Some of our joy turned to concern, however, when we learned that both little boys were having difficulty and were placed on breathing tubes. Knowing that Dana-Farber and Brigham and Women's were fast becoming my second home, Mom asked if I would go to the babies and to pray for them when I returned to Boston on Monday. At the time, I didn't know that she was asking me to perform a small miracle just to get past security and into the intensive care unit for newborns.

Chapter 17

Settling into the Protocol

From across the ocean, Tracy was like a combination mother hen and preseason coach, calling me at every opportunity that presented itself. She was nonstop at cracking the whip making sure I walked and exercised. She was pushing me toward the best physical condition I could obtain preceding the chemo. Tracy knew how difficult it is to exercise when your energy has been zapped by the effects of drugs as they kill cancer. She knew how quickly the chemo would bring changes and force me to slow down. Tracy was thinking months ahead, all the way to a future surgery date sometime in the fall.

Throughout the weekend and leading up to my first H/T/C infusion, Tracy and I talked several times on the phone. I felt some anticipation, and I wished Tracy was home instead of in Spain. She was the only one who understood exactly what I was feeling. I wanted to be with someone who had walked the miles and been down this path. She knew what it was like. She *knew* the journey I was starting. I needed her reassurance: Mom…it will be alright. You can do this.

What I didn't know until writing this book was that the day of my first H/T/C combination, Tracy was feeling all of the emotion for me that she had felt on her own first day of chemotherapy. Monday, July 2, 2007, was an extremely difficult day for both of us; we were separated by an ocean and thousands of miles. There was no way for her to call, no way for her to check with me during the course of the day. The appointments at Dana-Farber and at Brigham and Women's Hospital that Monday were grueling and in rapid succession; Grady and I spent fourteen hours at the two hospitals.

We stayed at Tracy and Antonio's apartment in Milton. Tracy was extremely concerned about how I might react to my first round of H/T/C. She wanted us to stay in Milton in the event there were complications and I needed to be rushed back to the hospital. Because of the length of the day and fourteen hours' worth of appointments, we spent two nights at the apartment, one night before and one night after.

The phone rang at 5:30 a.m., as we were on our way out the door.

I looked at Grady, puzzled. "Who…? It must be Tracy! … Hello? Hi, Trace…. We were just leaving for the hospital and my first appointment."

"Mom, I'm thinking about you…. I will be all day."

I could hear the concern in her voice. "I know you are, Trace. I know that you wish you could be here for me, but I'm sure I'll be fine. After all, you have paved the way for me. You and Tonx found Dr. Lin. How much better care can I ask for? Right? Trace, try not to worry; there are literally hundreds if not thousands of people praying. I've got a hunch God is walking before me this day and clearing the way of any obstacles. I have a strong peace, and I'm resting in that peace. It's going to be alright. We'll spend the night here at your apartment again tonight; it's going to be a very long day. You can call us in the morning…just not too early."

"I will call you, Mom. I love you."

"I love you too, Trace. Thanks for calling to 'wish me well.' I'm doing fine…honest. I'll tell you all about my day when you call tomorrow. Okay?"

"Okay. Bye, Mom."

I did have a peace, I was sure I was going to be fine…but I longed for Tracy to be home.

By 6:15, I had changed into a hospital gown and the surgeon installing my port came to the patient care unit several times to talk with me about the type of port I would need. He asked how long I expected to have the port, and how often it would be used.

I explained about the protocol and the number of months I would be on Herceptin; the port would be accessed regularly for a year. The surgeon decided on a port with two access heads that could be accessed simultaneously, if necessary. (As rapidly as things improve medically, a higher quality power port became available not long after my port installation. The port I had served me very well, but the power port would have been an even better choice, had it been available.)

On a scale of one through ten, if Tracy's surgery for her port installation was a "ten" for being a horrible experience, mine was a "ten" for being an excellent experience. My entire procedure was handled differently than Tracy's. (Tracy also had lymph nodes removed, and that required her to be unconscious.) I was awake during the procedure, yet felt nothing. The surgery was over in an hour. As I was rolled from the operating room, I was asked if I was ready for breakfast. Shortly after eating, I was on my feet, feeling fine and on my way to the maternity ward to find my niece, Amanda, and her babies.

The Lord opens closed doors. Literally!

It was nearly 11:00 when I found my way (with Grady's help) to the maternity ward and the nurses' station. I asked which room was Amanda's, and I was told she was not in her room but with her babies in the neonatal intensive care unit. That area of the maternity ward is closed to visitors. In fact, there is no visitation with the new moms and the premature babies until after 2:00 p.m., not even for grandparents. But there I was!

The nurse sat silently, looking at me for a few "long" moments. I stood and waited. (I was sure I needed to see the babies; I just didn't know *how* it was going to happen.) Finally, she spoke. "Go down the hall and press the buzzer outside the double doors." When I did as I was instructed, the double doors opened and I entered the unit where Amanda and her newborns were. The entire little family was there with a maternity nurse.

The new dad sat in a rocking chair with tiny Aliya resting on her "daddy's chest" and snuggled against his flesh. I was in complete disbelief that I was allowed into this restricted area...but I knew exactly why I was there. Two tiny baby boys were on breathing tubes and laboring with each breath. As I stood at the incubators of each of the little boys, I silently asked the Lord as the Great Physician to touch and heal these little ones.

Before leaving, I chatted with the new parents, and as I was leaving, I softly rested my hand on Aliya's back as she slept in her father's arms, her head nestled near his heart.

Lord, call this little girl to be Your own. Let it be Your heart that she learns to hear as she grows. Draw her mom and dad to know You. Gently guide them to raise these children in Your wisdom and truth. Unite this family in You, Lord Jesus…. Bless this little child.

The Lord had opened doors that under normal circumstances would have been closed. He opened them that I might pray for three tiny premature babies. I had a peace that little Jayce and Kaidan would begin to respond and their breathing would improve. I trusted that God would enter in where He was invited.

The very next day Jayce's lungs were strong enough for him to be removed from the tubes that had been supporting his breathing. Kaidan began to improve, slowly, but grew stronger over the next several days.

Grady and I hurried to Dana-Farber for my appointment with Dr. Meyer after making a quick detour en route to the parking garage to retrieve the gift bag of freshly baked cookies. We arrived in the Radiology Department promptly at 12:15.

Something else I did not know until after the fact: not only did Dr. Meyer come in especially for me, the actual time for the appointment was "special," too. Ordinarily, biopsies are scheduled in the early morning only. I praised God, for He worked out the timing of the entire day. I could see His fingerprints all over the daily planner!

I was taken to a room where Dr. Meyer would perform the biopsy for the protocol. Once again I was positioned on my side, facing the wall, with my immobile left arm stuck in midair and held steady by a nurse so that Dr. Meyer could take tissue samples from the mass in my breast. "So, Dr. Meyer, are you able to see any difference in this tumor as you are looking at it on the monitor?" I nearly came straight up off the table with his response.

"Oh, yes…there is clearly a difference in this tumor. The edges are changing. It's slightly smaller. How many days ago did I see you?"

"June 21… Eleven or twelve?" I answered.

"We will need to look at the MRI report. But I can see a definite change."

I was *ecstatic!* One dose of Herceptin and already a change was visible! Maybe that explained the pain I had felt a day or two after the loading dose of Herceptin...the drug was at work and killing cancer cells.

With the biopsy finished, I handed Dr. Meyer the bag of cookies and the "Thank You" note I had written. I could tell my gesture of appreciation caught him off guard. As he stood reading the card, I thought to myself, *Here is one of the unsung heroes in this hospital. He quietly does his job with excellence...and beyond the call of duty (in my case). Most patients who see him are probably scared, only see him once, and never know what a truly wonderful, caring doctor he is. I'm so thankful that he is here.*

The smile on Dr. Meyer's face assured me I had done the right thing. I was happy that I had taken the time to express my gratitude to him in such a small way...cookies!

As I left Dr. Meyer and the Radiology Department on the lower level of the hospital, I reflected on how rapidly my life had changed in four short months, beginning with the surgery to my left shoulder.

Physically, I had felt nothing that would have given me any cause at all to even question that a cancer might be growing in me. If I felt any difference, it might have been that I was slightly more tired than usual. However, my body was healing from the surgery to my shoulder; I should have felt tired.

It truly amazed me when I thought about how clearly I could see God in the smallest details leading up to my diagnosis, starting around the time of the attempt to correct the miserable frozen shoulder and before the ominous "worrisome" mammogram. Looking back, I could see God's hand releasing me from my responsibilities at church. A few weeks before my shoulder surgery, someone much more qualified was hired to direct the sound team.

After my diagnosis of breast cancer, the sound and worship teams faithfully lifted me in prayer. For eight months I had spent every Friday night and Sunday morning with them. Now, when I truly needed prayer support, they were praying.

If I thought I was tired as I healed with my shoulder, when Herceptin was added into my body, I was ready for a good long snooze by early afternoon. After my appointment with Dr. Meyer, I was exhausted and ready for that nap.

On Dana 9, my brand new port (only hours old) was accessed for the first time. It worked perfectly! For the nearly bazillion times I would need to have a vein accessed for blood profiling or for chemo, having the port made things much easier. It was an excellent decision.

I was to see Dr. Lin at 3:00. As tired as I was, the electricity in the air when she and Peg entered the room brought me back to life. Although there hadn't been time for Dr. Meyer to update my computer file and document his findings, Dr. Lin did have my MRI report. When I told them what Dr. Meyer had just finished telling me about the borders of the tumor and that it did, in fact, appear to be shrinking, they could not hide their joy. This was new ground and discovery about breast cancer treatment. We were part of science and research. Odd…at the time I was delighted the Herceptin was already attacking the cancer, but I hadn't put all of the pieces together. Exactly how important were these new findings? I didn't see how important my part in this was. At least not yet.

Before Peg released me for my infusion, she went over instructions to make sure I understood the order of taking the anti-nausea medications for the study. She checked and double checked, and when she finished, she checked again. Had I taken the first corticosteroid pill on Sunday night? And again this morning at 6:30, just before having my port installed, had I taken my next dose? Was it exactly twelve hours after my 6:30 Sunday night dose? It seemed as though there was an endless rambling list of "remember this, did you do that, take this if…, and don't forgets"!

I know she was only doing her job (or at least trying to), but there was simply too much to absorb and keep track of; my brain was about to short-circuit and explode from the overload!

Finally, I blurted out to Peg, "Can you make a chart or a list for me? Then you'll be sure you haven't forgotten anything, and I'll remember the order of the instructions."

That was a truly brilliant idea!

With the flow chart Peg produced, I realized for the first time how perfect Peg was in the research field. Peg's charts had the times for all of my appointments (which were many) and the times of each of my anti-nausea medications…all highlighted beautifully in pink and yellow. Charts were Peg's strong point without question; communicating clearly and precisely without the aid of the charts was perhaps where she was challenged. But everything made perfect sense when presented in colors. I often found myself praying for Peg, and for my ability to understand her instructions when she didn't have a chart. Peg was an expert chart maker!

Even though the chemo ward on Dana 10 had everything a patient might need to make the experience as pleasant and comfortable as possible, I had read what makes "you" comfortable as a patient is what counts. For me, that meant having my own soft blanket, slippers, and a book.

Grady and I entered the elevator for our second trip to Dana 10 and my first experience with all three of the drugs that I would receive every third week. This drug combination, Herceptin, Taxotere, and Carboplatin, not only needed to kill the cancer that was in my breast, but lymph nodes were diseased. In my appointment with Dr. Lin, Grady and I learned that two of the lymph nodes under my arm tested positive for cancer, a third node appeared "suspicious," and at least two lymph nodes under my collarbone appeared "questionable" for being cancerous. This was definitely not news that I wanted to hear and not a good situation at all. Even with these findings, however, I was at peace. I realize now more than ever that the peace I felt was not a natural reaction to what was about to happen to me. It was *super*natural.

As Jade, my oncology nurse, attached a small bag of clear liquid labeled CHEMOTHERAPY to the line that accessed my port and set the volume of the flow, she commented, "First of three. It looks like we will be closing the ward together." It was already 4:00, and after Jade handed me the Benadryl to combat possible allergic reactions, I could not stay awake. I was glad I had my blanket and slippers, and I drifted off to sleep as Grady sat nearby.

I awoke to the beeping of the monitor as the first chemo bag emptied and the last of the fluid it contained dripped from the tube and into my port. Grady was quietly reading, and as I began to stir from my nap, he quickly came to attention, asking if there was anything I needed.

"Are you hungry?" he asked.

"I am. But I'm a little bit afraid to eat. Have you looked to see if there are sandwiches in the canteen area?" I wasn't certain how my stomach might react but decided on a grilled chicken sandwich. The only way to find out what works and what doesn't is trial and error. I was walking through unknown territory—now, even food was a new experience.

The sandwich was satisfying and settled just fine; the anti-nausea medications did their job in combating any feelings of illness. This definitely gave me some confidence about food. Part of the discovery was to understand how well the combination of anti-nausea drugs worked, after all. I did need to eat for this part of the research.

By the time the third and final bag of chemotherapy was finished, it was after 8:00. The ward was empty of other patients. Most of the nurses had left. The last of the cleaning crew were disinfecting the chairs in the stations, preparing for a repeat of the day tomorrow.

We closed the unit together, just as Jade had predicted.

I was glad we were spending the night at Tracy's. I was fatigued not only from the length of the day but from the emotional energy. Twenty-five percent of my long treatments were now behind me. My first milestone had been reached.

Through the night, I had no ill effects from the drugs that had been infused into my body. I did, however, wake up in the predawn hours with pain to my neck. I had a surgery wound below my collar bone on my right side for the port, and a small incision had been made to thread an access line from the port into my jugular vein. The discomfort was a small price to pay for something that had already served me so well during my first four-hour infusion of H/T/C.

As I lay in bed, I began to consciously inventory how I felt. I felt fine! I was clearly aware there was no nausea. The only thing that hurt was the tiny incision that had been made on my neck during surgery.

When I awoke in the morning, I felt so good I was almost afraid to move for fear that something might change. By mid-morning, after hearing from Tracy, we left Milton and headed home. The only thing that seemed different to me was how extremely tired I felt.

Until I knew what to expect, I ate conservatively, choosing foods I might select after having a stomach bug. Tracy's awful reaction to chemo during her first infusions was still fresh in my mind. But honestly, I felt so good, I almost felt guilty.

On Thursday, I finished my anti-nausea pills, and that was when I discovered how I *really* felt. I became jumpy and less sure about what foods might settle.

Emotionally, I began to feel like a complete flake!

Subject: 25% Finished!

Hello Everyone!

It's been 12 days since my "tough" week of treatment, and I've got to say I'm feeling pretty good about how my body has taken the blow from the drugs it has been assaulted with.

From the steroids and anti-nausea meds I was taking, I felt like the host battlefield for an internal "civil war"! I have a new appreciation for people who are bipolar.... It was weird! But, hey, the drugs did their job and you can put up with almost anything when your head is not in the toilet! Praise God!

I did have a few reactions that need watching. I developed a very bizarre pattern of rashes on my neck and upper chest and shoulders. I looked like I had been painted by aliens with circles, spots, and stripes. There were other strange side effects that have at this point subsided. I felt like I had a mouth full of Novocain and my teeth were ready for extraction. I had slight balance problems, all sorts of weird things.

Four days after my treatment, I totally crashed and finally slept. And slept and slept!

While on the meds I was hyper and exhausted at the same time, but really couldn't settle down to sleep for more than a few hours when I did go to bed.

At this point, I'm feeling really good! An afternoon nap is pretty much a physical requirement, but even they are not as long as they were a few days ago.

I have so much to be thankful for. Considering what Tracy went through while she was in treatment two years ago, my experience has been a cake walk. I am so thankful to be a part of this research protocol. I'm doing something for other women as I'm being used for science; this treatment seems to be really working. It was exciting to know that eight days after my loading dose of Herceptin, and again at eleven days, there was a change in the texture and size of the tumor. This will not change the fact that there will still be surgery, but **I am still praying that it will change my treatment beyond surgery.**

The Lord has already provided some very cool opportunities for me at the hospital to encourage others.... When you first learn that the tests show "it is cancer," you feel like you are a water balloon that just got splattered. I was in Radiology when a young woman had just been given that news. I was able to reach out to "Elsie" and encourage her with the Hope and the Way to get through this. My own daughter is proof, God does heal, through medicine and supernaturally, and life continues. Fifteen minutes that are behind you are fifteen minutes closer to your healing. And give thanks....

I am thankful that I have such an incredible support system with friends, church family, prayer warriors, people from Grady's office, and business friends...so, so many volunteers ready and willing to help. God bless each and every one of you!!!!! I could not go through this as easily as I have thus far if not for your love and support (and food!). I praise God for you.

It seems the week that I have my chemo infusion of the three drugs, I can pretty much expect to be wiped out for about eight days. But that is every third week of my treatment; my other two weeks, when I receive just the Herceptin, I'm pretty normal and I feel good. I'm just tired.

...Yes, I will lose my hair.

Last week I had my appointment to pick out my new "hair do" for the next year. As Grady and I arrived at the hospital, a young woman was exiting the building donning a wig that was straight, shoulder length, and very pink! Grady promptly suggested to me, "You're not getting *that!*" ...But one of the first wigs I tried on was equally hysterical. It was *identical* to my sister-in-law Caron's hair on my head! I almost fell out of the chair laughing to see Caron's hair on me. I love Caron, but no, her hair did not work for me!

This is going to be a long journey. You've got to find humor where you can. *And give thanks....*

Blessings and Love,

Kathy

Chapter 18

"The Moo-o-vie Star..."

I question if Tracy ever really liked her wig. She seldom used it after she lost her hair. Instead, she wore scarves most of the time to cover her head.

Tonx was with her when she made her selection, and being the upbeat, zany, and crazy kind of guy he is, I think he might have been thinking a little more along the lines of "Trick or Treat" instead of hair replacement. At any rate, his influence was there in the wig that Tracy chose.

Tracy's normal hair color is light brown sugar with sunny highlights. Her wig was platinum blond! It was a beautiful wig, and she did look like a knockout (!) wearing it, but every time she put it on she broke into the theme song from the old *Gilligan's Island* series as she dramatically took a pose imitating Ginger, the movie star. The wig did not match her slightly less flamboyant personality.

I made an appointment to pick out my wig while I still had my hair. Dr. Lin told me well in advance that because of the way my chemo treatments would be given, I would not only lose my hair once, but twice. After finishing my last round of H/T/C on September 3, and after having the mastectomy in mid- to late October, the break would be long enough that when I started A/C in late November, my hair would begin to grow only to fall out a second time. She strongly suggested that I pick out a good-quality wig, one that I would enjoy wearing for most of a year.

While Tracy was fighting cancer, with the sheer stress of being her mom and emotionally going through cancer with her, a lot of my hair fell out—maybe as much as 20 percent. I knew when my hair began to thin after starting chemo, there would not be much to debate; I would have to shave my head soon after the first signs of shedding.

On the morning of my appointment to select my wig, I was completely preoccupied and lost in thought as we arrived at Dana-Farber. But when someone walked out the front entrance while we were walking in, wearing a screaming pink wig, the ice was broken. Grady began to tease me about not getting my heart set on a cotton candy pink wig, and I began to laugh. The sadness and apprehension about losing my hair took on new "color."

When we arrived at the Friends Place on Dana 9, I was taken into a room that was filled with boxes of wigs in every style and price range imaginable. I had brought some pictures of a few different styles that I thought I might like and asked the pros who were helping me for their opinions. I appreciated their guidance while learning about the advantages and disadvantages of synthetic wigs over wigs made from natural hair. I learned what to look for in quality, comfort, and style, and how to care for my wig. I had no idea there was so much to consider.

As the two assistants listened and learned about me and my normal routine, a stack of boxes were selected from the shelves and placed beside me.

One of the first wigs I tried on was an exact replica of my sister-in-law Caron's slightly bouffant blond hair. I broke into hysterics to see Caron's hair on my head!

Grady was "helping" and as he voiced his opinions, I began to understand how Tracy ended up as a platinum blond with Antonio's help and suggestions. I tried a short, auburn brown, spiked wig and Grady loved it. I looked like a refugee from a punk rock band! (The cotton candy pink wig we had seen earlier that morning as we were entering the hospital was looking better by the minute!)

As I tried different wigs in the private salon, I not only had the expert advice of the woman who works at the Friends Place, but I also had the input from a hairdresser who volunteered on Mondays. (Thank goodness!) I was interested in why the hairdresser volunteered at the Friends Place on his day off, and so I asked.

He told me that some of his clients had been diagnosed with breast cancer. After hearing their stories, he understood what it was like for them to lose their hair. Volunteering his talents to make the process a little easier seemed to be the natural way for him to give back and bless others.

Together (excluding Grady's ideas) the suggestions that were made were fantastic! I was guided into buying a beautiful new "do" and selected a color that would compliment my complexion as the chemo began to drain my face of its natural health tone. As difficult as I thought finding the right wig might be, the process was easy and fun thanks to the great advice I received.

The following Sunday at church, our youth pastor, Pastor Kevin, had the honor of addressing the ladies of the church about a women's retreat. Knowing that I could take a joke, he sashayed onto the platform at the front of the church wearing a spaghetti mop on his head with his voice raised a few octaves. He encouraged the ladies to attend "a weekend of fellowship, teachings, and fun" as he dramatically posed and brushed his "spaghetti locks" from the side of his face.

I was in the back of the church with Grady, laughing hysterically. When Pastor Kevin finished his invitation, he came to join us in the back of the church and where we were standing. Slowly I leaned toward him and quietly asked, "Can I borrow your wig?"

Imitating my slow and calculated move toward him, he leaned past me and directed his response to Grady. "No! I'm still voting for you to get the pink one!"

Each day my hair seemed to shed a little more as I neared the date for my second H/T/C infusion. We had two weddings to attend that were a week apart and coming up soon. I began to wonder if my own hair would be going to either of the weddings!

Much to my surprise and delight, the two wigs (that had been ordered) arrived at the Friends Place in less than a week and before either of the weddings. After I paraded around modeling the wigs in front of the staff, they cast their votes and helped in my final selection for color and the subtle difference in style.

The morning of July 21, while getting ready for the first of the two weddings, my hair began to fall out in gobs. I really wasn't expecting this to happen so soon. Here I was hoping (at the least) to look presentable, and instantly and overnight I was taking on the appearance of a molting chicken!

Only a few people attending the wedding knew I had been diagnosed with cancer. If I wore my new wig, it might be obvious to others. I certainly did not want to upstage and outshine the bride with my lovely new "do," nor did I want any of the attention to be on me as friends learned (by my appearance) I was fighting cancer. Then again, I did not want to be socializing at the wedding looking like I had an incurable case of mange!

Knowing that the day would arrive and we would face the inevitable, I had Antonio's hair clippers. I hinted to Grady that maybe I should wear my new wig for the first time. Carefully he surveyed my head from every angle, declaring, "It doesn't look *that bad*."

His words didn't make me feel much better. Clearly, he was the one who was not ready for me to shave my head, and he was not volunteering for the job. *Great! Now what? Lord, do you think we can make it one more day with my hair?*

The wedding was at an outdoor setting overlooking Lake Winnipesaukee. Each time there was a breeze, I held my breath hoping that my hair would hang on until this day ended. Despite the fact that I had adorned and taken my hair to some of the finest places, now when I needed it most it seemed determined to leave me!

During the reception, I noticed a few strands hanging that seemed to have *two ends* instead of just one, and with every person who greeted me with a hug, I only hoped that when the embrace ended they wouldn't have more of my shedding hair on them than I had left on my head.

On Monday morning when we went to Boston for my infusion of H/T/C, I wore a hat to cover my thinning hair.

I prayed about who I should ask to shave my head, and Cherie came to mind. She has such gentleness about her. The Lord had used her to confirm that this diagnosis of breast cancer would be used for God's glory the night I had shared about my diagnosis in our small group meeting. The gentleness that is so much a part of who she is made the words she spoke easier to accept; God was allowing this illness, and He would be glorified through this trial.

On Tuesday morning after Grady left for work, and after praying that she would be at home and able to help, I called Cherie. As I heard the words coming from my mouth, it felt like the request was being asked by someone else. "Cherie, would you help me… Cherie, I need to… *Cherie, my hair is falling out and I need someone to shave my head.* Can you help me?"

Leading up to this time, I knew it was important to have the right person for this task. I just didn't realize how important. Cherie was comforting and perfect for this moment. Graciously, she came to my rescue.

The last thing I needed was to have anyone cutting off my hair that I would need to console and reassure. And I didn't want my head to be shaved in a hair salon. I wanted this to be done privately and at home. This is something a lot of women diagnosed with cancer don't think about, something they don't know how to prepare for unless they have been through it with someone they love, as we had with Tracy two years earlier. For a woman, it is an extremely intimate and vulnerable moment when you are bald for the first time since birth and making your grand entrance into this world. Cherie has such a tender servant's heart that out of all of my friends, I knew she was the person I needed for support and for this moment.

I placed a stool outside on our back patio and laid the clippers and a pair of shears on the step. The sun was shining. The day was beautiful. I slipped on a rain slicker to substitute for a hair salon cape. As Cherie picked up the shears, she asked if I was ready. "Do you want a mirror?"

"No. I can't watch. Let's get it over with."

She began to cut at what was left of my shoulder-length medium brown hair. Next she picked up the clippers and shaved what the shears had left behind.

"You have a perfectly shaped head. No divots, no bumps!"

I felt slightly weepy, but I began to laugh at Cherie's comment about my "perfect" head…. Who would have known!

"Wow! This really makes your eyes stand out. I never realized how green they are. You look great!"

"Yeah, Cherie, sure I do."

"No…really! You look *really* beautiful!"

It was a traumatic moment. Once the decision was made, it was much like diving into an icy cold lake. When you are in mid-air and before impacting the water, it's too late to turn back. Cherie made the moment of the icy cold impact easier.

I had not told Grady that I was going to call Cherie. When he came home from work, he found me fixing dinner and wearing a scarf covering my shaved head.

Tracy had gone before me; the path she had so recently walked was still fresh in my mind, and I knew how to be as prepared as one can be for the day when scarves, hats, and wigs replace hair. It was time, and I had everything I needed. Tracy had told me where to find all of the scarves that had come from Spain. She had packed them and they were ready for me to retrieve from her apartment. To lessen the trauma of the moment, I had picked them up weeks before I needed them.

It was obvious that Grady felt sad for me, but I know he was glad for Cherie's willingness to do something he would not have been able to do. He can be such a mush-ball during emotional moments.

My first public appearance wearing a scarf to cover my head was the very next evening when Grady and I attended our small group meeting from church. Again, I was happy that Cherie had been the one to shave my head. She arrived at Wendy's house ahead of us and told everyone about our preceding day together as she clipped off my hair. Everyone was prepared for my entrance, and there was no shock at my appearance when I walked through the door. There was only love and support.

That evening our discussion was about Pastor Peter's Sunday morning message entitled "How God Grows Us." The teachings were based on the Scripture from John 15. Jesus is the "Vine." We are the "branches." What does that mean?

During our small group discussion, one of our questions was: **If it's all about fruitfulness, what is it that you can do to be in a better position to produce fruit for the Lord?**

As different ones in our group shared, I listened. I was wondering about what God had in store for me as I went through cancer. I knew that this journey was going to be a long one, but I had not really thought much about how this would put me "in a better position to produce fruit for the Lord."

Our discussion went deeper. What does it take to produce a successful harvest? It takes soil preparation, fertilizing, and watering. Trees, shrubs, and vines require careful pruning, cutting, and reshaping to produce fruit.

We applied the principles we were discussing to our own lives. What did we expect the Lord was doing in us personally? What stage of "growth" were we facing during the next 6-12 months? Were we allowing God to produce good fruit in our lives?

In my heart, I knew I was in a painful stage of growth with the Lord. My next year would be filled with "pruning." Nine sets of eyes looked in my direction when it was my turn to share. For several moments, there was silence at my response. From the corner of the room a single word from Bill broke the stillness as he plumbed the depths of the year ahead of me that would revolve around hospitals and cancer. "Wow…"

With each round of H/T/C, I reacted differently. I never knew what side effects to expect, which is to say life became interesting! Violent diarrhea can follow chemo treatments, and that can lead to dehydration and an imbalance of electrolytes; a proper fluid intake was something I had to watch closely. I learned that lesson well from watching Tracy and the number of trips she made to the hospital because of dehydration.

Fortunately, the week of my brother's wedding, and five days after my infusion, my side effects were miraculously few and short-lived.

This was David's second marriage, and he and his bride planned an outdoor wedding at our family farm. I had been given the order to pray for clear skies, since scattered storms were in the forecast. I guess everyone thought that would be just about the limit of my capabilities, since I had just had another heavy round of chemotherapy.

Three days before his wedding, Dave called. "Ah-h-h-h, Kath, how ya doin'?"

I could tell by his tone there was something concerning the wedding he had forgotten to do. "I'm okay. What did you forget?"

"Ah-h-h-h-h, music???"

"DAVID!"

"Look, I'm not worried. You and Grady are pros at this. You just pick something with nice words that Grady already knows on guitar, and I'm sure we'll all love it!"

"David! NO! I will pick out some music for you, but I insist that you and Lori decide which pieces you want and how you want them worked into the service. This is your wedding, after all. Fair?"

"Okay."

The following evening while David and Lori selected their wedding music with Grady, my sister, Barb, called and she was frantic. "Kath, Mom's driving us all nuts! SHE has decided to make chicken pie for the rehearsal dinner. She says you're the only one who can make the biscuits light and fluffy. What do you do that the rest of us can't?"

I began to laugh. "Barb, the biscuits are pretty easy. I think I can handle making them. Actually, I'm still feeling pretty good. The meds for the nausea are doing a great job, and my energy is surprisingly good. I'm a little worried I may crash on Saturday right after the wedding ceremony. But I'm really doing okay."

A few days after the wedding, I shared in my email "updates" all that had transpired during that week, including the importance of where my prayer focus was as we passed the halfway mark of being in the research trial.

Date: Tuesday, July 31, 2007
Subject: Halfway into this phase!

Hello Everyone!

I can "officially" say I have now passed my halfway mark. Hurray! A milestone! (Someone gather stones and build an altar to "remember.") I need to approach my treatment plan in segments. This is only the beginning in this process, but still a significant point.

It is time to seriously pray that these drugs that are being put into my body are attacking and killing any and every

cancer cell (or fragment of cell). These cells travel through the blood stream. Please pray for the effectiveness of the chemo treatments...that every "abnormal" cell or fragmented cell is killed off.

All of my treatment beyond surgery will be determined by how effectively the chemo drugs have killed ALL abnormal cells that will be examined in the pathology after surgery. I'm still looking for my Heavenly Father to **create** medical history through me!

*[*At the time, I had no idea how that request to the Lord would be met!]*

I have shared with most of you that I have been emailing with Kelley Tuthill of Channel 5 News since her diagnosis of cancer. "Chronicle" did a half-hour program about the women Kelley has met, sharing their stories. A follow-up program is being planned.

A week ago, "Chronicle" was there to record Kelley's last A/C treatment, and the producer had hoped I would arrive in time (for my infusion) to meet and discuss the follow-up program.

Overall, this last round of H/T/C was harder in some ways, easier in other ways. It has been eight days, and it seems that when I returned to the hospital for my Herceptin on day seven, my side effects were worse for about twenty-four hours. That is nothing compared to some. I am Praising Jesus!

These drugs do affect the heart. Man! Am I aware of that! Yesterday at the hospital when my pulse was taken "at rest," it was 118 beats per minute! I looked at Shannon, the medical tech taking my pulse, like she had three heads! Normal for me is around 52!!!!!!! Whew!

Pray that the Lord would be Lord of all...including protecting my heart from damage; the Herceptin is the chemo that can cause damage. I have learned this change is usually temporary and the heart usually regains strength once the Herceptin is stopped.

I did feel less intense mood swings and goofy thoughts this time. I felt like I was right out of my tree and completely nuts after my first round of H/T/C and taking the anti-nausea combination of meds.

Last Saturday I attended, enjoyed, and fully participated in my brother's wedding. My wig was an absolute hit! My younger sister,

Barb, was so impressed she's all set to shave her head and get a wig just like mine. (I'm sorry, Pastor Kevin; the pink wig would not have matched my outfit.)

It was a wonderful day. My job was to help Grady select music, work it into the service, **and to pray that the Lord would "part the clouds over the farm," since the wedding was outdoors at our family farm.** I did my job well, and so did the Lord.

It was lightly raining as Grady began to sing and the bride was to make her entrance. As if on cue, suddenly the rain stopped and the sun came out.

This interesting little parting of the clouds gave way to an incredible opportunity to witness for God's power and grace. God is so amazing! The things He uses to bring attention to His power.

I am doing so incredibly well. I know it is because of the prayer support from the "warriors" who have been so faithful in prayer.

I cannot end this without bragging about my pastors and tell you about their encouragement and support. My pastors offered up prayers for my health and requests for my healing and took them to the Wailing Wall in Jerusalem while they were there for a conference. WOW! God bless you, pastors. God bless you!

Jesus has surrounded me with the best of the BEST!!!

Blessings and Love to each of you,

Kathy

Grady and I were among the last guests to leave the wedding celebration. I thought of Tracy and Antonio at her cousin Amanda's wedding two years earlier, and how they were among the last guests to leave that wedding. I thought about how Tracy looked that day—just like a "movie star"!

The good days are more than good; they are *Great!*

While going through cancer, laugh.

Special days are *more* special. You want them to never end, even into the night. And Tracy taught me it's okay to go through them with joy, grace, and elegance.

Chapter 19

Looking for Answers

I wore the many scarves Tracy had given to me as often as I wore my wig. Usually when I was grocery shopping or visiting friends, I wore a scarf rather than my wig. At first I felt uncomfortable about my appearance and the reactions from others, but eventually those feelings changed as friends treated me like "me."

Going through chemo, there were days that it wasn't safe for me to drive because of medications, but nine or ten days after a round of H/T/C, life was normal. I socialized, drove myself around, cooked, and cleaned; it was just at a slightly slower pace.

One morning my friend Deirdre (who had helped me decide upon the research protocol) asked if I could drive her to a doctor's appointment. She had injured her back and could not find anyone else who was able to take her to the appointment. I felt well, and I was more than glad to help. When I arrived at her house and watched her as she walked toward my car, I could tell Deirdre was in agony.

After her doctor's appointment, we drove to the supermarket so that she could fill her prescriptions at the pharmacy in the store. She didn't think it would take more than fifteen minutes to have the prescriptions filled, so I took advantage of the extra stop and hurried through the store to gather a few groceries I needed and paid for them.

We agreed on a location to meet just beyond the checkout. I stood and waited for Deirdre.

And I waited. And I waited. And then...I waited some more.

I began to notice that some of the other customers were looking at me strangely. Some were staring or looking away, some were looking at me in disgust, and others would drop their gaze to the floor and walk past. I couldn't figure out why.

Suddenly, I realized the reason for the reactions. Here I was, looking like a cancer poster child on an anti-smoking billboard, and I was waiting for Deirdre in front of the glass cabinet where the cartons of cigarettes were under lock and key!

With my head wrapped in a scarf, I can only imagine what was going through their minds as people buying cigarettes saw me standing post beside their favorite brands.

With each week, our routine of driving to Boston became more and more integrated into our lives and I became more and more accepting of this new way of life. As I became increasingly familiar with my surroundings at Dana-Farber, a strange thing happened. I began to look forward to trips to the hospital and who the Lord might bring to my attention. It never failed. There was always someone. My heart became more and more sensitive to how great the need was to be compassionate and bring encouragement to others who were also there.

It started to become a secondary concern that I was a patient fighting cancer. What mattered first was having the perfect peace and the joy of the Lord in my life, despite my condition. The pruning God was doing in my life was starting to produce spiritual fruit. How God grows us...

Whenever an opportunity presented itself for me to share about the Lord and the peace He had given me, I shared. I found it to be an incredible place to reach out to others, and it became an extremely unusual blessing to be at Dana-Farber.

I shared about my experiences at the hospital with those on my email list. Something amazing began to happen in the lives of many of the people receiving my updates. Several felt impressed by the Lord to pray for the people I met. My friends were praying for me, and they began to pray for other patients whose stories I shared in my email updates. It became an adventure unfolding as the Lord provided opportunities.

The more prayers that went out, the more opportunities I had to share my faith with others, including some of the medical staff.

Date: Sunday August 12, 2007

Subject: Heading for 75%!

..."I praise you, for I am fearfully and wonderfully made. Wonderful are your works; my soul knows it very well." Psalm 139:14 ...And when I write my paraphrased version of the Bible, right here I would add: "Therefore do not despise *your nose hairs!*" (Anyone who wishes to know "why"...just ask! I'll tell you this: When you don't have them because of chemo, YOU MISS THEM! They serve a purpose!)

God is doing so much. I can't believe all that has happened in the past few weeks. Since I am at the hospital every week, I see lots of patients waiting for their treatment.

Two weeks ago, the Lord drew my attention to a young couple. They are probably only thirty years old. Last week it seemed the Lord deliberately delayed my thirty-minute infusion of Herceptin so that I would be given the opportunity to speak to this couple.

"Shannon and Todd" were brought to our private infusion pod, where there were just two infusion chairs! Some of the infusion pods have as many as ten chairs. But there I was with Shannon in a pod for just the two of us.

She shared her story with me: She had finished her chemo treatment for breast cancer last January 2007. (She had not been treated at Dana-Farber originally.) When she returned for her six-month checkup after completing chemo treatment, it was discovered that the cancer had metastasized in her breast bone and lungs. As we talked, her eyes were filled with hope when I told her I would keep her in prayer....

They are so young. She is such a gentle and sweet girl. Her husband is so attentive and, I know, very concerned for his young wife. Please remember them in prayer with me.

This past Friday I had a phone interview with the producer of "Chronicle." Kathy Bickimer would like to interview me at the hospital for the upcoming segment of "Kelley's Story." I really want to honor the Lord through this illness. If you have to go through hell, it may as well be for a heavenly cause. Here is a *BIG* way for that to happen and to impact lives. I just want to be an instrument in His hands.

Kathy (the producer) would also like to interview Tracy. Our story is unique: Tracy's diagnosis June 2005, my diagnosis May 2007... two different types of breast cancer...two different modes of treatment.

My surgery is scheduled for: OCTOBER 15.

Please pray for wisdom for my doctors. So many decisions need to be made in the next few weeks. Pray for wisdom in the choices Grady and I will be faced with in the options put before us before going into this surgery. Pray that we will be guided by the Lord as the doctors help us make some very tough choices. One of the key things that we need to know is, will I definitely need radiation? **This will matter for some of my surgery decisions.**

...A note of praise! The tumor continues to shrink thanks to the chemo drugs I am getting **AND, WITHOUT DOUBT, ALL OF THE PRAYER!!!!!!!!!!!!**

Tracy is FINALLY home from Spain. Hurray!!!!!!! We are on our way to her house in a couple of hours for my tough treatment tomorrow morning.

Tracy lives so close to Dana-Farber, I clearly see God's hand in opening that position for her to teach at Milton Academy. It has been such a blessing to be so close to the hospitals that we *both* have needed.

After tomorrow's chemo round of H/T/C, I will have 75% of my tough treatment in Phase 1 behind me. My last thirty-minute infusion of Herceptin for this first phase is on September 17.

Grady and I are hoping to take a break from everything related to cancer and go away for some snorkeling before my surgery. The swimming would be such good exercise and conditioning leading up to the surgery. Plus we all know I'm a "snorkel-aholic."

I continue to thank God for each of you and remember to ask God for His blessing upon you.

By His Grace,

Kathy

It had been more than ten weeks since Grady and I had seen Tracy and Antonio. Trace and I talked on the phone every chance possible while she was in Spain, but it was hard (especially for Tracy) for us to be apart during my first several weeks of treatment.

Every Sunday afternoon we packed an overnight bag and spent the night at their apartment for my Monday morning appointment. On Sunday, August 12, I couldn't get there fast enough! Tracy and Antonio were finally home.

I was at the point in my treatment that I needed to make some very tough decisions. I needed Tracy's support, her opinions, and her experience as I made those choices.

When we arrived, Antonio greeted us at the door. "WOW! You look really 'hot' in that wig! You look terrific!"

"You mean this really was the better choice over the pink wig??? It was a hard choice, you know? That pink wig had some serious interest."

We all laughed.

I turned to Tracy. She was smiling, but there was a sad, almost melancholy look in her eyes as she looked at her mother as the one bearing the effects of breast cancer. We embraced and did not say a word.... We just "understood," in the quiet moment of holding each other, something that most mothers and daughters will hopefully never experience.

"Hi, Trace..."

"Hi, Mom..."

"I'm glad you are home. I've missed you."

"I know; I'm really glad to be home and to be here for you."

Tracy accompanied her father and me to Dana-Farber in the morning for my appointment with Dr. Lin. I wanted Tracy there for some of the things I planned to talk to Dr. Lin about. Something had been haunting me for months about Tracy's diagnosis and then my own.

Dr. Lin greeted the three of us with a big smile as she walked into the exam room. "Tracy, you're home! I'll bet your mom is glad to have you back."

We chatted briefly and then moved on to something that had been on my mind and troubling me for several weeks.

"Nancy, every time I ponder what Tracy and I have in common with our diagnoses of breast cancer, I keep coming back to two things. Prior to our diagnoses, we both had abnormal and intense stress for two years or more, with little relief from the emotional pressure we were under. Tracy had been in turmoil as her first marriage failed. Marrying Antonio brought its own level of emotion as she broke ties to permanently live in Spain.

"Before I was diagnosed, I faced some very significant losses including my Dad's passing. Tracy's diagnosis would have been traumatic enough, but I was worried about my mom's ability to adjust to life without Dad.

"The second thing I have questioned is an event that happened in June 1979."

There was intensity in Nancy's expression as she leaned forward in her chair.

"In June 1979, we attended an outdoor Christian festival called 'Creation '79.' On March 28, and shortly before Creation '79, there was an accident at the Three Mile Island power plant. The accident was serious enough that the surrounding area was evacuated. Three Mile Island wasn't far from Buck, Pennsylvania, where the Creation festival was being held.

"About five thousand people were registered for the festival, and almost everyone who attended camped. It rained at least part of every day, most of the week, making it impossible to avoid exposure to the elements. The camping area was called 'Muddy Run,' and after being at Muddy Run we knew how the campground got its name."

I could tell Nancy was thinking through this information that I was sharing with her for the first time.

"Nancy, I'll always wonder if Tracy and I developed breast cancer because we were exposed to something that rained down on us or because of eating something that was locally grown. Was there something that was still in the atmosphere from the nuclear accident at the Three Mile Island power plant?"

I told Nancy that when the festival was over, and we were packing to leave the campground, I saw notices posted in the restrooms. Warnings. The notices said to refrain from having x-rays unless they were completely necessary, because of questionable exposure to radiation from the steam that escaped from Three Mile Island and may have been in the atmosphere.

Nancy's response gave me even greater reason to question. "Now that would be an interesting study. The female population who would have been most likely to develop breast cancer after such exposure would have been between the ages of ten and twenty-five."

I looked at Tracy as I spoke to Nancy. "Tracy was weeks shy of turning nine. I was a few weeks from turning thirty.…. We were both on the cusp of the most vulnerable ages for the women who might develop breast cancer from radiation."

Nancy had a long list of things to discuss. Our conversation moved on. She started by telling me Dr. Golshan needed to know who my plastic surgeon would be and the type of reconstruction I was planning. I was discouraged after meeting two different plastic surgeons and researching the surgeries that had been presented to me.

"Nancy, I was settled on having a TRAM flap reconstruction, but I've ruled that procedure out. I do not want to compromise the stability of my lower back by taking the abdominal muscle that is used in a TRAM flap surgery to supply the blood flow to the reconstructed breast. I believe it will seriously and adversely affect my lifestyle.

"I do not like what I have read; maybe I'll be stuck with prosthetics. I'm not happy with my choices so far. And I didn't feel the plastic surgeons I have spoken with were right for me."

I sighed as I slouched forward in my chair. "I wish there was some way to simply use belly fat to reconstruct a new breast and leave the abdominal muscle intact and where God intended it to be."

Nancy suggested a new procedure that very few plastic surgeons were trained to do. The surgery, called DIEP flap reconstruction, is very complex, but Brigham and Women's had recently hired the best DIEP flap surgeon north of New York City. "Her name is Stephanie Caterson. I'll give you her number."

The process of finding the right plastic surgeon was not an easy assignment. If there was ever a time when I needed to know what I wanted, it was on the topic of reconstruction. This was a time when I listened closely to the women in my life that had faced the decisions I was now facing. Pat,

Mary Kathryn, Claire, Claire's sister, and Pauline all played a part in helping me through this time. They all had experiences to share about mastectomies, either from personal experience or information from women in their families. And some of those experiences were not good and led to further surgeries later on, because of choices made hastily and under pressure.

My health insurance company had assigned an oncology nurse to my case. Through our many phone conversations, Helen and I became friends. One of the interesting facts she shared with me is this: few women do the kind of research I did before determining what they will do after having a mastectomy.

I can understand that. Some women are so traumatized by the diagnosis and treatment for breast cancer, they are swept into making decisions they later regret. They do not (or cannot) take the time to understand the number of different types of reconstruction options available. There are choices, and the first choice is not always the best choice!

Many women are so stuck emotionally on the fact that they are losing a breast, they forget they are saving their life, and there *is* life after breast cancer. I have heard horrible stories about women who could not think beyond the word "mastectomy." Frozen in their terror, or because of reasons of vanity or fear that their husband or boyfriend would leave them, they refused treatment. I have to voice a reality check. If an entire relationship is contingent upon breasts.... (You complete the sentence!)

Tracy shifted in her chair and addressed Dr. Lin. "Dr. Lin, if my mother is going to have radiation, do you have an opinion about reconstruction at the time of the mastectomy?"

Nancy skillfully sidestepped Tracy's question and told her that she would know what was happening as decisions were made, but this was something for my plastic surgeon and my radiation oncologist to agree upon and work through together. She told Tracy, "We still need a plastic surgeon to be selected. We all have a part in this, and we need to make the best decisions for your mom as her team. Nothing will be overlooked as the whole picture is considered."

Then Dr. Lin turned to me and asked if I had met with Dr. Jennifer Bellon, our radiation oncologist. My appointment with Dr. Bellon was on the calendar; I only hoped that Dr. Golshan would be satisfied by that.

Slightly forlorn, I said to Nancy, "I feel like I'm barely used to my chemo routine, and here we are facing the next phase of treatment. I understand the reasons, but as a patient, it feels like curing breast cancer is a little like getting swept up in a rip current." (You can see the shore, but you just have to keep going with the current until it ends.)

My analogy reminded me of something I needed to ask her. I wanted her permission to take a vacation before my surgery with Dr. Golshan. I knew it would be a very long time before I would feel well enough to travel if we did not take time immediately after my last Herceptin infusion. Grady and I both needed another mental escape from cancer.

Dr. Lin looked at me like I was just a little crazy. "Well, if you are physically up for it, I have no medical objections."

Tracy redirected the conversation and brought us back to where she was still fretting about the reconstruction and radiation. What I didn't know was Tracy had emailed Dr. Bellon for her opinion. She was hoping Dr. Lin would say something that would support Dr. Bellon's views. Trace knew plenty about survival rates. She had some very definite ideas about the best course of treatment, and those opinions included postponing reconstruction. And I was glad she was determined enough to voice those opinions. This was "all about" her mom surviving!

Together, Grady, Tracy, and I headed to Dana 10 for my infusion. It felt good to have our daughter's support. I was comforted by her presence. Since it was a little past lunchtime, we were hungry and ready to check out what was left in the canteen. The sandwich selection had been picked over, and the remaining choices were meager.

Once I was settled and Jade had the first of my three infusions started, Tracy and Grady went scouting for food. When they returned, they were beaming with delight. Not only had they found that the cafeteria was serving my favorite chicken soup, they had made a detour on their excursion and discovered that the hospital had a lottery for Red Sox tickets. Four tickets for three different games were going to be given away. Together Grady, Tracy, and I decided which of the three Red Sox games would be our first, second, and third choices to attend, and we entered the giveaway.

A few weeks later I received a letter of congratulations. I had won tickets to the September 10 Sox game against Tampa Bay!

There is a longstanding connection between the Red Sox and Dana-Farber. I have so much appreciation for the Sox charity work for the hospital and their support in finding a cure for cancer.

When I was a little girl, one of my TV favorites was a kids' program with Big Brother Bob Emery hosting the show. As a child, I didn't understand the meaning of the coin canisters with a little boy's picture on them and Big Brother Bob's plea to support the "Jimmy Fund."

At Dana-Farber, I experienced firsthand what I could not understand but had heard about on a children's program some fifty-odd years earlier. There is an historic "Red Sox baseball wall of fame" on the lower level of the hospital. As I looked at and read the memorabilia along the wall of the corridor, I learned about a little boy and his fight to survive cancer, Dr. Farber, and the hospital's connection to the (then) Boston Braves.

I never could have imagined as a child how a little boy from Maine and known only as "Jimmy" would impact me as an adult. Much of what is done at the hospital began because of his diagnosed leukemia in 1948, and a caring, dedicated research doctor in Boston named Dr. Sidney Farber.

Chapter 20

Like Running a Marathon

My third round of H/T/C hit me like a steamroller. Suddenly, I knew why Dr. Lin had looked at me like I was crazy when I asked for her permission to vacation and snorkel. *I* was beginning to think I was crazy!

After my other infusions, my energy level returned pretty well, but after the third H/T/C infusion, I could hardly manage to put one foot in front of the other.

Subject: August 25

Hello Everyone!

I'm discovering that it is taking me a little longer to rally after my three infusions. The "sick" part of this wasn't too bad: the waves of mild "queasies" lasted a little longer than after my second H/T/C dose when I finished my anti-nausea meds. I'm definitely more tired and weaker. I'm trying very hard to get back into an exercise routine, after requiring eight days off to recover from my infusion. It's a huge effort.

Tracy is being a slave driver! It's important for me to be in the best physical condition I can be in before going to surgery in October. I'm still walking an hour a day. It's uninterrupted time with the Lord in prayer, and *that* is motivation for me to continue to walk. But I have a different kind of weakness and tiredness that I have never experienced. With the exception of the worst of my days, **I am walking!**

I can say, without doubt, the Lord really was gracious to me, considering how well I felt for my brother David's wedding on July 28. I didn't nap that entire weekend, and that was only days after my second H/T/C infusion.

With my third H/T/C, a couple of weeks ago, I crashed exactly the way I did with my first experience. I couldn't even pick my head up off the pillow from Friday at noon until Saturday late afternoon. Yet, the weekend of my brother's wedding I did *excellent!* Wow! I am so grateful!

Two weeks ago I met John, a man seventy-ish, and his daughters, Evelyn and Jeannie, as I was receiving my H/T/C. John is very definitely "from the *old country*"...I don't know which one...but one of those old countries (Greece, Cyprus...one of those).

I watched as one of the oncology nurses unsuccessfully tried to access the vein in John's arm. I had the same experience myself during my MRI in June. It was awful.

I began to talk to the three to distract them and help break the tension of the moment. After about three minutes, Jeannie looked at me and said, "You're a Christian, aren't you?" I told her I was, and she began to tell me all about her Dad. John has bladder cancer and is scheduled to have his bladder removed on September 7.

Last Monday, I was in my infusion pod and waiting for my Herceptin to arrive from the pharmacy. John and Jeannie walked past the area I was in. I went racing after them to see how he was and to tell John I had been praying for him. I shared with him that through the week I had spoken with two different people who knew others who had bladder reconstruction. They were both doing very well. I assured John I would continue to pray for him. His eyes welled up with tears as he gave me the biggest, most genuine hug and just kept saying, "Thank you, thank you, thank you."

Over the next few weeks, my doctors will be making decisions concerning radiation and my surgery. **The tumor continues to shrink. Please pray that ALL cancer cells in my lymph nodes are killed! So much of my continued treatment will be based on pathology.**

Please pray that God would guide their decisions and grant wisdom to all of my doctors.

On Monday, I will have the weekly dose of Herceptin and my "best" week physically.

Then...I have one more H/T/C dose on September 3, and two final doses of Herceptin for the protocol! My last dose of Herceptin in this first phase of my treatment will be on September 17.

I have been given the okay to take a vacation. Grady and I will take a week to snorkel before I face surgery. This has been mentally exhausting...all of the decisions wrapped around the surgery, as well as the physical aspects of running back and forth to Boston every week. It's been a giant juggling act to meet all of the requirements for the research protocol. You really have no idea! Grady has been so supportive and incredible through this. He needs some fun in his life before we start all over again for the next phase of treatment.

In October, Tracy will join in the "Making Strides Against Breast Cancer" walk. On her personal page there is a photo that was taken at the end of the walk last year. Tracy is wearing a "survivor" ribbon....I'm so proud of her. This year she is dedicating her walk to me. She's my hero!

Blessings and Love,

Kathy

On Tracy's personal page for Making Strides Against Breast Cancer, she shared about her victory as a cancer survivor. She also shared that she had an even greater cause to raise funds to support research for breast cancer—I was fighting the disease. She ended her personal page encouraging me and cheering me on. She dedicated her walk and the quest to find a cure for breast cancer to me. What an honor!

As Tracy trained for her walk as a pacesetter and fundraiser, she was relentless as she pushed me harder to be in top condition before my surgery. "Mom, you have to walk." "Mom, you have to keep trying." "Mom, if you have to, break up your routine. Walk thirty minutes in the morning and thirty minutes at night." "Mom..."

I continued to walk as though I was in preparation for a marathon, even though each day I felt worse. Finally, out of fear of collapsing a mile from home on one of the hills on my route, I decided it was in my best interest to walk back and forth on the road in front of our house. It is pretty flat. It was boring but safe and flat. I set a goal to walk for an hour, and most days I was successful, but I was physically spent and rubber-legged when I finished.

Each day my breathing was more and more labored. At the end of my walk, I thought my heart would explode in my chest as I climbed our two-hundred-foot driveway. In my mind, Tracy was cracking the whip moving me forward. During the previous weeks of treatment I needed naps. But now, it was ridiculous! I required two or more hours of sleep during the day. I was falling farther and farther behind and could not keep up with simple household duties. Until now, I had been able to pace myself and able to do the laundry and most of our cooking (with the exception of my worst days). But I lost all energy after my third infusion of H/T/C. I was a useless slug, curled up in the recliner for days on end.

Dr. Golshan was pressing for a firm surgery plan to be established. Was the reconstruction going to be done at the time of the mastectomy or later? What type of reconstruction? Would he need to place a tissue expander into my chest? He wanted answers I didn't have, and I didn't feel well enough to even care! I was exhausted and overwhelmed by the demands and frustrated to tears by how I was feeling physically, especially after my fourth and final H/T/C on Monday, September 3.

We had made arrangements with Kathy Bickimer, one of the producers for "Chronicle," to film during my September 10 Herceptin infusion. Kathy wanted to capture the hospital experience during the interview. As Grady and I had done so many times, we stayed at Tracy's the night before the interview. We had a full day of activities. My first appointment was at 9:00 with Dr. Stephanie Caterson to discuss reconstruction. There was just barely time to meet with this new doctor before my interview for "Chronicle," and there were no extra minutes to spare. I was excited and looking forward to this day. However, there were a few surprises in the making. A whole new dimension was about to be added into our plans.

Our day would end with the Sox playing Tampa Bay. We were going to historic Fenway Park and living the experience: the roar of the crowds, the lights on the field, the "crack of the bat hitting the ball," the famous Fenway franks…we would be in the stands behind home plate together… me, Grady, Tracy, and Tonx.

I woke up irritable the morning of this nonstop day of events and completely frustrated by how odd and woozy I felt. I literally stumbled to the bathroom to shower.

I was ghastly pale. Unlike Tracy, I never completely lost all of my eyebrows and eyelashes, but they were very thin, and without makeup I looked plain and sickly. This morning, I could not have looked worse.

As I hurried in slow motion to dress and put on my makeup, I discovered I had forgotten half of my cosmetics at home. I could not possibly be interviewed for a program to be aired on television looking this bad. It was out of the question! I had to buy foundation and blush someplace before my interview and attempt to make some improvement to my "death warmed over" appearance.

We arrived at the Faulkner Hospital, where Dr. Caterson's office is located. If we were late for our appointment because we got lost on the way, it didn't matter; Dr. Caterson was running even later.

Walking into the hospital, I was hanging onto Grady's arm to keep from falling. I was faint, stumbling, and grumbling about my physical condition, my appearance, everything planned for the day, and now having to shop for makeup before meeting the crew from "Chronicle." My heart was not at all feeling thankful.

Within minutes of meeting Dr. Caterson, I knew THIS was my plastic surgeon. This was the doctor I had been looking for! Although I was painfully short of time, Grady and I spent almost an hour asking questions about DIEP flap reconstruction as Dr. Caterson performed an exam and explained the surgery.

Deep inferior epigastric perforator flap surgery is excruciatingly long— from nine to twelve hours on average. Dr. Caterson had the answers for some of the most critical questions I had been wrestling with concerning the various types of reconstruction. Most importantly, she was willing to surgically work with whatever my radiation oncologist decided. If that meant my best success for killing cancer was to have radiation before reconstruction, she would do the plastic surgery after radiation.

Depending upon the angles of the radiation beams, Dr. Caterson felt radiation might jeopardize the integrity of the transplanted tissue. It might be better to wait and have reconstruction a year after the mastectomy. She spent time explaining the effects of radiation on the skin, a reconstructed breast mound, and (in logical terms) what needed to be considered. This was about saving my life, first; the quality of my life, second. And cosmetic appeal, third.

I knew she was right. Our first objective was to kill any stray cancer cells that might still be present in the skin or the tissue surrounding the area where the cancer had been. Optimistically, I said, "Well, if we have to wait for a year that will give us one more year of knowledge and experience from other women's surgeries. DIEP flap is still a relatively new procedure. I'm sure there is still much that could be learned."

Dr. Caterson looked at me as she seemed to ponder my statement. "Well, I suppose that could be true."

Meeting Dr. Stephanie Caterson completed my medical team. My final doctor had been found. I left our appointment late, still wobbly and pale...but very satisfied. And so thankful!

We made a brief detour for me to buy and apply the makeup I needed to improve my gray-white appearance. As we rushed for our appointment on Dana 10, I clung to Grady's arm for the sake of staying upright and walking straight. We exited the elevator, and we were told the film crew from "Chronicle" was waiting.

Gallantly, and with my head held high, I released my grip on Grady's arm, straightened my posture, and walked through the doors into the infusion ward. An attractive young woman standing beside a man holding a large TV camera approached me the moment I entered the ward.

"Hi. I'm Kathy Bickimer. Are you Kathy Crews?"

"Yes, I am."

"Wow, you look fantastic. If I didn't know you were battling cancer, I never would have guessed. You didn't lose your hair???"

"I did. Usually I take off the wig once I am settled and wear a scarf during my infusions. For the interview, if you like the wig, we'll keep the wig."

Shannon politely excused herself into our conversation to whisk me into the private infusion room to take my vital statistics. Both my pulse and blood pressure were elevated to levels we had never seen.

"Are you a little nervous today?" she teased.

"Well, a little. But I really am not feeling well at all; I'm feeling dizzy, weak...exhausted."

"I'll tell your assigned nurse. Your regular oncology nurse, Jade, is off today."

"Thanks, Shannon."

Shannon helped me to the bed in the private room, where the door could be closed and we would not disturb others. She invited Kathy and the camera man into room.

Tracy's oncology nurse, Connie, was assigned to me. Connie is such a wonderful and experienced nurse, but she was as nervous as could be with a camera in the room.

Everything connected to the interview was going beautifully, while on the other hand, everything connected with the real reason that I was there was not. Filming and the interview had to stop at one point because Connie actually had a job to do and needed to question me and diagnose why the entire area surrounding my port was red and inflamed.

Was it infected? Did I have an allergic reaction to laundry detergent? Or new clothing? What was going on?

As an oncology nurse of many years, Connie never saw such problems as she had with Tracy, and now here she was with "Tracy's Mom" trying to solve the mystery behind some renegade rash. To me it didn't seem like a big deal, but no chances were about to be taken, and my port could not be accessed for the infusion until the mystery was solved and Dr. Lin was consulted.

I addressed my patiently waiting spectators. "I apologize, Kathy. I guess this is just the real life stuff that goes with fighting cancer. You said you wanted to film at the hospital to capture the reality of what it is like, well, this is what it is like. Nothing is ignored. Everything is examined closely. I may be here for a lousy reason, but Dana-Farber is a wonderful place to be for such a time as this."

As filming was interrupted and Connie worked, Kathy and I chatted about my schedule for the day. At last, Connie accessed my port and the interview resumed. I was asked what it was like for me as Tracy's Mom, hearing those words, "Mom...it's cancer." How did I manage to encourage her, when she was so sick, discouraged, and at her lowest point emotionally?

Kathy asked about my first contact with Kelley Tuthill (from the Channel 5 News team) and why it was so important for me to encourage Kelley in her fight against the disease. And then she asked about the shock of my own diagnosis so soon after Tracy's, and while I was encouraging Kelley.

Kathy asked, "What was it like to take the words of encouragement you had given to Tracy and then to Kelley and apply them to your own diagnosis and treatment?"

I answered that the advice I had given both women was sound. There are plenty of times when the entire process of dealing with breast cancer feels endless. "Early in the process, discouragement can creep in. But with each infusion that is behind you, you are that much closer to your goal. With each fifteen minutes that is behind you, you are fifteen minutes closer to the finish line and being well. That's what you need to focus on; that's the goal you need to set: winning the marathon—fifteen minutes at a time."

She finished my portion of the interview and turned to Grady. "Both of the ladies in your life were diagnosed with breast cancer. What was that like for you, first as Tracy's 'Dad' and then as a husband facing those words a second time...'it's cancer.' How did you feel?"

Grady's eyes began to tear as he answered, "Both of my girls facing breast cancer: the immediate response is denial. It was like living a bad dream, something that could never happen in our family...first Tracy, and then Kathy."

He fanned the air with his hand, signaling he needed a moment before he could go on with the interview. The past feelings of how helpless he felt to protect his family from this awful thing were again fresh with the same newness of hearing it for the first time.

Grady had been such strength to both Tracy and me, but he suffered every step of the way with us. Indeed, the caregivers in our lives are the forgotten victims of cancer. Those of us who have survived the disease know the sacrifices of our loved ones.

As the interview ended, the Herceptin that had been dripping was nearly finished. The camera gear was packed, and Kathy filled me in on her plans to finish the interview with Tracy's part of our story filmed at Milton

Academy. The program would be telecast in October during Breast Cancer Awareness Month. She would call as soon as she knew the exact date. "I'll be in touch. Have a great time at the ballgame tonight."

"Thanks, Kathy. I'm sure we will. This will be Antonio's first major league baseball game. He and Tracy are so excited."

Connie was acting a little unusual. I thought it was because of the filming (she did say it made her nervous). As soon as the room was emptied of all but me, she came in and announced, "You need a blood transfusion."

My mouth fell open in shock. "Ah, ah, ah, transfusion? ...Blood?" Suddenly I felt submissive, vulnerable, and helplessly bound by Connie's words. "Well...I have been feeling discouraged and awfully tired. I guess that explains why?" I thought about our plans. "Connie, we have tickets for the Sox game. I won't be able to go. My family will be so disappointed."

"You should be okay to go to the game."

"I can?"

"Sure. You will be finished with the blood transfusion around 5:30."

"*Five-thirty!* It's barely noon! What takes so long?"

"Well, we need to put in the order, have the units couriered from next door, and then..."

"*Units!?* Did you say *units* with an "s" on the end of that word...as in more than one? Well, *how* much blood do I need?" I was now horrified as I thought about the downward spiral I had experienced physically. Possible low blood counts never crossed my mind.

"We are going to give you two units, and that will bring you to a point of being just on the edge of an acceptable level."

"You mean I actually could use more than TWO? Oh, my word! No wonder I felt half dead. I was! Good grief! And here I have been desperately trying to walk three miles every day, and Tracy has lectured me when I told her it was killing me to walk that far. It was!"

Picturing the daughter lecturing the mother, Connie laughed. "Well, we'll have you feeling better in a few hours."

A flood of questions began to pop into my mind and I asked as they arose. "How did this happen so quickly? I've been feeling awful for more than a month, I think. What happened? All of a sudden I need this transfusion?"

"Your blood counts have been watched closely. This isn't exactly sudden. You are right; you have been dealing with this for a while. The infusion of H/T/C last week was the one that made the final difference."

Connie continued with her explanation as she made preparations for the blood transfusion. She checked the flow rate of the saline drip that had been started after my Herceptin infusion had finished. "Apparently, you are going away on vacation before your surgery? Ordinarily, we might have 'encouraged' your body to rebound on its own by using medication. Your body doesn't have enough time to do that if you are going away. The only way we can bring you back to normal levels quickly enough is by a transfusion."

Connie exited the room to order the blood that I needed to feel human again and revive me from the walking dead. I had never had a blood transfusion. Even with all of Tracy's difficulties, she never had a blood transfusion. As I sat waiting alone, from the depths of my soul a chorus of praise came from my mouth. "He makes all things new...." Suddenly, the thought came, if blood is the vehicle cancer cells use to travel systemically, perhaps this was God answering prayer as I prayed in great detail that He would destroy every fragment (down to the last molecule) of cancer that might have traveled from the tumor.

My mind raced back to a cold winter's day the previous January: at Grace Capital Church we organized a blood drive for the Red Cross. A blood drive was much more work than I had ever imagined. I arrived at 11:00 that morning as the Red Cross truck was unloading portable gurneys and supplies.

It was after 8:30 p.m. before the Red Cross workers finished packing the units of blood that were donated and their truck rolled out of our church driveway. They were pleased. We had an excellent response to our blood drive. Nearly eighty units were added to the blood bank supply. Even then I thought to myself, *Wow. This is a lot of work for just eighty units. It took us all day and into the night!*

Connie walked into my room, bringing me back into the moment. The first unit of the precious blood was hung on the IV pole, and I watched as the steady drip, drip, drip and the color of "red" slowly overtook the saline and filled the length of clear IV tubing that was accessed through my port and into my chest. Connie set the volume of the flow.

Quietly and respectfully I asked, "Connie, what does it say on the IV bag?"

"Well, the blood type, of course; the volunteer's identification number; and this unit came from northern Michigan."

"Really? Northern Michigan? Wow, there's someone in northern Michigan who is now connected to me, as I receive their blood here at Dana-Farber in Boston. They have no idea who I am, or where their blood went. And here it is helping me to regain strength as I fight breast cancer. I never thought about donated blood being used in this way. I always thought about accidents or surgeries, but not breast cancer."

After Connie left the room and I was alone again, I dropped my head in prayer. I prayed for someone I did not know but that the Lord knew in northern Michigan. My mind revisited the experience from the previous January, and I prayed for every person who had come to Grace Capital Church on a cold and wintry day to share the gift of life. I didn't realize until this moment how important their unselfish act of giving was.

Many, many months later, I was still wondering why my blood counts were allowed to decline so drastically and why I received the blood transfusion at the moment I did.

While I was talking with another woman who was in chemotherapy, we were discussing low blood counts and how her chemo treatments were altered to allow time for her body to recover. She asked about blood transfusions and was told that they were given for the purpose of increasing blood counts only in "uncommon" cases. I have to wonder if I was one of those uncommon cases because of the research protocol.

I'm sure there must have been some discussion among my doctors concerning exactly where the line should be drawn for the sake of science and research and a patient's safety.

As time has passed, I have to laugh at how tenaciously I walked and exercised when I was in such terrible condition. I can still remember Dr. Lin blinking in amazement when I told her before I received my last round of H/T/C that I was very tired but still walking an hour each day. Knowing what I know now, my complaints were very legitimate considering my activity level and my frustration with fatigue. I can only imagine what Dr. Lin and Peg the research nurse were thinking!

Tracy and Tonx arrived at the hospital shortly after Connie had announced that I needed a blood transfusion. At first they were extremely concerned; not quite so much about me...but about possibly missing the game! After being assured by Connie I would be fine (once I had a "few pints"), Tracy, Tonx, and Grady walked to Fenway Park to claim the tickets that I had won in the raffle. They returned just in time to find Connie adjusting my second unit of blood on the IV pole. I asked again, as the slow and steady flow from the second bag entered into my body, "Connie, where did this unit of blood come from?"

"Western Pennsylvania," she answered.

Thank you, Lord, for this person in western Pennsylvania. Thank you, not just for their willingness to give their blood, but for the effort and the time it took. Thank you, Jesus. I appreciate their sacrifice, and I ask that You would bless them in abundance for their kindness....Bless them, Lord.

Tracy examined the rich, dark color of the blood in the transparent bag that hung from the IV pole. As she studied the precious gift, she announced, "I think this donor must have been *very* healthy. I'll bet they ate lots of spinach. As soon as you are finished getting *this* blood, I'll bet you'll be ready to walk *all* of your three miles!"

I think Tracy was so convinced of her own words, Grady and Tonx believed Tracy's declaration too. Somehow the three of them talked me into believing that since I was now feeling *so* much stronger after receiving two units of blood, we should *walk* the "short" one mile *to* and then *from* Fenway Park!

Chapter 21

The Countdown to Surgery

I completed my last round of Herceptin, the final chemo requirement for the research protocol on September 17, 2007. For twelve consecutive Mondays, Grady and I had been at Dana-Farber for the purpose of killing cancer and furthering research on HER2/neu breast cancer. As we were leaving Dana 10 after my infusion, Connie asked about the baseball game.

"Tracy figured that the units of blood I received should have made me as good as new. She convinced us all that we should walk to Fenway Park from here."

"They made you walk? I don't think that was exactly what I had in mind when I said you would be fine to go to the game."

"Well, I told you I have felt like Tracy has had me in training for an Olympic marathon, especially as my surgery date nears. I think walking to and from the baseball game immediately after a blood transfusion proves it."

Connie laughed and wished me well as I faced my upcoming surgery.

We exited the elevator on L1 to meet with Radiation Oncologist Dr. Jennifer Bellon. I was nervous; this appointment was going to set the direction for my surgery. So much depended upon Dr. Bellon's views and what she prescribed in my radiation treatment. It was really her decision if immediate reconstruction should even be a consideration.

Dr. Bellon was Tracy's radiation oncologist first. Again, I was grateful Tracy had made a path of medical support for me to follow. Thanks to Tracy, I knew how wise and excellent Dr. Bellon was.

During my appointment, Dr. Bellon listed the reasons to consider having reconstruction before or after radiation. Purely from the radiation oncologist point of view, she had sound reasons for suggesting that reconstruction (in my case) should be postponed. She asked, "How does your plastic surgeon feel about working on radiated tissue? Some plastic surgeons have a very definite position on this."

The previous week, I had discussed this question with Dr. Caterson. "She's okay working on radiated tissue."

"How are you going to feel waking up after a mastectomy and not have a breast mound?"

"Well, obviously not thrilled. But I think I feel this way: this *is* about saving my life."

I paused for a moment and thought realistically about the question I had just been asked. *How would I feel? What would that **look** like? Would I feel repulsed by my own body? Or worse, would Grady be repulsed by my appearance?* Fear began to lead my mind down an undesired path. I took a stand of determination as I looked at Dr. Bellon. "I am *more* than a breast. I am not defined by my body."

I continued. "I liked the idea of going through just one surgery and having everything done at once. I mean, I really liked that idea! But I think your opinion should carry the greatest weight as we decide whether the reconstruction should be done at the time of the mastectomy or done later. It's your call. You are the one who knows best how the radiation should be administered with the greatest effectiveness for that part of my therapy. I'm willing to accept whatever you tell me is best."

"You are a strong woman. I think psychologically you will be fine if we postpone reconstruction. We can do a better job during radiation if there is nothing in our way for how we angle the rays into the surgery site. A new breast mound would make the job a little more challenging. If you are okay with this decision, I'd like you to wait. I will let Dr. Golshan and Dr. Caterson know that you will have reconstruction done later, if you are sure this is what you are willing to do."

Another piece of the puzzle was added. Reconstruction would not happen for a year.

Dr. Bellon turned to me. "Where are you (timewise) in chemotherapy treatments?"

I explained Dr. Lin's expected treatment plan beyond the research protocol: chemotherapy would resume a month after my mastectomy, and I would have four rounds of A/C over eight weeks, and maybe Taxol depending upon the pathology.

"That should have you starting radiation sometime around the first or second week of February? I'll stay in contact with Dr. Lin to know the exact date you will finish. We will begin radiation four weeks after your next regimen of chemo is finished. Your 'mapping' tattoos will be done a couple of weeks before we start radiation."

"Dr. Bellon, as much as I would like to have my radiation done here, I cannot imagine how that is possible…to travel here every single day for seven and a half weeks during the winter? My husband can't take that much time away from the office. I don't know *how* this can happen. Can you write the radiation program, and can I have the radiation treatments closer to home?"

Her response was so true and honest. "I can write the program. But another facility may not choose to follow it."

Oh, Lord. I know this doctor is one of the best in her field. I need You to work out the logistics. How can I possibly receive the radiation I need and be under this doctor's expert care and supervision through my treatment? Lord, show me how this can be done.

The following Monday, I did not have an appointment at the hospital. When Grady and I woke up, we were not in Tracy's apartment, nor were we facing the madness with other commuters in the Monday morning traffic going into Boston. Instead, we slathered our skin with sunscreen, dressed in our swimsuits, grabbed our snorkel gear, and headed for the warm tropic ocean whose gentle waves beckoned us, *Come.* If this was not heaven, it was by far the closest thing to heaven I had experienced on a Monday morning in the past three months!

It's strange how over time the abnormal becomes normal. Monday mornings at Dana-Farber had become my normal. It felt strange not being there. (I certainly could get used to this change, however.)

As two of the regulars who had discovered this charming little Bajan resort and repeatedly vacationed during the low season when rates are a bargain, we had become familiar with the staff. We were always greeted warmly with "Wel-comb home Mis-ta and Mis-is Cr-oos!"

Heather, the head chef for the morning and lunch crew, stepped out from behind the grill and greeted me with a hug when we arrived for breakfast. "What haa-pin to yoo, Darr-ling?" she asked in her melodious Bajan dialect as her big brown eyes searched my face and shock filled her expression.

Heather had been accustomed to seeing me arrive for breakfast with my hair pulled back in a ponytail. But this morning I arrived for breakfast wearing a blue and white bandana to cover my bald head. As I told her about my past several months fighting breast cancer, she quietly listened. Like a favorite girl friend (or sister), she put her arm around my shoulder and pulled me close. "Well! You ah hee-a now. Yoo go-in to feel ma-aa-ch bet-ta! Yoo tell Hea-tha wat fish yoo wont for lunch, I'll gat it foe yoo. Yoo tell me now, Darr-ling."

Heather was right! Being there I did feel much better. And at lunchtime, my every fish (on the grill) was Heather's command.

I had brought my wig and scarves, and I wore them in the evening to the open air dining room that overlooked the surf that gently surged over the breakwater a short distance from the shoreline. The island ladies working in the restaurant loved the scarves. There was a freeing feeling of acceptance wearing a colorful scarf on my head in the islands. It felt so good to be there.

God has graced this world with such beauty. My senses were soothed by warm island breezes, and for a perfect week, I was cradled in His goodness.

For a week Grady and I swam, walked the beach, enjoyed the amazing food, and napped under the palm trees that surrounded the pool. We enjoyed snorkeling and watching the bountiful, beautiful fish that swim the reef. There were so many reasons that *this* tiny resort had become our favorite.

The repeat clientele affectionately describe the little resort as "4 star rustic." But in so many ways the warm greetings from the staff describe it best: "Wel-comb home!" Emotionally, it was exactly where the two of us needed to be as we enjoyed a break from cancer before facing surgery.

Far from hospitals and cancer, our week passed by much too quickly. The morning we were packing for our flight home, my eyes began to fill with tears as I dreaded the mastectomy. I didn't want to face the weeks of chemotherapy *yet* ahead of me and beyond the surgery.

Oh, Lord, I wish I could stop time right here. I don't want surgery....I don't want to go through A/C. I just DON'T want to continue treatment! I don't want to face the horror that Tracy went through. She was so sick.

Jesus, I sense how much my body has been changed by the chemo that I have already had. I have been active enough to realize how weak I am. I have felt the difference in the efficiency of my lungs and my heart as I have swum. I am not as strong as I was. I beg You to restore my health and heal my body.

Lord, I beg You, spare me from eight more weeks of chemotherapy and the drugs that made Tracy so ill. I pray for my healing. I pray for wisdom for my doctors. Lord God, I beg You for mercy.

I could not stop the tears that formed and started to roll down my cheeks.

It seemed that once our vacation was over and we returned home, half of the demons from hell were commissioned to our case. Grady returned to work to find management changes and chaos in full swing.

My surgery date (that I thought was set) suddenly was *not!* Dr. Golshan was going to be away from the hospital. I had no set surgery date!

The Monday we returned from our trip, I was scheduled for the last MRI before surgery and for the protocol findings. The surgery had to happen! If that wasn't enough anxiety to face, within days of our return, our beautiful Siamese cat, JoDee, somehow slipped through an open door one evening, never to be seen again. Our hearts were broken and our grief over her disappearance magnified everything else that seemed to be going so wrong.

I had not seen Dr. Golshan since he had turned my care over to Dr. Lin in June. With my surgery date again an unknown, I began to question if Dr. Golshan *was* the right surgeon. *Lord, why would he be not only unavailable but out of the country the week I had been scheduled for surgery? Is the date wrong or the **doctor** wrong? Father God, I want to be in Your will and Your timing. I am trusting You to make the plan clear and the path straight.*

The next time I saw Peg, the research nurse, even she was discouraged. "You are not Dr. Golshan's only patient finishing a protocol and in need of surgery. You were, however, the only one who I thought was set with a surgery date. I don't know what we are going to do. I guess, Kathy, the only thing you can do is to keep checking with Linda at Dr. Golshan's office for a surgery date."

After seeing Peg, I felt worse. Everything related to the research had to be done just so.

*Lord, this isn't anything I can fix. I'm asking You to work this out. If it means a different surgeon, You need to direct me to that doctor. If Dr. Golshan is my surgeon and hand picked by You, I pray that **You** would lead him and **schedule his time** in compliance with the research study. Guide his footsteps and his calendar.*

Within days, Linda called. I had a surgery date with Dr. Golshan: Monday morning, October 22, 2007.

With Tracy's words ringing in my ears, I stepped up my exercise pace and walked rain or shine, praying and singing praises to the Lord with every step I walked.

Days before my surgery as I was walking, singing, and praying, I felt strongly impressed by precisely how I was to ask others to pray for me. It seemed especially critical for the lymph nodes removed during the surgery to have absolutely no sign of live cancer in them. I had prayed that there would be no live cancer cells in the pathology, but suddenly in my spirit I felt more impressed than ever to pray fervently and in earnest for this result. I shared my prayer request with those who had been faithfully praying with me and for me.

Sometimes the Lord asks us to do things more than once. And sometimes, more than twice. While we pray for those things that are impressed upon our hearts to pray, our faith is challenged and it grows. I felt my willingness to be obedient and to ask again was being tested.

On October 17, 2007, I wrote to the ever-growing list of people on my prayer list.

Hello Everyone...

As I face surgery next Monday, (first of all) **please pray for Dr. Golshan, the surgical support staff, and my caregivers.**

Pray for Grady and Tracy and that the Lord would give them His peace as we go through this next week.

Pray that the Lord would strengthen my body and I would face this surgery in the confidence that Jesus has my life in His hands.

And please pray that the pathology would reveal a miracle and that NO cancer cells would be found to be alive in any tissue OR IN ANY lymph nodes that are examined!

...Pray that the Lord would cover me from harm spiritually as well as physically.

...And please do not forget my mom. Pray for peace for her. She worries about everything.

Grady will have his computer at the hospital next Monday, and he will send out an email to all of you to let you know what the doctor reports to him after the surgery....I guess that means you'll know how I'm doing before I do!

Tracy thinks she will be able to meet Grady at the hospital to wait with him while I am in surgery. I am scheduled to go into surgery at 7:30 a.m. at **Brigham and Women's Hospital**. We have been told to arrive at 5:45. Ugh!

We still do not know how many days I will be in the hospital...two nights, I'm sure. I have been told the recovery is not as bad as I had thought. I will have many restrictions; Dr. Golshan wants me to rest as needed, but also be as active as my body permits, within reason.

My surgery is on the horizon! One of the things I am looking forward to most about this surgery is having **four more weeks** that I will not have chemo before I have to start in again for "Phase 3," which will be eight weeks of chemo. Praise God for the little breaks in between!

I'm like the little boy who always wanted a pony and one day awoke to find that a manure truck had tipped over and dumped its "load" in his front yard. Frantically, he began digging through the manure. When he was asked what on earth he was doing, he replied, "With all of this manure in my yard, there's *got* to be a pony in here somewhere!"

Optimistically I have to say, *"There's got to be a pony in here... somewhere...."*

Blessings and Love,

Kathy

Chapter 22

I Found That "Pony"!

It seemed hell was nipping at my heels almost up until the minute before I was wheeled into surgery. I caught a cold days before my surgery, and as I sat dressed in a hospital gown and on the gurney, I did not know if I would be taken into the operating room. My lungs were checked for clarity in the patient care unit at 6:15 a.m., and only then it was declared I was well enough to continue and have the surgery.

Grady stayed with me until it was time to be rolled toward the operating suite. Tracy arrived to wish me well moments before the IV drip took effect and I was unconscious.

Through the haze of grogginess, I awoke just enough to know the surgery was over. As my bed was wheeled into place in my hospital room, both Grady and Tracy were waiting. I began to breathe deeply to oxygenate my blood in an attempt to rid my brain of the anesthesia.

Dr. Golshan appeared shortly after coherency began and pain set in. "How are you feeling?"

I looked at him like he had to be kidding. "Like I've been kicked in the chest by a mule."

He began to chuckle at my apt appraisal of my condition. "Well, that's the first time I've heard that for a response!"

"This hurts. My ribs feel bruised. On a pain scale of one to ten, I'm a fifteen."

"Let's increase your pain medication and see if we can't get the pain under control and make you a little more comfortable....Ha! Kicked by a mule. I won't forget that one!"

As he walked from the room, I felt grumpy and I thought to myself, *I guess he must have grown up in the city.*

As the shadows of the late afternoon sun began to lengthen on the wall in my room, Tracy and Grady kissed me goodbye. Their day had been long as they waited for my surgery to finish, and then as they sat with me in my room. I wasn't very good company (for certain), and what I needed most was rest and to escape the discomfort that the pain medication did not completely cover.

Brigham and Women's is a teaching hospital, and early rounds are made by those doctors who are "just practicing" their medical training. Most of the new interns are excellent, astute young doctors under the expert supervision of some of the finest doctors in this country. On occasion, however, you will meet an intern and wonder if maybe they are really a janitor who stole a lab coat to take a break from washing bathrooms!

The morning of my second day, I was awakened before sunup by two *young* interns. I wasn't in any mood for company of any sort—especially at such an early hour of the morning! My night had been disastrous!

During the night, we discovered the hard way that I was allergic (and had a miserable reaction) to the compression boots that covered my legs from foot to mid-thigh to prevent blood clots. I had spent half of the night itching and feeling like what I needed most was to be transported to the nearest veterinary clinic for a "flea dip"!

When the compression boots were removed, I began to scratch and rub my legs, tearing at the red welts that covered the skin that had been in contact with the boots. I was miserable as I waited for medications to arrive. Once the anti-itch lotion was applied, and with the addition of Benadryl on top of my IV pain meds, I fell back asleep. But the night had been short, and rest had been anything but restful.

Before dawn, I opened one eye to see who was there and turning on the switch that flooded my room with unwelcome brightness. I thought to myself, *Oh, brother!*

The intern who was taking charge of my care was an overconfident young male. He was followed by this *very* adorable pretty little "young thing." They were both dressed in their *brand new* glowing white lab coats.

As drugged as I was, even *I* could see the writing on the wall for this one! His entire demeanor shouted, *I'm in charge here, Sweetie. Let me show you how this is done.*

Upon making his bold, grandiose entrance into my room, he said, "So-o-o-o, we'll be going home today."

My mood was evident as I replied, "I don't think so."

As he walked toward me, "Sweetie" peered out from behind his shoulder with a shy, nervous smile. She reached for examination gloves from the box attached to the wall as she followed "Dr. Cool" and then dutifully reached for a second pair and handed them to him.

(Oh, Brother!)

"How are 'we' feeling today?"

I thought to myself, *Lousy, Doc. How do you think you would feel if you were a woman and someone cut off half of your chest less than twenty-four hours ago?* But politely I lied and managed to say, "Okay."

The "sweet young thing" was still "smiling" and "peering," and I was feeling more and more irritated with each second these two were playing their cutesy character roles as doctors.

I looked at "Dr. Cool" and thought to myself, *Tell me, Doc, are you a* **real** *doctor or do you just play one on TV?*

"Let's take a look here and see what we have."

*(You mean no one told you what **we have**!?! Go away! Send in a **real** doctor! How about one with gray hair and wrinkles across his brow?)*

Suddenly, and almost without warning, "Dr. Cool" grabbed my surgical bandages and tore them back to expose my chest minus one breast.

Whether it was because he had no idea what to do or because he saw that the fresh incision line across my chest looked perfectly fine, as quickly as he had torn back the bandage, he slapped it back down on my flattened chest. The bandage hung limp and open as the adhesive refused to stick to my skin a second time. *(Brother, oh, brother!)*

"Okay; everything's fine." And he made a beeline for the door. (Perhaps he raced to the nearest bathroom to vomit after seeing his first mastectomy patient??? I'll always wonder.) Whatever happened, I did not see "Dr. Cool" and "Sweetie" during the remainder of my hospital stay.

In the months that followed, and as I developed greater familiarity with Dr. Golshan, I recounted the story of seeing my mastectomy scar for the first time and that it was at the hand of "Dr. Cool" as he attempted to impress "Sweetie." Patient comments are important at a teaching hospital, and I know that Dr. Golshan appreciated that I was not angry. Instead, I saw humor and I suggested that "Dr. Cool" somehow missed class the day that patient bedside manner was being taught. Dr. Golshan laughed with me as I told him about the melodramatic young doctor's attempt to appear knowledgeable.

There is a great deal of controversy about how long patients should stay in the hospital after a mastectomy. Some insurance plans only allow a one-night hospital stay, which is dubbed a "drive through surgery." Personally, I think that a second night should be mandatory.

I ran a fever my second night, and had I been discharged twenty-four hours after surgery, I would have faced a trip back to the Emergency Department and re-admittance. I am thankful to have had a surgeon who allowed me to voice how I was feeling and express an opinion and an insurance carrier willing to allow attending health care experts the final word in my care. I knew I didn't feel well enough after twenty-four hours to be released. After a second night in the hospital, I was up, showered, and dressed by 10:00 and waiting for Dr. Golshan to discharge me. The difference of one extra night in the hospital truly did put me on my feet.

Before my surgery, I had visited the ladies in the Friends Place on Dana 9. I was guided in selecting the mastectomy undergarments, the special camisoles (that I would need for the next several weeks as I recovered), and "puffs" to give my flattened chest form. I was prepared for my exit from the hospital and back into the world still looking like a lady.

For the next week, a visiting nurse came to our home daily to monitor my progress and help with my wound care. I left the hospital with two drainage tubes attached to my side, under my left arm. Grady and I were both instructed about my care and how to drain the abnormal apparatus that was hanging from my side, and I adjusted quickly.

The Friday after my surgery, Dr. Golshan called me at 5:30 p.m. Immediately after his call, I sent out an email update. This is a portion from that email.

Dear "Prayer Warriors,"

The Scripture tells us that we are to weep with those who are weeping and to rejoice with those who are rejoicing.

Well, everyone...**dig out your party duds, confetti, and streamers! WE are rejoicing!**

I just received a phone call from my surgeon. My pathology report is in. **There was absolutely NO SIGN of live cancer cells in the tumor OR in the lymph nodes!!!! ALL CANCER WAS *DEAD!!!***

I am so excited; I'm practically doing back flips! There was indication that three of the fourteen lymph nodes that were taken *had* been affected with cancer. But there were no live cancer cells in ANY of the pathology. Glory to God!!!

Dr. Golshan said, "You could not get a better pathology report than what we have just received!" I could hear the joy in his voice as he shared this news.

I have no idea if this will change the course of treatment from here.

Please pray for continued wisdom for my doctors in how much or how little follow-up will be needed. We still very much need the Lord to be in charge of my treatment plan.

I can't tell you how excited I am. This is **exactly** how we have all been praying. God bless you! God bless you all and *big time*.... God is so GOOD!

Please pass the news along. I know most of you who have been so faithful in praying have asked others to join with you in prayer for me. I can't even begin to imagine how many have been storming the gates of heaven with prayer.

...All I can say is I am *so blessed!!!* "Thank you" doesn't begin to express my gratitude for your support.

Rejoicing in His Grace!
Kathy and Grady

One week post-surgery, I saw Dr. Lin and Peg, the research nurse. There is no way to reflect back and capture my emotion and that of Dr. Lin and Peg other than to share the email I wrote after that appointment.

It was one of those moments of "do you believe that?" I mean, "DO YOU *BELIEVE* THAT?" THAT'S STUPENDOUS! AMAZING! ... UNBELIEVABLE!

Subject: Oct.29 Appointment

Hi All!

I've got to say my appointment with Dr. Lin on Monday was one joyous occasion. Tracy and Grady were with me and we all came away from the appointment with an even greater understanding of breast cancer.

I want to thank those of you who have emailed saying that my pathology report was only confirmation to what the Lord had already revealed to you ahead of time. And a special thank you to Mike. On Sunday (before my surgery) he joined Pastor Peter and others to pray over Grady and me, and the Lord spoke to Mike's heart as we prayed.

Mike "saw" the surgery outcome. He *saw* "no cancer" and how surprised the surgeon was! Again, the Lord confirming through him what we all had been praying. ...By the way, Mike didn't know the details of my surgery and had no idea that this has been our prayer focus for weeks.

I had what is referred to as a "100% response" from my chemo treatment. Exactly as we had been praying, **there was not a live cancer cell to be found anyplace!**

Peg was *beaming* with joy with my results. During the appointment, we were told this outcome happens **less than 20 percent of the time**.

When I found this out, I stopped the dialogue about the pathology right there and told Dr. Lin, but mostly Peg (the research nurse), that because the findings in my pathology would be used for research, **it was important for them to know this: literally thousands of people across the country have been praying for that "exact" outcome: ALL CANCER CELLS TO BE DEAD... and specifically, no live cells in the lymph nodes!**

I think for the first time, Peg saw how seriously I relied upon the Lord with my life and my real fight against this disease, and the outcome has been fought for on a spiritual level. Grady backed what I was telling Peg and Dr. Lin and told them that I had prayer warriors interceding who didn't take this sort of thing lightly. As you prayed, you were "asking" God and "believing" God "in faith" for specific prayer requests! ...**ALL cancer cells dead! IT HAPPENED.**

As I was asking, *I had no idea that the cancer cells in the lymph nodes ARE NOT USUALLY COMPLETELY KILLED BY THE CHEMO.* The Lord impressed upon my heart the importance to pray in detail for this outcome. (Maybe as a testimony to the power of prayer to my doctors?)

This was God answering our prayers, specifically!

The next thing Dr. Lin said was, "This kind of success doesn't happen often. It is unusual that all the cancer cells in the **lymph nodes** would be killed. This was an amazing result."

God bless you guys for being so diligent in praying for me. We have an amazing God...and an amazing victory. Praise Jesus!

Where from here? On the last day of our vacation, I was telling the Lord how much I did not want to go through A/C in my next stage of chemo treatments. I am filled with thanksgiving for His mercy: **I will not have A/C!!!!!!!!**

Dr. Lin has opted to give me two more rounds of a known success and that I have had 100% results with already! On November 12, as I begin Phase 3 in my treatment, I will have my fifth infusion of H/T/C, and on December 3, I will have my sixth and final infusion of the three chemo drugs in this next phase of treatment. Phase 4 will begin in January as I start my seven and a half weeks of radiation and continue with seven more months of Herceptin. Radiation MUST start thirty days after my final round of H/T/C. The time frame of things has just moved up by more than a month.

We have prayed for God's wisdom for my doctors as they chose my course of treatment. I have a real peace with this course.

Somehow I had the cart in front of the horse concerning this research protocol. I thought what I was doing was *finishing* the research. Duh!!! *I've been a pioneer!* This was just the first step in this research trial. If the other thirty-nine women who have joined me in being a "lab rat" do as well as I did, this will be tried with a larger group of early-stage HER2/neu-diagnosed women; according to Dr. Lin, maybe as many as four thousand to find out if those numbers compare to my small sample group of forty! **LOOK what God has allowed me to be a part of!!!! WOW!!!!!** What a "needle in the haystack" opportunity the Lord has blessed me with! And look at the result I had and what a HUGE opportunity to give Him the praise for the outcome! WOW! Just plain *Wow....*

There is one more "coincidence" I'd like to share (and we all know I do not believe for one second this is a coincidence!) that has happened to my surgeon, Dr. Golshan.

This past week...he was promoted to the position of "Director of Breast Surgery Services for DFCI-BWH Cancer Center."

Hmmm... As I have asked for prayer for my doctors, and I have continually prayed for God's hand to be upon Dr. Golshan, I wonder if there's a connection here????

In All Praise,

Kathy

When Dr. Lin walked into the exam room where I was waiting with Grady and Tracy, she was beaming. My pathology report was in her hands. When Peg entered the room, she was practically in tears of joy. "Oh!" she said. "Let me give you a hug! How are you feeling? Your pathology report is SO exciting! Oh! You have done so well. You're our brand new breast cancer research poster child!" And she laughed.

As if suddenly the Lord revealed what had been hidden from me before, I realized I WAS ONE OF THE FIRST "RATS THROUGH THE MAZE"!

"Oh my goodness! You didn't know this was going to happen! What about the other women in the study? Has anyone else finished? What can you tell me about the others?"

My questions did not receive a direct answer. Then Peg said, "The study is still open. We will not have all of the information compiled for a few years."

"Well, tell me what you do know," I said as reality began to set in.

Dr. Lin answered me. "You have had a '100% response'—no evidence of live cancer cells in any tissue and none in the lymph nodes. This happens less than 20 percent of the time."

I momentarily lamented for my breast that had furthered science—and had been deemed to be free of cancer after chemotherapy. From my perspective it seemed it had faced a state of execution and on further examination been found innocent! "Tell me about the pathology and the sections of breast tissue examined."

Dr. Lin read from the report in her hands. "There were fifteen cross sections of breast tissue examined. Of the fifteen slides, eight revealed some sign of ductal carcinoma in situ."

Maybe my breast wasn't so "innocent" after all! "Nancy, hypothetically, does that mean if the tumor had been in a location in my breast where a lumpectomy could have been performed and I had gone that route, I might have developed breast cancer a second time?"

"Hypothetically, that is a possibility."

Silently I sat and pondered what I was learning. Nancy broke the silence with excitement. "Did you hear about Dr. Golshan?" And she told me about his promotion.

As Nancy spoke about Dr. Golshan's promotion to Director of Breast Surgical Services for Dana-Farber and Brigham and Women's Hospital, immediately I thought about my list of prayer requests prior to surgery. Prayer for him was *first* on my list.

Praise You, Lord, for blessing my doctor so specially!

Chapter 23

Giving Thanks in ALL Things

Far too quickly the recovery from surgery and my break from chemotherapy were over. It was time to begin the third phase in my treatment, and emotionally, I was not ready. I was beginning to enjoy *not* having my port accessed on Dana 10, and it was harder than being a kid facing school after a terrific summer's vacation. (Even if in my case a "terrific summer's vacation" was recovery from surgery.)

Upon seeing Dr. Golshan for my first office visit after surgery, I could not resist the opportunity to put him on the spot about "a rumor about a promotion of some sort?"

Acting a little surprised and taken aback by my query, he said, "Oh. That." He paused before commenting further. As if making an excuse and downplaying his own excellence and worthiness for the promotion, he justified, "Well, all it really means is more work."

I couldn't resist the opportunity. Softly, I spoke what I knew to be true. "Dr. Golshan? Do you know that last week there were thousands of people praying for you? As I faced surgery, *you* were at the top of my list as I requested prayer. The email updates that I have been sending out have been forwarded to friends of my friends and their friends. Everyone had been asked to pray for you. I needed the Lord's hand to be upon you, *first*."

After examining the surgery site, Dr. Golshan provided a quick lesson on reasons to call and problems to watch for. "On occasion after lymph nodes are removed, fluid collects and causes a bulge. Now you need to call me if you begin to grow a 'new breast.'"

I looked at him, puzzled and unsure I understood what he was saying. I began to laugh. "Call you? I think if I begin to grow a new breast I'll call Ripley's Believe It or Not! I think I need further clarification."

Dr. Golshan began explaining how the lymph system works and how mine had been altered when the entire chain of lymph nodes were removed from under my arm. The body's means of purification and producing infection-fighting white blood cells (that had previously been under my arm) was now missing. It would take time for my body to readjust. Other lymph nodes under my collar bone and around the surrounding area would compensate. New pathways and channels to expel the waste carried in the fluid would take over. (At least that's how I understood the explanation.)

Approximately 25 percent of the time when lymph nodes are taken from under the arm, issues can occur and need medical attention. One of the first indications of a problem is swelling in, around, by, or under the surgery site.

For weeks, everything seemed just fine. Other lymph nodes that were near the surgery site took over and seemed to be doing the job for the nodes that I no longer had.

On November 8, a few days before receiving more H/T/C and advancing into *more* uncharted territory beyond the research protocol, I sent this email out to the ever-growing numbers of those who were following my progress. By this time my friend and supporter Pauline had coined a name for my email list: "Kathy's cancer groupies!"

Subject: "Phase 3"

...So much to be thankful for!

Blessings All!

On Monday we will be back in Boston to begin "Phase 3" of my treatment. I'm doing well and recovering, but I'm not sure I *feel* strong enough to try to stand up to chemo so soon.

I knew that dealing with recovery after having lymph nodes removed was no picnic. And *this is NO PICNIC!* Friends who have been through this (including Tracy) tell me things will improve.

From surgery, half of my side and underarm is completely numb... no feeling whatsoever. It's weird to shower and be washing your body and not feel the water from the shower or the bath puff on your skin. Bizarre!

I have been reading *WHY?* by Vernon Brewer...a book that he wrote after he survived lung cancer. At the end of each chapter he writes a little review, "Life Lessons Learned." One of the things he learned was this:

"You must go through the process to receive the benefits.

"There are no shortcuts through tough circumstances. It is in your circumstances that you will find out what you are made of!

"Know that there is a purpose for your trial and a plan for your life. God wants to develop in you the patience, perseverance and endurance you need for victory." (Used with permission from Vernon Brewer. *WHY?* "The Reason for the Trial," page 65. Copyright 2006, World Help Inc.)

...I think I can say with greater certainty than ever before, he's absolutely right! None of this has been fun. But you know what? If I could have been separated from the physical aspects of battling cancer, the spiritual side of this has been a total kick!

It is so cool to watch God work and to be used by Him: the new people God has brought into my life, my attitude toward prayer... and how I have grown personally in trusting Him with my life.

My update emails began (as a means) to keep friends and family informed. And people have been added and added to the list and forwarded, and somehow God has used my experience of going through cancer to encourage SO many others and to truly bring glory to His Name.

And you know what (again)? It's been the "eternal circle" of God working in my life encouraging you *through* my trial, and you encouraging me with your notes, gifts, cards, prayers, FOOD!, flowers, and love, that *draws God closer into all of our lives! In*

Christ, we are of one Body. Thank you for ministering healing to me.

Please pray that I will be strengthened and able to endure the chemo on Monday. ...I'm still recovering from the surgery. ...I'm tired, already.

Please pray that even if there is the tiniest fragment of cancer ANYPLACE in my body, these last two doses of chemo (H/T/C) will find ANY cancer or pre-cancer cell and kill it!

This may sound a little silly...but my hair is *just* beginning to grow back. I surely would be grateful to the Lord if I could keep it. I have a whole new appreciation and compassion for bald men! Br-r-r-rr-r-rrr. It's really cold without hair.

Begin to compose your "Thanksgiving list." I hope you will find this Thanksgiving that you have as much to "give thanks" for...as our family does. Sometimes you don't know just how much you have until you come close to losing it...*hair included!*

Blessings and Love to each of you...

Kathy

To give "thanks"...thanksgiving... To new heights of gratitude I had never experienced, the Lord was leading me.

"Rejoice in the Lord always, again I say rejoice. Let your reasonableness be known to everyone. The Lord is at hand; do not be anxious about anything, but in everything by prayer and supplication with thanksgiving let your request be made to God. And the peace of God, which surpasses all understanding, will guard your hearts and your minds in Christ Jesus.

"Finally, brothers, whatever is true, whatever is honorable, whatever is lovely, whatever is commendable, if there is any excellence, if there is anything worthy of praise, think about **these** things." (Philippians 4:4–8)

If the Bible offers a "how to survive cancer" passage, I think this is it!

Up until this point, my side effects had been comparatively easy to tolerate. My final two infusions of H/T/C were about to change that; and for a time, I thought it might be the chemo I was given as a final precaution that might kill me! My entire immune system seemed to fall apart almost overnight. My local pharmacist became my new best friend!

I was glad that before I had even had my first round of chemotherapy, I went to my local (and small) pharmacy to get to know the head pharmacist, Mike. I told him what I was facing and about my needs (including the Neulasta shots that I required exactly twenty-four hours after each round of H/T/C). He was interested in the clinical trial at Dana-Farber and in me as a patient.

Introducing myself to Mike was a brilliant idea! I was always, always, *always* cared for on a priority level of service because at the pharmacy they knew I was a cancer patient and often (and sometimes on the turn of a dime) had immediate need of medications.

Subject: Re: "Phase 3"

Hi Everyone...

I made it through my chemo treatment on November 19 and actually felt fine for a couple of days before the effects really slammed me hard. I had thought since it had been two months since having chemo, maybe it wouldn't be quite as cumulative. WRONG!

I spent five days barely able to move from the recliner, zapped of all energy. "Sloughing" has become a huge issue for me. ...All of the soft tissue areas in my body are "sloughing" off the new fast-growing cells. This has caused "thrush" in my mouth and my throat, and a nose that feels like I've just gone twelve rounds in the boxing ring with Rocky Balboa! I had no idea a nose could hurt THIS much.

There really isn't much that can be done to relieve the pain, and I've got to go through *another* round of chemo *again in a week!* Good grief!

Please pray for rapid cell growth and healing to the areas that are so fragile and raw.

...I honestly cannot imagine losing any more tissue in these areas that are so painful and bleeding.

It's amazing what the Lord protects us from seeing, sometimes. Going into this experimental chemo program, for some dumb reason I thought what I was doing was for the **end** of the research and then it would be used as a common treatment plan.

I'm still trying to absorb what I now understand. I was one of the **first** to complete this research study! Me and thirty-nine other women will contribute a potential new model in the battle against HER2/neu breast cancer. I can't wait to find out how we helped as our data is analyzed.

At this point, the study is still open for prospective candidates. All of a sudden "I get it!!" Now I know why my doctors were nearly doing back flips with my results. I still can't believe what I have done for cancer research. WOW!

I genuinely have been a "lab rat"...a very blessed and successful lab rat. Praise God! Once more I see His hand prints all over the timing of everything I've been through!

I have another story to share about an opportunity the Lord provided. A couple of weeks before my surgery (through unexpected circumstances), I took my mom to one of her doctor's appointments. I had not planned to be out in public, so it was one of my days when I sincerely was looking like a cancer patient and wearing a scarf to cover my head.

Mom's nurse had been through breast surgery four weeks earlier, and her pathology report had been misinterpreted and the poor woman had just been told she was facing more surgery. She had only learned this the night before I was in the office with Mom.

My appearance made it obvious that she and I had something in common. In three minutes or less, she poured her story out to me, and once more the Lord provided a wonderful opportunity for me, not only to minister His peace to her, but to help her to make connections with my oncologist, Dr. Lin, in Boston for a second opinion.

Dr. Lin has set a course of treatment far less radical than what she **had** been told.

Timing. God's timing. It is EVERYTHING!

I wasn't even planning to be at my mom's that day, and yet I was there and Mom needed transportation to an appointment she had forgotten about! God is so amazing!

I recently have come to understand that cancer cells can hide in the skin, and chemo works systemically; hence, the need for radiation. Recurrence with radiation is decreased by as much as 50 percent.

I need to remind all of you that as you have prayed for me, **YOU** have a share in the victories I have had! **YOU are a part of how women's health care will be approached in the future.** I was the "lab rat"...but you were the "prayer" behind my success as you interceded for me!

Thank you! May Jesus heap blessings upon you, 'til overflowing.

Blessings and Love,

Kathy

The changes in my body after my fifth round of H/T/C gave me a clear picture of how *murderous* chemotherapy is. The purpose of chemo is to kill all fast-growing cells throughout the body—including fingernails. It's one of the reasons that many chemo drugs cause hair loss within a very short period of time.

There are numerous cell types in the body that are fast-growing cells. Logically, moist tissue areas are compromised. I had some minor problems with soft tissue after my fourth infusion of H/T/C on September 3. The chemo also caused painfully dry eyes. As late summer/early autumn weather came, the humidity levels in the air decreased and my nose occasionally bled because of the combination of drier air and the moist lining in my nose being attacked by the chemo.

By September, and before my surgery in October, our vacation to the tropics, where the air was warm and moist, was a vacation for my nose! That may sound really silly, but when it was time to start chemo just before Thanksgiving, I would have given almost anything to be someplace in the tropics during my last two rounds of H/T/C and to escape the cooler, dry air in New England that compounded the problems. Tolerating my nose all but became one of the most painful experiences I had ever known. As the chemo killed the soft tissue cells in my nose, the fragile lining was frequently bleeding and infected. This was when the real fun began!

Having lived a relatively healthy life for fifty-eight years, most of the antibiotics I had ever taken were in the penicillin family. Not every infection or bacteria will respond to just any antibiotic. All of a sudden we were all learning that I was allergic to huge families of antibiotics, and the choices for treatment to combat infections were limited.

...And this was all learned because of sloughing in my nose! There is nothing that is minor when you are a cancer patient. NOTHING!

By Tuesday, December 11, I was so ill from infections and sloughing I bordered on hospitalization. I had my final infusion of H/T/C the previous week, and that was the round that nearly killed this poor lab rat (as I later reported to Dr. Lin).

I developed infections in my bladder, kidneys, urinary tract, and of course my nose. Physically I was miserable. I not only felt awful from the infections but also felt awful from the adverse reactions to antibiotics (and let's not forget the effects from chemo, for good measure!). As different antibiotics were tried, repeatedly I was allergic.

On the third try, my local doctor found an antibiotic my body tolerated. As my body fought to recover, I slept through several days. As the antibiotics worked, I was thankful for every small improvement that brought a little more strength and the hope for a better day tomorrow.

One of the things I discovered was how blessed I had been not to have the metallic taste in my mouth that often accompanies chemotherapy treatment as a side effect. That was not a problem for me until the very end. When it did happen, however, it was so intense I needed to keep mints in my mouth almost constantly. The mints were especially helpful when it came to my intake of water. The natural desire is to refuse water when it tastes like an old rusty bucket. The mints flavored the water and I kept dehydration at bay. I was thankful Tracy taught me this little remedy.

The final two rounds of H/T/C definitely answered the question "How much is too much?" Those last rounds were the ones that put me flat on my back and wondering if I would ever recover. It was several weeks before I genuinely improved, and as improvement came, I gave thanks at the end of each day. I was that much closer to wellness. I gave thanks knowing I had survived six rounds of H/T/C and soon new, healthy fast-growing tissue would grow and would be allowed to stay!

I gave thanks that soon my days of being "hairless" would finally come to an end.

And I especially gave thanks when on Christmas morning I awoke and felt well enough to cook Christmas dinner and invite family to join us at our table.

Chapter 24

Count It All Joy

Sent: Saturday, December 22, 2007, 10:45:40 PM
Subject: Phase "4"

Greetings All!

Although Phase "3" was my shortest phase of treatment, it came with the most difficulty and side effects. ...It was only two rounds of the same H/T/C I had such success with. However, I hadn't fully recovered from my surgery when I was given the fifth and sixth doses. I took two steps forward and SIX steps back, with horrible side effects. I'm only just now beginning to feel well and regain my strength.

This week Grady and I were in Boston twice in preparation for Phase 4. On Monday, we meet with Dr. Bellon, my radiation oncologist. She is incredible at explaining the "whys and wherefores" and the course of treatment that we are on. There were two very important things that we spoke of on Monday. The first is a real "praise." Dr. Bellon said my pathology is an excellent indicator for my long-term prognosis. If I read between the lines of what she said, it is the opinion of my doctors that this is the first and last time I will deal with cancer that is in any way connected to this incident!

I also asked about two lymph nodes under my pectoral muscle that were thought to be "suspicious" when I was given my CT scan in June.

Dr. Bellon pulled up my CT scan on her computer and we took a tour inside my body, and she showed me the nodes I was asking about. (It was really cool!) These nodes could not be removed during my surgery. This is part of the reason I need radiation, if I understand correctly.

I believe in diligence in prayer. Please continue to offer these petitions to the Lord.

Please pray that all cancer cells in these nodes *have been killed by the chemo I have received!*

Please pray that the radiation that I am about to go through only acts as an insurance to make doubly sure that ALL or ANY unhealthy cells in these remaining nodes are KILLED!

Please pray that this radiation treatment plan is fully successful in every sense of the word, and that the Lord would guide EVERY radiation beam that enters my body. Both my heart and lung will be at risk to some degree of getting some unnecessary rays.

Because I had a "100% response" to the chemo, Dr. Bellon did not seem concerned about these nodes having any live cancer cells. However, without removing them (and it would not have been the best choice, apparently), there is no way to be absolutely sure about the cells in the nodes. ...So, we'll blast with radiation.

On Thursday, December 20, it was back to Boston for my radiation "mapping." It was like being in a "Star Trek" episode! There were people hovering over me, talking in code, writing coordinates on my body for the radiation rays and waving strange guns at a computer I could not see, but I could hear it speaking out coordinate codes to the techs. It was bizarre!

I came away from all of this with eight small tattoos that will be used to set up the angles for the radiation rays. I have two things to say about being tattooed, and I hope I don't offend anyone.... People who pay money to be tattooed either have a thing for pain, or they are just plain numb to needles. Tattooing **hurts!!!!!!!**

Phase "4":

On January 1, 2008, Grady will be bringing me to my new home in Boston, for the next seven plus weeks. I will be living at the Hampton Inn and Suites on Mass. Ave during radiation.

I plan to come home on weekends, but I will miss the support and encouragement I have received from SO many of you by email. I will not have my computer.

Please pray that the Lord would "direct my path." I want this time in Boston to be fruitful.

...I'm going to be alone. I'm going to have a lot of time that I would not have had otherwise. My time commitment to my radiation appointments will last for less than an hour each day. That gives me a ton of time to spend with the Lord and be used by Him in whatever it is that He has planned. **Please pray that I would have "ears to hear," and I would have the courage and *physical strength* to follow in obedience.**

Thank you for the notes and encouragement you have sent. I have been so *blessed!*

Again, God bless each and every one of you and **Merry Christmas!**

Blessings and Love,

Kathy and Grady

The week after Christmas, and nine weeks after surgery, I began to grow a breast! Not only that, I began to grow a saddlebag on my side. Foregoing the urge to call Ripley's Believe It or Not, I followed Dr. Golshan's instructions and called his office.

Linda, Dr. Golshan's administrative and clinical assistant, answered the phone.

"Linda, this is Kathy Crews. I think I have a small problem. Dr. Golshan told me to call if I started collecting fluid around the surgery site. Well, I think it's happening. But isn't this late and awfully far beyond my surgery date for this to happen?"

Without hesitation Linda said, "Dr. Golshan will want to see you right away." "Linda, I start radiation next week. Can't this wait a few days?"

"Honey, this fluid can develop into an infection. He'll want you in here right away."

If I didn't understand the "how," I did understand the possible end result: infection! Yes! Linda was using a language I understood! I was still fresh from recovering after being knocked off my feet by the final rounds of H/T/C and an immune system that seemed to have been nullified. Finding antibiotics that worked was an experience I would be happier not to repeat by yet another infection!

Linda continued. "Let me talk to Dr. Golshan, and I will call you right back."

It was late Wednesday afternoon when I spoke with Linda. I began to mutter to the Lord that I really wasn't impressed that this had happened and I sure hoped that He had a good reason for this new aggravation.

As Linda had promised, she quickly returned my call. She had scheduled an appointment for Friday morning in the Comprehensive Breast Care Unit at Brigham and Women's Hospital. I just knew Grady would be thrilled when he got home from work to find we needed to make another trip into Boston, after just having been there for my radiation mapping, and only days before my move to the hotel. Great timing! *Lord, what are You thinking!?!?*

On Friday morning, I expected to be seen by one of the nurse practitioners. Instead, Dr. Golshan, himself—the newly appointed Director of Breast Surgery Services for Dana-Farber and Brigham and Women's Hospital—attended to my ailment personally! As he aspirated vial after vial of fluid, I wondered how much lymphatic fluid I had pooling in these strange new bumps.

"It looks like that's the end of it...180 cc. I hope this will be the only time we need to do this, but don't be surprised if fluid does collect again. Eventually, your body will absorb the fluid naturally."

I was horrified when, within days, fluid began to collect a second time and I was calling Linda to have another 180 cc aspirated.

The area filled again and again and again. I lost track of how many times I reported to the Comprehensive Breast Care Unit to have the area examined and/or lymphatic fluid aspirated from my chest or from under my arm. Conveniently, at least I was living at the hotel during the worst of it. The fluid became a major nuisance. I called Karen, the nurse practitioner assigned to my case, with ridiculous frequency. To this day she says she never saw another patient more than she saw me. Each time I reported to the Comprehensive Breast Care Unit to have more fluid drained, Dr. Golshan was notified, "Kathy's coming in again."

I was astounded by Dr. Golshan's attentiveness. If he was anyplace around and knew I was in the Breast Care Unit, he appeared to learn firsthand how I was feeling and how much fluid was being aspirated. My respect and prayers for him as my doctor multiplied.

My body refused to learn to make new channels to other lymphatic chains. After each visit Karen would say, "Well if that doesn't do it, you know where to find us."

Moving to the hotel in Boston for my radiation treatments meant I had easy access to the Comprehensive Breast Care Unit. That became something to be thankful for! All of my medical team was beginning to express concern, however, about possible infection from needle sticks to aspirate the fluid and the frequency of my trips into the Comprehensive Breast Care Unit as I began radiation. It was a delicate balancing act as Karen, Dr. Golshan, and Dr. Bellon watched and made decisions about the ongoing fluid buildup.

On the day Grady was moving me to my new quarters in the hotel, a major snow storm was blanketing the East Coast. It was forecasted to strike New Hampshire and the Boston area midday on New Year's Day. The trial run to test the tattoo mapping for my radiation coordinates was scheduled for Wednesday, January 2, at 9:00. As I had already learned from Tracy, nothing altered radiation treatment schedules. Absolutely no excuses!

Grady and I nervously watched the local news and the reports of the approaching New Year's Day storm as it intensified and the winds rapidly moved the blizzard in a northerly direction and toward New England. Hours before we had planned to leave, I rushed to finish packing and we made a mad dash out the door with hopes of reaching the hotel before the storm enveloped Boston. We weren't on the road for more than fifteen minutes before we saw the first snowflakes in the air, and minutes later we were driving with the full force of the storm bearing down on us.

The winds drove the snow into the windshield of the car as the wipers fought to clear it away. The pavement turned white as the inches of snow quickly began to accumulate. It seemed that every Christmas vacationer who had spent the week skiing in the mountains north of where we live was trying to outrun the storm as their holiday vacation ended with the arrival of the new year. The highway was congested with travelers as we all pushed through the blinding storm to reach Boston and points south.

It took hours to travel the eighty miles and reach the hotel. Grady was exhausted from the tedious challenge of staying on the road in such adverse conditions. Together we moved my belongings into my temporary home as the wind wildly swirled the snow that formed a small drift on the sidewalk at the entrance of the hotel.

As we finished moving my last suitcase and food into my room, Grady turned to me. "I'm not going to stay. I want to get back on the road before I'm too tired to drive. Are you okay, Kath?"

"You mean there's a choice?" Bravely, I tried to smile. "I'll be fine. God would not have allowed any of this if there wasn't 'a pony' in this mess someplace."

Grady smiled at my courage as he comforted me with a hug. Hoping that maybe he would change his mind and stay for just a little while, I asked, "Would you like to have something to eat? I have brought extra food to heat up for dinner." The rooms reserved for the hospital patients were equipped to prepare simple in-room meals.

"I'd like to, but I really need to get on the road. I have a driveway to plow when I get home."

Clearing the driveway with the snow blower had been my job. He was one of the few husbands on our street who came home after a stormy day to bare pavement. I kidded with Grady about living in the only house visited by the snow removal fairy.

I didn't want him to leave but knew he was right. "I'll walk with you to the elevator. Call me as soon as you arrive home safely."

"I'll be back on Friday right after you finish your radiation treatment."

"Yup! I can make it that long. Friday! ...One week at a time."

When the elevator doors closed, I turned and stood in front of the wall of glass that overlooked the hotel lobby entrance. In the shadows of the streetlamp, I watched as Grady hunched forward into the cold and trudged through the blanket of white toward our SUV. He disappeared from my sight and slowly the car crept forward, creating a new path through the ever deepening snow. I never felt more alone than at that moment as I stood motionless and watching as the taillights of our car vanished into the night. In the almost deafening silence, I questioned my own courage to face the days ahead without Grady beside me. I'm not a city girl. I easily become disorientated and lose what sense of direction I do have. Living in a hotel for so many weeks felt scary.

Lord, I know absolutely nothing in this life passes through Your fingers without You knowing what will happen. I'm here, and alone. I'm willing to be used as I seek You in this. Let's press on and into this mission. I choose "joy." I choose not to be embittered with self-pity. ...Lord, lead me. There must be a reward as I look for Your purpose in this. ...Where's that "pony"!

Several weeks of radiation treatments were finished before I sent another email to tell everyone what God and I were doing in Boston.

Subject: Radiation—Jan 20, 2008

Blessings and Happy New Year!

On New Year's Day I moved into my new quarters in Boston to begin radiation; at this point I am a third of the way into my treatments.

Radiation isn't painful, and the actual treatment only takes about fifteen minutes. What has been painful (or is a pain) is the shuttle service from my hotel to the hospital. Because my radiation schedule does not mesh well with the shuttle schedule, I spend about four hours at the hospital for my fifteen-minute appointment. However, the praise is this: with all of the extra time at the hospital, the Lord has provided some incredible opportunities to hear the stories that other women have to share about facing cancer...all kinds of cancer.

Last week I was talking with a woman about how effective my chemo treatments had been. There was a lady named Janice, who was just beginning radiation. She was listening to our conversation. Suddenly, she began to weep. She said, "Are you a 'plant' the hospital has put here to encourage us and give hope?" Janice's fear was evident as her tears flowed.

She had surgery just after Christmas for brain cancer and is only beginning the next steps of her treatment. She is terrified of chemotherapy, which is still weeks away.

The Lord gave me a perfect opportunity to share "the HOPE that is within me" with Janice and others who were close by and listening in on our conversation.

This poor lady. She has teenagers at home and who need their mom.

People who love Jesus: they're everywhere!

My first week at the hotel, I met a young college student who was staying at the hotel. His girlfriend, Daphne, was having her foot amputated. Cancer. He was there to support her through the surgery, until her parents could be with her. As I talked with him, I found out that they were both Christians (as well as Daphne's parents), and it was only through prayer and God changing the "unchangeable" that Daphne was being treated in Boston at Brigham and Women's Hospital and Dana-Farber.

She is from northern Maine. Daphne's doctors in Maine didn't have an accurate diagnosis for three years (!!!), and insurance was refusing treatment for her in Boston. It was nothing less than a miracle that the cancer remained encapsulated and did not spread. Exactly one day before she was scheduled in Maine for her surgery (which her surgeon had never done before), her insurance carrier granted permission for treatment in Boston.

...This past week I met Daphne and her parents in the lobby of the hotel. Although I had not met them or Daphne, I recognized the Maine accent, and from the description I had been given, I recognized Daphne instantly.

"Hey!" I said. "I know who you are! You're Daphne, aren't you? I've been praying for you. How are you?"

What a beautiful spirit this young woman has! What incredible faith! Daphne was given choices, but she was the one to make the final decision for amputation. Her doctors in Boston gave her other options.

God has supplied me with fellowship while I have been away from home.

The general manager of the hotel is an incredibly vibrant, praying Christian man. It's nice to talk with him about some of the people who are staying at the hotel for medical reasons and know he is praying for them also.

I have met people from California, South Carolina, Bermuda, Maine, New Hampshire, and even ENGLAND...all here for medical treatment. And so many want someone who can understand and just listen to the pain they are going through as they look for reassurance and hope.

I'm one third of the way through radiation. It's usually at the halfway point that fatigue sets in and the skin that is being radiated needs to be watched closely for radiation burns and cracking.

I've been pretty good about exercise while at the hotel. I've been told exercise helps combat the fatigue factor.

Although my treatment schedule Monday through Thursday keeps me at the hospital for several hours because there is no shuttle bus back to the hotel between 12:00 and 3:30 p.m., on Friday my schedule is great!

My treatment is at 7:45 in the morning, and Grady has agreed to let me give him a break and try using the bus to come home for the weekends. By 9:00, I'm at South Station, on the bus, and heading home. It's almost like getting a day off and having three-day weekends! I really can see how the Lord has arranged my appointments. I am home by 10:30 on Friday morning and do not return to Boston until Monday morning in time for my afternoon radiation appointment.

I think my only prayer request would be that my surprisingly good energy level would continue. Ask that the Lord would continue to use me to bring "hope" to some of the people that I meet...and "wisdom" in sharing His Love.

...Please continue to uphold Grady. I think my being away is harder on him than it is on me.

I REALLY miss being home.... But I do believe that God is using this time for his glory.

I continue to give thanks for all of you and uphold you in my prayers.

Blessings and Love,

Kathy

Chapter 25

The Stories

Moving to the hotel proved to be a true blessing. The 2007–2008 winter was a "humdinger." With 100-plus inches of snow, it came close to breaking records as the snowiest winter in recorded weather history in Concord, New Hampshire. As the weather patterns formed, it seemed there was at least one major snowstorm that buried Concord every week.

For years I gladly had taken on the task of snow removal. Blowing light, fluffy snow is great winter fun! (Wet, heavy snow is a different story, however.) Without my presence, and as the winter storms continued, Grady came home from work most Mondays to a snow-filled driveway. I teased him relentlessly that just like the Easter Bunny and Santa Claus, there wasn't a "Snow Blowing Fairy" after all. Another chore that was mine (that I did begrudgingly) was retrieving the dump barrel from the bottom of our 200-foot, uphill driveway after the waste management truck had collected the trash. It wasn't that the task was difficult; I just didn't like the chore.

The second week that I was away from home for my treatments, our dump barrel mysteriously appeared at the top of our driveway after the dump collection. It was weeks before Grady and I figured out that it was Mike, our neighbor, who was our "Dump Barrel Fairy." What a blessing of kindness. You cannot imagine how much we appreciated Mike's thoughtfulness as he took on this menial task while I was away. For months after radiation as I slowly regained my strength, Mike remained our "Dump Barrel 'ANGEL'"!

As the weeks of radiation became my routine, I chose to be content in my circumstances and embraced each day as a day with opportunities to reach out to others. I looked forward to the opportunities God provided on this journey. I prayed as the Lord brought people to my attention. There was always someone new, and a different story. Yet, there was usually a common thread with almost every person I met. I don't think I met anyone who didn't start with their diagnosis being made at a local "Pretty Good Hospital." It was beyond that commonality that individual stories took shape.

"Cathy" was from upstate New York. It was a Friday morning, and we were in transit to the area hospitals when we struck up a conversation. Cathy was on her way to Brigham and Women's Hospital. As we rode she told me about the diagnosis of cancer in her knee and the final surgery she would have this very morning.

An active woman in her thirties, she and her husband were board-by-board, nail-by-nail building a house together. After running a backhoe (of all things), Cathy had some pain in her knee. She blamed it on the repetitive moves with her feet on the pedals while using the backhoe, but the pain did not go away.

Cathy made an appointment with her local doctor, who ordered x-rays and came up empty handed as to why there was pain. He ordered physical therapy to see if that would bring some improvement.

The building project continued for several more months before the pain increased to a constant throb; she returned to her doctor. Further testing revealed "good news" and "bad news." She was given the bad news: there was a tumor. But the good news was that it was not cancer (according to her local doctor).

The couple spoke with Cathy's parents about the diagnosis and together decided they would not take any chances on a wrong diagnosis. At the least, it was definite that Cathy needed surgery. When her medical information was sent to Brigham and Women's Hospital, enough red flags were raised that further tests indicated the tumor *was* cancer.

Cathy was a very fortune young woman. Aside from some weakness in her knee, she came through all of her cancer treatment with no problems thanks to her quick action and courage to seek a second opinion about her surgery from a larger hospital more experienced in diagnosing cancer.

"Laurie" was a beautiful woman with two adolescent daughters. She was from Atlanta, Georgia. Just as Tracy had experienced, Laurie found a lump in her breast. Without any thought at all that it might be cancer, she called her primary care doctor for an examination. Later, a biopsy revealed it was cancer.

The lump was removed at her local "Pretty Good Hospital." When the pathology reports came back, shock set in. Laurie learned three things. The tumor was 2 centimeters, it was triple-negative breast cancer, and the surgeon had not removed enough tissue surrounding the cancer for clear margins when he removed the mass.

A second surgery was performed to remove lymph nodes, and an attempt was made to retrieve more tissue to obtain the critically necessary clear margins at the tumor site. Pathology revealed she was stage II; the sentinel node did reveal fragmented cancer cells (just like with Tracy).

Laurie was assured at her local "Pretty Good Hospital" that chemotherapy would kill any cancer cells that might have been missed; there was still some question whether they truly had adequate clear margins.

After the standard treatment of chemotherapy and radiation, Laurie returned to her doctor in Atlanta for her six-month checkup. Her checkup showed something Laurie could not even imagine. The cancer had spread to her breast bone and had metastasized in other organs.

As Laurie tried to deal with her new diagnosis and prognosis, she scrambled to research where to go to increase her chance of survival. She found Dana-Farber to be her best choice medically.

One morning while I was finishing my forty-five minutes on the treadmill, two women with distinctly British accents came into the fitness room. At first they seemed reluctant to stay. For the sake of giving them the opportunity to each use a treadmill, I told them I was just finishing if they wanted to walk. The offer opened up dialogue.

"Gee, the two of you definitely don't have a Boston accent. Where are you from?"

They chuckled as they told me they "definitely" were not from Boston but from England.

"Well," I said, "January isn't exactly our high tourist season around here; what brings you to wintry *New* England?"

It had not occurred to me that they might be staying at the hotel to receive treatment at Dana-Farber. After all, only a percentage of the rooms at the hotel were set aside for hospital patients and families. I was shocked to learn that Dana-Farber and Brigham and Women's Hospital were precisely their reason for being in Boston.

I learned that the women were close friends and one of the ladies had been treated in London for a small tumor in her mouth. She was in Boston because her treatment had not been successful and Dana-Farber was recommended to her by doctors in London!

There was a pattern that began to emerge. Many of the stories ended the same way. When local "Pretty Good Hospital" ran out of answers, patients were referred to Dana-Farber Cancer Institute in Boston, Massachusetts! However, by the time referrals were made, many of the people I met had a recurrence of cancer. Many were late staged with the disease, lessening the chance for survival. Several were there to receive experimental treatment or research protocols because they had no other options.

As I listened to other patients tell me their stories, I came to my own conclusion. No cancer is minor. No cancer can be taken lightly. Pure logic should dictate that the first step in battling cancer is this: find the best *research* cancer hospital in the country that is accessible, and start with a phone call to that hospital. A cancer research hospital (or hospital with high grades among the published *Best Cancer Hospitals*) is going to have the most experience and knowledge.

Carolyn, Dr. Bellon's administrative assistant/scheduling coordinator, has said, "Circumstances should not dictate the course of treatment and where it is done."

"Information" should dictate the course of treatment. Where are you going to find better informed, more experienced doctors than at the top-ranked cancer research treatment facilities? If cancer is the diagnosis, all hospitals will not have the same success at curing the disease. It's easy and comforting to stay close to home after a diagnosis and receive treatment at local "Pretty Good Hospital." However, is that the wisest choice when there is an alternative, albeit inconvenient?

The second logical point that began to come into focus as I talked with different patients was how many times patients were referred **specifically** to Dana-Farber when their local doctors and hospitals were out of answers.

As I have stated earlier, Dana-Farber is a *cancer **research*** institute. I was part of a research protocol and had a 100 percent response to the chemotherapy treatment that I received. That fact alone should shout volumes to any person reading the printed words on these pages. I am so thankful that in absolute ignorance and God's guidance, both Tracy and I started our chemotherapy treatment with oncologist Dr. Nancy Lin, at Dana-Farber. I think it is fair to say that medically it was her guidance as a doctor that made the difference in our outcome. God bless, Nancy! The Lord does not always choose to heal miraculously but uses medicine and doctors to accomplish His purpose also.

On Friday, January 25, I was tired after my week of radiation. I had a love/hate relationship with my Friday schedule. There were always families who needed affordable hotel rooms as they visited their loved ones who were in treatment. The hospital subsidized a block of rooms for long-term care patients. Each weekend, I evacuated my room so that the hospital could offer the space to weekend visitors. This meant rising at 5:00 and moving my belongings to the luggage storage room before grabbing some fruit, a bagel, and coffee from the free buffet breakfast and catching the 6:45 a.m. shuttle to the hospital.

The second morning shuttle returned to the hospital for patient drop-off and pick-up at 8:20. I was finished with my appointment by 8:10 and ready to go home for the weekend.

Each Friday, the shuttle bus driver transported me directly from the hospital to South Station to catch the northbound 9:00 a.m. bus. By 10:30, I was at home and very ready for a nap.

On this particular Friday, as tired as I was and try as I might, the Lord would not allow me to rest until I sent this email. Someone on my email list needed this word of encouragement about how God intricately is at work in our lives. Our part is to simply pray and trust Him with the final outcome.

This is a portion of what I shared.

"Connecting the Dots"

...I hadn't planned on sending out an email this weekend. But as a word of encouragement from the Lord specifically for one of you who receives my email updates, I am writing.

I need to remind you of events leading up to the continuance and the sharing of this story:

Two years ago, our son-in-law, Antonio, was a teacher for the public school system. Many of the students were from an area where young people and drugs were common and crime was normal activity.

I began to pray for these young people. I didn't know any of them... but I began to pray.

Three months into my prayer vigil, (if you remember) I shared about watching the Boston local news, and the pastor at Jubilee Church in Mattapan was being interviewed about the young people around his community. He spoke about the need for the church and community leaders to take an active role in the lives of the youth. He was praying for mentors to come forward and make a difference in the lives of these kids. This was confirmation to me that I *was* hearing the Lord as I prayed for this community of young people.

I continued to pray for our son-in-law as a teacher, the youth...and now Jubilee Church.

This week at the hotel, Phillip, the general manager, and I were talking about the Lord. I felt compelled to ask him where he attended church. (As if I'd have a clue about any of the churches in or around all of Boston!)

Guess where he attends church??? JUBILEE!!! And, yes, it's the same Jubilee Church the Lord has had me praying for these past two years!

...Okay. What are the odds? All of Boston...all of the different hotels.... All of the churches...all of the "Christian" general managers??? And me living at *THAT* hotel as I'm going through radiation?????

Trust the Lord in the impossible.

...The Lord has a "word" for you:

Jesus cares about the smallest details in our lives, and He has a way of "connecting the dots" that we ourselves cannot possibly connect on our own.

"Rely" on the Lord and he will make your pathway straight.

Blessings and Love,

Kathy

During the weeks of radiation (and the number of hours I spent at the hospital), women came and went as they started and finally finished treatment. When I was in my fifth week of treatment, Lorraine, a woman in her early forties from Denver, Colorado, started radiation. Although many of the women were receiving radiation because of breast cancer, Lorraine was not. Lorraine had been diagnosed with tonsil cancer!

"Well, that's one I haven't heard about before." I asked, "What is the profile for someone diagnosed with tonsil cancer? Is there one?"

Lorraine's answer set me back on my heels. "There is a common profile. Most cases of tonsil cancer occur in middle-aged, beer-drinking males."

"Good grief! You don't exactly fit the profile." And then I asked, "Why did you come to Boston for treatment?"

"Because tonsil cancer is not common in women, I did some research and found that MD Anderson in Houston and Dana-Farber Cancer Institute in Boston were my best choices for treatment. I flew to MD Anderson and saw a group of specialists at the hospital. The doctors scoped and examined my throat individually. All of them did the same painful exam and separately came up with pretty much the same treatment plan.

"Then I flew to Boston to compare the two hospitals. A group of doctors consulted about my case. The team scoped my throat *once* and together examined and came up with a treatment plan. The doctors at Dana-Farber made me feel like a real person that mattered. There is something different about this hospital—a warmth and compassionate attitude by the staff. Dana-Farber won my vote hands down, even though MD Anderson is one of the best cancer hospitals and would have been a closer hospital for me to receive my treatment."

I was surprised to learn that three of the women I met in radiation were in the medical profession. All three were in treatment for breast cancer.

Judy was a nurse at Boston Medical Center. The other nurse I met was the head cardiology nurse at another Boston hospital.

At my Friday morning appointments I had met and talked with a third lady in the medical field. She never had an abundance of time to chat, and one day I asked, "Where do you work? Each Friday you have said that you need to hurry to get to your office."

The lady looked a little shy or embarrassed by my question. And my mouth fell open when she answered, "I'm a cancer research doctor."

As I fought to close my gaping mouth, I responded quickly to try to hide my shock. "Thank you. All I can say to you is 'thank you.' You are doing an incredible job, and as survivors, my daughter and I both appreciate what you are doing in cancer research....I'm so happy to have the chance to tell you how grateful I am."

She replied, "You are right. I've been over the microscope looking at cancer and under the microscope as a specimen. I've seen what we are doing here as a doctor and now as a patient. We *are* doing a good job! It makes me proud to be contributing as a cancer research doctor."

One morning as I was waiting for the shuttle bus and on my way to the hospital, my attention was drawn to a man who appeared to be around my age and a younger man. The younger of the two was very tall—more than six feet, and he was thin, weak, and very sick. For several days, I watched the wall that was building between the two men, and I felt the Lord sensitizing my heart toward them.

As I watched the two, I began to put the pieces together. They were father and son, and the son was so ill that the father had begun to withdraw emotionally. He watched his son, David, valiantly fight against the cancer that was slowly winning the battle. "Ron" had lost all hope and no longer knew what to say to his son. I could see what was happening, and my heart ached for both men.

During my weekend at home I could not stop thinking about these two men that the Lord had brought to my attention. I began to pray for an opportunity to speak to them if I could be used in some way to give a word of encouragement and soothe their wounded hearts.

On Monday, something very unusual happened. When the shuttle bus came to Dana-Farber, I was the only person waiting for a ride. Gregg, the shuttle driver, opened the door of the van for me. He took a final look to make sure no one else was waiting inside the hospital lobby and then drove next door to Brigham and Women's Hospital, where Ron was waiting for a ride back to the hotel, and he was alone!

Before I could stop myself, the words flew from my mouth. "Is your son okay? I prayed for the two of you all weekend long while I was at home in New Hampshire." After addressing him so boldly, I was embarrassed that I had not so much as said "hello" to Ron before now.

For a moment Ron appeared startled, but then he broke into a warm smile, and his face softened with an unspoken *thank you for being someone caring enough to speak.*

"My son, David, is in Intensive Care, and his lungs are filling with fluid. His stepmother is on her way here from Honolulu. The doctors have done everything possible to save him. My son is dying."

Ron and I were the only two passengers as the shuttle made its way back to the hotel. It was rare that the van wasn't at least half full of passengers as the rounds were made to the Longwood area hospitals. As the van wove through the side streets and alleys of Boston, Ron and I talked about what it was like to have a child—even a grown child—diagnosed with cancer. When we arrived at the hotel, our conversation continued.

Honolulu, Hawaii, was his home. A year earlier, David had a small growth inside his nose; a biopsy was taken, and it came back positive for cancer. At their local "Pretty Good Hospital" the tiny growth was removed, and David endured the recommended chemotherapy, only to return for his six-month checkup and find the cancer had spread to his bones and spine. David's doctor in Honolulu suggested the only hospital where David's life might be saved was a research hospital—a hospital like Dana-Farber; but the cancer was very advanced. The tone in Ron's voice was desperate. "David is only 31. How did this happen?"

I felt so helpless to respond. What could I say to him? Ron's eyes were pleading for answers—any answers from someone who knew what it was to experience cancer as a parent but also as a cancer patient.

"Ron, I can't tell you why this has happened. I can't give you the reason why some of us live through cancer and why some of us die. But I can tell you this from firsthand experience: God loves you, and you can respond to this painful experience in one of two ways. You can surrender and trust the Lord in this or you can become despondent, angry, and bitter. The

Lord uses the most painful times in our lives to build hope in our hearts and draw us to His side and into a deep and trusting faith."

I allowed Ron a few moments to take in the words that seemed to flow so freely. *Oh Lord, inside I'm shaking. I give You my tongue; I pray for Your wisdom as I speak. Comfort this man's hurting heart. We are talking about life and death and this man's son!*

Gently I asked Ron, "Tell me what it is that you see happening with your son."

"He's fighting. I think he is afraid."

Again I paused. "Ron, does David have a faith that there is something more than just this life?"

"I'm not sure he does."

I took in a deep breath. This was such a sensitive topic, but one that at some point most cancer patients and families face even when the prognosis is hopeful: the "what if" questions. What if the doctors are wrong? What if I don't get well? What if...I die? What if there really is a life beyond this one? How do I know for sure?

Ron was squarely looking at the inevitable with David. David was in Intensive Care and struggling for every breath as his lungs filled with fluid.

My heart was filled with compassion as we spoke. I thought about Tracy and how terrifying "the unknown" felt with those first words, "Mom...it's cancer!" I knew as a parent what it was to want to give her the depth of my faith in the Lord Jesus Christ, as shaky as I felt at times in that faith. I knew what it was to have a child fighting cancer and living in fear.

I also understood on a personal level the stunned feelings when hearing the words "It's cancer...." *Lord, what words of comfort can I offer?*

"I only know one answer. Trust in the Sovereignty of God and His love for you. Despite how things look, by faith we must 'surrender' and place all of our hope in the Lord. Jesus knows your pain. And David's. Let him know how precious a gift he has been in your life. Open up your heart to David as his father. Let him know *his Father's love.*"

Our conversation was cut abruptly as the announcement was made that Ron's shuttle was departing for Logan Airport to meet the flight on which his wife was arriving. As Ron thanked me, I told him I would continue to pray for him and for David.

Faithfully, I reported to the fitness room for my afternoon exercise on the treadmill. While walking, I prayed for David and sang to the Lord.

I was returning to my room when I saw Ron and his wife walking in my direction as they started down the corridor. Our rooms were across the hall from each other. His wife looked worn out after her long flight from Hawaii. Both she and Ron seemed to perk up when Ron spotted me at the door to my room.

"Oh!" Ron said. "This is my wife. I was just telling her about you. I was telling her we have to have faith, just like you said."

Praying for David that day, I felt certain his lungs would clear and he and his family would be given the time Ron needed with his son to simply love him.

The next week when I briefly saw Ron, he told me David had been moved from Intensive Care and was in less distress as his lungs cleared! God is gracious.

Several months later I stayed at the hotel while attending a women's conference. I learned from Gregg, the shuttle bus driver, that the week after I last saw Ron, David died.

Gregg said to me, "Miss, I always knew when I picked you up at the hospital that you were 'different.' You never got mad when the shuttle was late picking you up from your day at the hospital. I knew your days at the hospital were long and you were tired, but you accepted things the way they happened. You always had *peace.*"

Gregg continued. "When I heard you talkin' to Ron that day that I was takin' just you and him back to the hotel, it was like you were an angel sent just for him.

"He was different after you talked to him. You helped Ron a lot; he told me so. But I could see the change in him. It wasn't so hard on him when his son died. He had a couple of weeks while David was in the hospital to say his 'goodbyes,' and I guess what you told him helped him to come to peace.

"...You were sent to talk with him; just like an angel."

Suddenly, as I listened to Gregg, the lessons in Acts 16:25, of Paul and Silas singing hymns and praises as others looked on, while they were in a deplorable condition, impacted my heart like never before. As my eyes took in the familiar sights from the window of the van while we traveled to the hotel, things were a little clearer. I understood something I had not fully grasped before. I saw what the Lord was opening my heart to during my months of radiation.

I had learned to sing hymns and praises to the Lord during difficult and painful times. But I had not truly connected with the importance of being transparent to others—especially people who were searching for the answers—as I rested openly in God's supernatural peace *"as others looked on."*

Chapter 26

Home Sweet Home!
(Well, for a Little While)

My final radiation treatment was on a Wednesday. After so many weeks of being in Boston for radiation, it felt strange boarding the bus and knowing it was for the last time.

I stared out the window at the crowded southbound highway and the cars streaming toward Boston. The bus sped north and toward home; I reflected on the experiences of the past several weeks. I looked back over my shoulder at the ever- shrinking skyline of the city. Soon, it was far away and in the distance. There was something bittersweet happening in my heart. Funny. I had expected to feel only joy at this moment. One more phase of my treatment was finished.

A blur of events in time-lapsed image took form in my mind. As much as I had wanted to have radiation treatments closer to home, God knew I needed to be in Boston…not only for my health but for my spiritual growth. I'm so glad the Lord guided me through the right channels and made it possible for me to stay at the hotel.

I was alone for many hours with only the Lord for company. What a blessing! But there were plenty of opportunities to be with others who were going through cancer and for me to share: *You, Lord, are my Strength.*

"My flesh and my heart may fail, but God is the strength of my heart and my portion forever." (Psalm 75:25)
Jesus, You are so good.

Sent: Tuesday, March 4, 2008, 9:16:42 PM
Subject: Radiation...FINISHED!!!!!!!!

Hello Everyone!

...And another step toward being well is finished!

I had my last radiation treatment on February 20. I think this is how it must feel when you have been released from prison...but are still on parole. I've completed the "hard time" but will remain under the watchful eye of my doctors as I continue to regain my health over the next MANY months. I still need to be in Boston every three weeks for Herceptin until late summer (I think). So, I'm not completely free from treatment.

I've been asked by many of you, "How are you doing?"

The short answer? "Pretty good!" I did super well until my last ten radiation treatments of the thirty-three that I received. Then I developed radiation burns.

Originally, I was told they would be like a really bad sunburn; mine were more like stove burns, and some blistered. I'm still healing; but everyday they are a little more gone.

I have a praise of thankfulness to share. Remember how I said that I was completely numb under my arm and down my side after my surgery? Well, that's where the worst of my burns were, and I couldn't feel the pain! Praise God or what!?!? I am so thankful for not being able to feel.

I'm noticing some of the physical effects from the chemo rounds which ended on December 3. I have muscle and joint pain...ankles, knees, hips.

Please pray that the Lord would restore my strength and flexibility. Even though I was walking on the treadmill at the hotel forty-five minutes each morning and an hour each afternoon, it *was* and has been a painful chore to walk. I was doing well energy-wise

222

until I got back home and started to resume a more normal life. At the hotel, I was on an excellent exercise and sleep schedule, but now that I'm home, there is just so much to do and too many distractions.

Living in Boston at the hotel provided countless opportunities to talk with so many people. I had two weeks where it seemed my path crossed with people who were truly in the battle of their lives. So often I could hear their fear as I listened to their stories. Time and time again the Lord opened the door for me to share.

There really is a God in this universe who has a very personal interest in everything that we go through. He knows our thoughts, our fears...and He cares.

He knew, before the foundations of the earth, when we would be born...and the day that we will die...and we are not going to die one day sooner or later than that day. We can rest in that knowledge, and if we fully trust in that truth, we can release the fear and find peace, even as we battle cancer. The Sovereignty of God: there is nothing we can do to change what He has seen our lives **to be**, since before time began. Allowing Him to use the trials in our lives to draw closer to Him can completely change how we go through the experience.

I have one more story: One morning at the hotel I met Emily. She was a little doll! ...About five years old. When I asked her where she was going dressed up so pretty, she told me she was going to see her doctor. I asked her if she was going to Children's Hospital, and her dad answered they were going to "Children's" and then to Dana-Farber.

Emily had been diagnosed with cancer when she was three. She's doing well...but still being carefully watched by her doctors.

I turned and directed my conversation to Emily. "I go to Dana-Farber, too!"

Her eyes got so big and filled with expression as she said, "Do you have a 'port'?" (For infusions.)

I wanted to burst out laughing at her question; she was so adorable! When I told her, I did(!) we connected and were instant friends.

...It's so hard for little kids; they feel they are different, and they gravitate toward anyone who understands what it is to be just like them.

As Pastor Kevin (our youth pastor) has been sharing a recent series of messages on "Being a Lion Chaser...Facing our fears," I've reflected on how this entire experience of going through cancer has changed me. I think I could come up with quite a long list. Again, this has not been a path I would have chosen, but it's been the "best" "bad" experience of my life! I could never have met and shared the Lord with SO many people who are literally facing life and death. I have met people from all over this country and beyond. What a HUGE blessing!

As a result, I've drawn even closer to the Lord. Was I perfect in how I used my time in Boston? Not by a long shot!

Could I have had a better attitude? You bet! I had one desire in my heart on Monday mornings as I traveled on the bus to Boston heading for my week of treatment. I was already yearning for Friday to arrive and my weekends at home. But still, even though I know I missed the mark on so much, there was good to be gained.

...Thank you, Jesus, for extending so much grace to me.

It has been so evident to me how strong my prayer supporters have been as I have been faithfully held before the Lord in prayer; I have been so blessed through this experience.

Thank you. Thank you for being there with me as I have been on this journey through cancer. "YOU" share in the glory of my healing and for every opportunity I've had in Jesus' Name....

Blessings and Love,

Kathy

The entire time I was having radiation treatments, specially trained nurses examined the condition of my skin. I was watched closely for any indication that special care was required to protect the radiated tissue from permanent damage.

Each week Dr. Bellon came into the exam room as the skin was being evaluated. Upon seeing her, jokingly I'd ask, "How'm I cookin' Dr. Bellon?"

One week after completing all of my radiation treatments, I returned to the hospital for a skin examination. Dr. Bellon was amazed at how quickly and remarkably I had healed. I jumped at the chance to push the equation and I asked, "Does that mean the area is healed enough for me to have lymphatic fluid aspirated?"

Although I still had no feeling, I did have the sensation of the skin being pulled taut as fluid filled the bulging pocket on my chest that had developed...again.

Soon after beginning radiation, Dr. Bellon announced it was too risky to aspirate the spot that continued to be problematic. As a temporary solution, I was referred to the Friends Place and to Mary, who was so knowledgeable and helped me with the undergarments I needed after the mastectomy. Mary suggested a compression bra with a "Jovipak" that gently massaged and moved the lymph fluid that repeatedly pooled under my arm and on my chest.

This bra was not designed to be modeled by the "Ooo-la-la" lingerie models! I'm not exactly one to gravitate toward sexy French undies, but this "thing" was butt ugly! It was a cross between a form-fitting vest and a granny bra with hooks in the back and the front to tighten the garment and create compression against the tissue that repeatedly collected lymphatic fluid. The only time I was allowed to remove it was for showers and when it became so raunchy it required laundering. To help keep the garment clean and to protect my radiated skin (which required oceans of Lubriderm and was glopped with Aquaphor ointment), I wore a soft, thin cotton sleeveless tank under this lovely $240 bra! What an attractive underwear fashion statement I was!

Even while confined to this contraption, fluid pooled. When Dr. Bellon seemed impressed with my healing, I wanted to move the process along and have the spot aspirated and hopefully shorten the time I would need to wear the compression bra getup.

Dr. Bellon responded to my request with a short and definite "NO."

I pleaded my case. "Dr. Bellon, will you call Karen, in the Comprehensive Breast Care Unit? Could we ask for her opinion about how much fluid has collected and if the fluid might be a reason for concern?"

Dr. Bellon looked at me as I attempted to bargain, but stood strong in her decision. "You are at too great a risk for infection. I'm not willing to consider allowing the site to be aspirated unless Mehra Golshan steps in and feels it is necessary. I will call Karen and explain my position. I will yield to Dr. Golshan and only him."

I had been through this enough times to know that the bulge needed to be drained. It was just a matter of my medical team agreeing if the tissue was healthy enough to risk the possibility of infection. It was a flip of the coin. The area was at risk for infection if the fluid was *not* aspirated, and was at risk if it was!

Karen paged Dr. Golshan as soon as I arrived and like so many times before, he came to the exam room and inspected the site that, indeed, needed to be aspirated for the sixth time!

"Yeah," he said as he looked closely at the skin that was swollen with fluid near the base of my sternum. "The skin is well healed, and that spot looks like it is pocketing a good amount of fluid."

Sympathetically, Dr. Golshan looked at me. "Someday this will stop. Honest. Sooner or later your body will absorb this naturally. Let's hope it's 'sooner.'"

Karen aspirated the site while Dr. Golshan looked on and asked if we had made any exotic travel plans in celebration of finishing radiation. Then Karen sent me on my way with her usual "Well, if this doesn't do it, you know where to find us."

For the next few weeks all was well on the home front and life almost appeared normal. Grady and I were about to celebrate our fortieth wedding anniversary. For years I had wanted to see the production of *Phantom of the Opera* in Las Vegas. Our friends Dan and Gayle loved the idea of going to the show, and so we began making plans to celebrate our anniversary with Dan and Gayle.

I was due for an infusion of Herceptin on March 10, and just as I had been doing every three weeks since the beginning of January, I reported to Dana 10. Everything seemed to be fine immediately after the infusion, but later that night my temperature rocketed to 103 degrees. My first thought was, *Could this be an abnormal reaction?* My second thought was, *The flu!*

By 4:00 in the morning, I was sure it was the flu. All of the symptoms were there: violent vomiting and diarrhea, and severe body aches. As soon as Grady was sure Dr. Lin was at her office, he called. Nancy agreed that it did sound like the flu, and she had not heard of any other patients reacting adversely to the Herceptin. She was concerned about dehydration and strongly urged Grady to take me to our local hospital for IV fluids. When

Grady finished the call, he told me we needed to go to the hospital. I was so weak and sick, he was requesting the impossible!

"Grady, I'm too sick. I can't do it. Please call Deirdre. Let me talk with her about her patients and find out how long this flu has been lasting."

Grady was apprehensive but called Deirdre and handed me the phone. "Deirdre, I had a round of Herceptin yesterday, and I came down with the flu last night. Dr. Lin wants me to go to the hospital for IV fluids. There are two things I'd like you to tell me: How long have your patients with the flu been sick, and how much liquid do I need to drink and keep down to avoid dehydration?"

As a medical professional, Deirdre immediately pushed for me to follow Dr. Lin's instructions and receive fluids intravenously. After promising Deirdre anything at all that she wanted to hear, I insisted upon first trying to hydrate with liquids at home.

Reluctantly, she told me if I could successfully sip four ounces of liquids hourly and keep it down, I would hold steady and keep dehydration at bay. The flu cases she had seen at her office were lasting up to five days. Deirdre was also concerned about my runaway temperature that continued to spike beyond 100 degrees even while taking Tylenol.

I promised Deirdre I would stay in touch with her. Her other demand was that I was not to be left alone...something that concerned Grady. He had already seen the need to work from home until I felt better.

I managed to stay hydrated by following Deirdre's instructions. My temperature, however, continued to soar and never once dipped below 100. Food was out of the question, and by Wednesday afternoon, Deirdre was uneasy about the continuous 100 degree temperature.

At Deirdre's prodding, on Wednesday night I reluctantly agreed to try some broth and a few bites of dry toast. I was beginning to accept how awful I felt; what I wasn't accepting was how awful I was beginning to smell from perspiration and the never-ending fever!

On Thursday morning, sick or not, I couldn't stand "me" any longer! I had to shower. For once, I was glad I was still pretty bald; it made shampooing much easier! I removed the nightgown I had been in since Monday night, and to my shock the entire area that had received radiation was once again RED. I thought to myself, *Well, I was told how sensitive and fragile this skin is. I was instructed on being very careful about showering in water that was too hot, told to protect the skin from exposure to the sun's rays for a year, keep the skin hydrated with creams and ointments. Why shouldn't the skin be red—I've cooked it from the inside out with a raging non-stop temperature!*

As bad as I felt, it felt good to wash away the stench. I dressed in sweats and made my way downstairs and collapsed in the recliner. Grady had gone for an appointment, leaving me alone for a few hours. He was surprised to find me curled up in blankets and in the family room when he returned.

Gradually, I began to take some nourishment, and each day I was able to eat slightly more. But my temperature would not dip below 100.

Sunday evening, all of a sudden it dawned on me. *This is an INFECTION! OH MY WORD…THIS IS AN INFECTION!* That's why my temperature would not dip below 100. The entire area that was red began to swell suddenly with the infection that was brewing. *OH NO!*

Not wanting to panic Grady with my realization, as calmly as possible I said to him, "Grady, which will be easier for you: to take me to the hospital in Boston tonight or first thing in the morning?"

Grady looked at me like he had just been hit with a bucket of ice water.

"What's wrong?!"

"This is an infection."

Grady became very solemn. "I think we'd better call the hospital."

Calmly, I made the call to Brigham and Women's Hospital, and within minutes, the surgeon on duty returned my call. After I gave the doctor a brief history, in response she said, "Well, you have just finished radiation; are you sure the area is not red because of the radiation?"

"No. The skin was very clear and incredibly good the last of February and one week after treatment. This is a different red…neon red…like Rudolph's nose, red."

"Oh! …Well…Dr. Golshan is away until Wednesday. Ah…I will leave word with the Comprehensive Breast Care Unit, and I would like you to report there as soon as the Unit opens in the morning."

It was nearly 10:00, and my choices were like a coin toss. If I showered and packed a few things (in case I was admitted) and we drove to Boston, it would be after midnight. Then there would be the wait for medical care if the Emergency Department was busy. It was just as well to wait until morning when the Comprehensive Breast Care Unit opened at 8:00 a.m., and where I would receive immediate care.

"Okay. We will be there. Did you say Dr. Golshan is away?"

"Yes. He is out of town. He will be back on Wednesday."

For the first time since I had been diagnosed with cancer almost a year earlier, I was truly frightened. This infection was bad and I knew it. As I climbed into bed with my left arm supported by a pile of pillows to keep its weight away from my side and off the swollen and red area, I prayed. *Oh Lord, keep me until the morning and get me to the hospital safely. Calm my fears. And by the way, Lord, **where** is my Dr. Golshan?*

Chapter 27

Our Plans...God's Plans

I spent most of the night in catnaps. As I drifted in and out of sleep, I prayed for the Lord to keep me safe and for morning to come quickly. Just before 5:00, Grady began to stir ever so slightly. Immediately, I whipped around to look at him with pleading eyes. *Can we go to the hospital now?*

He opened his eyes to see the desperate look on my face.

"Let's get up," he said.

I immediately threw back the covers. Ordinarily, I was the one dragging behind for any of our early appointments, but this morning I was hardly allowing Grady time for coffee before I was in the car and ready to go.

We were outside the doors to the Comprehensive Breast Care Unit and waiting when the doors opened. Wouldn't you just know it! Karen, my nurse practitioner, was not scheduled until later in the day. I was escorted into one of the exam rooms, given a hospital gown, and told the usual instructions of what to leave on and what to take off. I changed into the hospital gown and sat. Soon one of the nurse practitioners that I had not met before came into the room.

"Hello. My name is Mary. I see you have been in before; what seems to be the trouble today?"

I told Mary the whole story about the infusion of Herceptin on Monday, March 10; the chills and the fever, the vomiting and diarrhea; and then the discovery of the red skin on Thursday; and finally, my call to the hospital Sunday night. I gave Mary a complete history based on what seemed to be endless detailed questions. At last Mary said, "Let's take a look at this."

I did not move to the exam table but stayed seated where I was and opened the hospital gown to expose my neon red chest. Instantly, Mary's eyes all but popped from their sockets! She sprang to her feet. "*WOW-ZAA!*"

Now this was a professional. She was trained to remain calm and not react adversely in front of patients. Mary tore from the exam room like she was on her way to a six-alarm fire! A few minutes later she returned as composed as she could fake. "Um…I have sent an email to Dr. Golshan's office and sent out a medical assistance page to request a doctor to come here to the Unit." She tried to look controlled and calm as she continued. "Unfortunately, Dr. C., who is usually here, has been called into surgery on another emergency; so we will have to wait and see who is free to come to take a look at this. In the meantime, let's move to the exam table and I will aspirate a specimen for the lab. Let's see if I can relieve some of the pressure that has been building from this infection."

By now the swelling was beyond ugly in appearance. But on the other hand, for the first time in about twelve hours I felt hopeful there was a chance that I was going to live, and I was at peace that I was in the right place if suddenly I died!

"Sure! Have at it, Mare. I don't have any feeling on that side (Praise God), so there is no chance that this will hurt. I just want to feel better."

The details of how hard Mary worked with minimal results cannot be put in print. In brief, because of the severity of the infection, Mary was barely able to aspirate enough of a specimen to send to the lab to distinguish the source of the infection.

After forty-five minutes, Grady was uneasy as he paced in the waiting room, worrying, and asked if he was allowed into the exam room. Mary had been in and out so many times, I welcomed Grady's presence so that I was not alone. I was glad he was not squeamish and could handle the sight of what was happening. During my year of treatment, he had developed an abnormal and almost scary interest in medicine.

Finally, with great confidence Mary entered the exam room where I waited patiently for help and announced, "Dr. Golshan is on his way."

"Dr. Golshan? Are you sure?"

"Yes. I just received an email from him saying he's on his way."

Again I questioned her. "Are you sure it's Dr. Golshan who is coming?"

Mary replied, "Yes, Dr. Golshan."

I lay back down on the exam table. *Hm-m-m. This is interesting. Dr. Golshan is away.*

Minutes later Dr. Golshan burst through the door. I raised my head with his abrupt and almost resistant entrance into the room. It all but appeared that he was being swept along by a giant hand that he could not see. As if in protest, he declared with a somewhat louder than normal tone, "I'm **supposed** to be in Dallas, Texas!"

He paused for just a second as if he was caught between reality and disbelief. "I woke up this morning and said to my wife, 'I'm not going!' Next, I emailed Linda at the office and said, 'Linda, cancel the trip. I'm not going. Don't call me or email unless it's a complete medical emergency.' The next thing I know I'm getting an email from Linda saying, 'Well… Kathy Crews is in the Unit with an infection.' I'm **supposed** to be in Dallas, Texas!"

From my reclined position on the exam table, I raised my arms in praise and brought my knees up as I semi-doubled in two with laughter. "My God is so great! Dr. Golshan, you are my super hero!"

Appearing as if he was caught in an out-of-body experience, Dr. Golshan refocused on the reason that he was summoned. "Let's see what's going on here."

He walked toward me, and as he came closer, he extended his hand to lift the side of the hospital gown that was hiding the hideous sight. A look of shock and compassion washed over him. "Oh, you poor thing! You poor thing! OH! You poor thing!"

I began to laugh. "It's okay. It doesn't hurt. And you are here. I'm fine!"

"Oh, you poor thing! Let me see if I can find some surgical 'jammies' and I'll be right back." Dr. Golshan and Mary disappeared from the room.

Within minutes, they were back and Dr. Golshan was mumbling something about the unavailability of supplies when you needed them most. His only option for covering his clothes (minus his suit coat) was a hospital gown identical to the one I was wearing!

Suddenly, the entire situation struck me as funny: Dr Golshan's unexplainable instantaneous change of plans to be in Dallas; how he blew into the room bewildered over why he changed his plans; and NOW he was at the hospital dealing with a very sick ME! He seemed completely baffled by the chain of events. And here he was looking hilarious, dressed in a hospital gown than matched the one I was wearing! If God doesn't have a sense of humor in the most serious times....

As I semi-disconnected from what was happening, my thoughts were philosophically centered on the subject of how we can make our plans (but God always has the last word).

As he prepared a sterile field, Dr. Golshan's compassion kicked in again. "You poor thing. You have been through so much."

I began to laugh. "I'm fine. I really am. I have no feeling in that area (thanks to the mastectomy), so do what you need to do; just tell me when you're going to do it. I don't think this is anything I want to watch."

He moved my arm into position to expose the spot on my side and under my arm that seemed to be the best place to lance and drain the infection. There is no delicate way to describe what happened when he pierced into the volcano of infection. There was simply an explosion of fluid that poured from under my arm as the pressure was released through the incision made by the scalpel. Dr. Golshan literally jumped back from the flood that erupted. As he and Mary cleaned the wound of infection, I was so thankful to the Lord that I was being helped. I was laying there and quietly praising God, barely aware of the conversation around me.

Later Grady asked if I had listened to what Dr. Golshan and Mary had said as they worked. There were comments such as, "I don't know how you made it through the weekend. ...I've never seen an infection any worse than this...." And repeated sympathetic choruses of the infamous "Oh, you poor thing! You've been through so much...."

Once the wound was drained and cleaned, Dr. Golshan did not stitch the wound but explained that it needed to continue to drain and heal from the inside out. He "packed" and dressed my wound. "I'd like to keep you here in the hospital for a few days. We need to keep an eye on this. I want you on IV antibiotics, and it will be at least twenty-four hours before the labs are back and we know the source of the infection. Are you okay with that?"

"Hey! Anything you say. Right now this is the best I have felt in a week! Let's blast this infection so that we can move on."

"I'm going to send you to Admittance. Hopefully we can have a room for you before lunch time. I will see you tomorrow."

From the flood that had occurred when Dr. Golshan lanced my side, the back of my sweatpants were soaked despite the best attempts to protect my clothing. Fortunately, I was taken to a room within minutes after reporting to Admittance. In my overnight bag I had fresh changes of clothing, and I was delighted to shed my wet things, clean up, and dress in my own pajamas and climb into my hospital bed. Despite my circumstances, I was *very* happy! ....And thankful.

Shortly after I was comfortable and resting, two nurse practitioners came to my room to access my port for the fluids and antibiotics that I needed. They mapped the red area that extended from my sternum to my shoulder blade with a marker. With the drawing on my skin outlining the infection, the effectiveness of the antibiotics attacking the infection could be visually watched as the borders began to shrink. The nurse practitioners were incredibly sweet and compassionate.

"Can I get you something for the pain, Mrs. Crews?" one of them asked.

"Please, call me Kathy. Oh, no, I don't need anything for pain; I'm fine. I am just *so-o* happy to be here." I was serious and meant every word I said.

The two women looked at each other, puzzled by my response, and burst out laughing.

"No!" I said. "I mean it. I am the happiest, most agreeable patient you've got! I was so sick, I'm delighted to be helped. I really am happy to be here!"

The two were still laughing as they left my room.

Dr. Golshan kept me under his care and in the hospital for three days as the IV antibiotics worked to rid my body of infection. Slowly, the perimeter of the area that had been neon red began to shrink and grew lighter in color.

The normal routine would have been for the interns to come at least twice a day to evaluate and repack my wound. Maybe it was because of my report to Dr. Golshan about the experience I had with "Dr. Cool and Sweetie" after my mastectomy, but Dr. Golshan came each day to appraise my progress rather than the interns. My wound packing was done by him or my nurse. At any rate, I was grateful to have the expert care and attention I received.

During my third day in the hospital, Karen, my nurse practitioner, came for a visit during her lunch break. "Mary said you were the most amazing sight she had ever seen. I just had to come and see this for myself. How are you?"

"I'm doing well now, Karen. Yeah, I was quite a spectacle. I thought I was going to give poor Mary a stroke!" I laughed with Karen as I retold the story of Mary bolting from the room when I opened the hospital gown to reveal my "glowing" red chest. Even after three days on IV antibiotics, the area was still quite impressive.

During our visit, Karen told me that I would again have a visiting nurse for my wound care, and she instructed me to call her with any questions as I healed. She offered some kind words for how quickly she expected me to recover from the infection.

Karen's visit and her words bolstered my hope!

Chapter 28

The Endless Infection

By Wednesday, March 19, and the evening of the third day in the hospital, I was improving nicely. I was released from the hospital with a massive bag of packing supplies for my wound and a list of instructions. I did feel considerably better, and armed with a ten-day prescription for oral antibiotics, I set my sights on our April 1 travel plans. I was sure I would be well.

It didn't take long before I realized I had set my sights a little too high. I was feeling better, but I was far from well. I had little energy and no desire to leave my recliner. As days passed, there was almost no improvement in how I felt.

I especially liked and trusted Melissa, one of my visiting nurses. After repetitive days of packing my wound, Melissa was beginning to question the speed of my improvement. As she examined and kept notes on how the infected site appeared, there was a spot at the base of my sternum that was still red and inflamed. Visually, it looked questionable, but I never once had any fluctuation or rise in my temperature. I hovered at 97.9, within a normal temperature range.

On my eighth day of taking oral antibiotics, Melissa felt some proactive measures should be taken. "I'm not sure about this. How many more days of antibiotics do you have? When are you seeing Dr. Golshan?"

"I was in Boston this past Monday to have the site examined. Mary, the nurse practitioner who had worked with Dr. Golshan, saw me. She thought everything was okay but did suggest I should come in once more before going away. I'm due for an infusion of Herceptin on Monday, March 31. I was planning to have the wound looked at then."

Melissa thought. "I'm getting mixed signals. Your temperature is normal, but that spot is awfully red. Maybe you should call and have Karen notify Dr. Golshan that the wound is still draining well and looks fine, but there is a secondary location several inches from the packing site that is very red. I wonder if the antibiotics are disguising more infection by keeping your temp in the normal range. It would be a good idea to ask for Karen's opinion. At the very least, I think you need more antibiotics."

Melissa's evaluation made my heart sink. With a possible secondary infection, would I be allowed to travel? What was I supposed to do? Take a nurse with me?

Our tickets to see "Phantom" were crumbling in my mind's eye. I had looked forward to this for such a long time. Suddenly, any hope that I might improve and feel better over the next few days seemed unlikely, especially if Melissa was right.

With Melissa there and my anniversary plans fading, I called Karen's voice mail and left a message. As always, she returned the call quickly. Karen asked me some detailed questions and agreed that it was probably best for me to remain on antibiotics. And then she suggested another visit to the Comprehensive Breast Care Unit tomorrow!

Grady and I made the trek back to Boston for the second time that week to have the site examined. Karen did not like what she was seeing.

Grady had a request. "Karen, it's pretty clear that the wound packing is going to be an ongoing thing for a while. Since we had hoped to go away for a few days, can you show me how to wound pack, or will I need to take Kathy to a medical clinic while we are away?"

"Not a problem. I can show you how to do this. It's pretty simple."

I was much more apprehensive about this than Grady. Karen actually taught nursing students, and Grady was an excellent student as Karen instructed him in the proper way to pack the wound with the sterile packing tape.

When Karen finished Grady's lesson, she said, "I'll email Dr. Golshan and let him know you're here again. He's in a class for the day, but I know him; he's checking email and he'll get back to me before you are dressed and ready to leave. We'll wait for instructions from him."

Dr. Golshan emailed back almost immediately and told Karen to schedule me back for Monday. That was his day for surgeries, but he would like to see me at twelve noon during his break.

I was filled with gratitude for how attentive Dr. Golshan was, but at that moment, I wanted to cry with frustration. I was at my wits' end. Poof! My hopes were gone…. Discouragement had packed its bags and was sitting on the doorstep of my life. I had had enough! I was tired of the endless and countless trips to Boston, tired of being a patient, tired of falling in the minority with so many abnormal ailments. I wanted an end to everything remotely connected to cancer and there was ***no end*** *in sight!*

I was quiet for most of the ride home. Spiritually, I was struggling to keep my focus, and I was feeling angry with God. *Enough is enough, Lord! This infection is so abnormal. Enough with the infections. How much more does my poor body have to go through?* **I want to be well!** *I am sick to death of being sick to death. If I haven't learned the lesson by now, if there is still something in this journey I'm not getting, give up! I've had all I can stand! It's been a year. Let me be well! Heal me!*

The next morning I was still despondent and angry. I was rebelling against feeling that I could not even have my morning shower when I felt like it. My entire day was wrapped around the time one of the many visiting nurses arrived. I could remove my bandages and shower, but because the wound was still draining, a nurse needed to examine and repack the wound immediately after I showered; my plans revolved around others!

Still dressed in the night clothes that covered the wad of gauze taped under my arm, I was having breakfast with Grady. I had been grumbling to him that I felt like I was being kept on an extremely short leash.

Twice each day I had to plan meals, activities—everything—around the schedules of the "strangers" who were coming to my home to plug the gaping hole in my side. ***I didn't like this one bit!***

The phone rang with the "twenty-minute warning" signaling me to head for the shower. As my foot touched the first step of the staircase, the

Lord broke through my grumbling. I began to sing the chorus from a song that I had learned as a baby Christian, so many years ago. The words were a reminder of some applicable Scripture: God **inhabits praise.** As we praise the Lord, the chains of despondency that we are shackled by lose their power. We are freed from oppression when we do the exact opposite of what we **feel** like doing and chose to praise God. The words I sang reinforced what the Lord had been pointing out to me at every turn as our family had battled cancer: the importance and the power of PRAISE.

...Just as in the Scripture...Paul and Silas...Acts chapter 16.

*Oh, Lord, I do "get it." I'm sorry. Forgive me for losing patience and grumbling. You do inhabit our praises to You. I **know** the power of praise. "The joy of the Lord is my strength." I see the connection.... I do need to be keenly aware of how easy it is to become self-focused, and lose sight of practicing this truth.*

Grant to me the will to remain steadfast and obedient to You, trusting You in all things. Even through the length of this endless infection.

As I made my way up the stairs, the Lord brought to mind an interesting parallel. More than twenty years ago, before we moved from Maine to New Hampshire, we rescued a beautiful, young blue point Siamese kitty. During the timeframe of the move, Tara escaped and disappeared. We hunted endless hours for her without success, and as she was a strictly indoor cat, we feared she wouldn't find her way back to us.

Tara had been missing for four days when our niece, Kelly (who was only about seven years old at the time), was playing outside in her backyard a few houses up the road. She heard a faint "meow" and followed the cry. She found our Tara in the woods and more than a quarter mile from where we were living.

Fifty-some-odd days later, Tara had a litter of two kittens. When it was time for their birth, Tara instinctively knew what to do for the kittens' arrival, even though it was a first-time experience for her. It was a difficult birth. I stayed with her, gently stroking her face as Tara and I waited for her long labor to bring forth new life. It was obvious how much pain she was in as her little body wrenched with each contraction.

As the contractions continued with no results, my concerns for Tara's life began to rise. It was late into her labor to attempt to bundle her up and race to our veterinarian's office, and it was nearly their closing time. I just had to stay with her and pray that she would make it through her labor, make it through the pain.

Finally, I saw the first evidence of the kitten Tara had been working so hard to push into the world. As soon as the shoulders were exposed, I carefully placed my fingers around the kitten. With Tara's next contraction, I gently pulled, and with a little more effort on Tara's part, the kitten was born. It was malformed and did not survive; the kitten was huge in comparison to Tara's small frame.

Thirty minutes later, the birthing process started again. My poor little mother cat had nothing left to give! I was talking to her, encouraging her to push "one more time." As the second kitten's head became visible and as Tara was pushing, I did all that I could do to help her in the birthing process. With a few more contractions, "Tigger" was born!

Through the long and painful birthing process, there was something that made an impression that I will never forget. Between every labored push, Tara purred. The entire miserable time, she purred! A hormone is released into a cat's system that calms them when they "sing." During extreme pain or stress (as well as when they are content), cats purr.

As I reached the top of the stairwell, I saw the lesson in remembering Tara's labor and how she "sang" through it.

If even in the animal kingdom there is a connection between purring and peace, I needed to remember that truth *as I labored through!*

Driving to Boston on Monday morning, I dreaded seeing Dr. Golshan. I could not help but feel anticipatory knowing I had another infection site! I was exhausted most of the time, but despite how I felt physically, my heart clung to a fragment of hope for our getaway; I needed something fun to look forward to.

After a few minutes of light conversation and telling Dr. Golshan about our plans to see "Phantom," he asked how I was feeling. He examined the red, swollen spot.

"You are gathering fluid…again. I think this infection originally must have been draining out through the opening we made a few weeks ago, but the channel must have sealed."

He looked at me with unspoken disbelief. "We've got to give this a way out. We need to lance this spot too. Oh! You poor thing. This has all got to come to an end soon. …This has to end."

I smiled at how sympathetic Dr. Golshan seemed. He appeared equally as pained and frustrated as I was. He prepared the area, and this time I watched as he worked. He was absolutely right. There was a considerable infection brewing under the inflamed skin. I was glad that he and Karen had questioned my symptoms even though I had not developed a fever. Antibiotics never would have cleared up the festering problem.

I continued to watch as he scoped the depth of my new wound and then packed the small hole. "Dr. Golshan, I want you to know how much I appreciate how good you have been to me. I have been so blessed by how caring you have been."

As he worked, I talked. "I know that you were a bit of a holdout and you wanted the reconstruction done at the time of the mastectomy. And yet, as a team of doctors you all came to agreement. Dr. Bellon was right, wasn't she? Considering the lymphatic fluid problems I have had, and now the infections, what would have happened if I had done reconstruction after the mastectomy last October 22?"

The expression on Dr. Golshan's face told me he was being reflective. "Yes, Jennifer Bellon was right. She had some definite opinions about your radiation script and she was right. I'm glad we waited. …But don't tell her I said so!" He was smirking and there was a twinkle in his eyes as he joked about keeping his confession a secret. Then his expression became serious. "There is a good chance that you would have lost the transplanted breast mound, and we would have had to start all over again with a different plan for reconstruction. Jennifer made the right call. Stephanie supported that decision, and she was willing to wait and work on radiated tissue."

He paused. "You have been through so much more than what we ordinarily see."

Dr. Golshan's comment gave me pause to consider the "what ifs." More than ever, I was thankful for Tracy's determination for me to see Dr. Lin. Tracy was right. I shudder to think what would have happened had I not chosen to follow her lead. Tracy's diagnosis and what we learned about cancer from her experience likely had saved my life!

As Dr. Golshan finished bandaging my new wound, I talked. "I've heard rumors that Dr. Bellon is extremely picky when it comes to details. I think I'm glad that she is."

He rolled his eyes and muttered something about "hearing that rumor, too." He was grinning. We began to laugh as seriousness and the business of medicine gave way to lighter moments of joy and knowing that right choices had been made. I was on my way to having the worst behind me. (At least we hoped so.) I thought this might be one of the last times that I would see him. I thought this might be "goodbye" to my wonderful and caring doctor.

"Dr. Golshan, I am so grateful to you. Thank you for all you have done."

Again he grinned with an impish expression. "Well, you've paid me well."

Grady was in the exam room, and he began to laugh.

"So," I asked, "when is it time for me to say goodbye as a patient and you release me from your care? When will I get my walking papers?"

He hesitated briefly before answering. "Well…this a lot like a marriage. You can divorce us anytime you like. But we would prefer that you *not* do that."

I was surprised by his response. But then I had such a feeling of security; my team of doctors will always be a part of my health care. I'm so glad I chose doctors that were young—and some of the county's most brilliant!!!

Dr. Golshan gave us his blessing to enjoy our planned getaway, after giving Grady a few pointers for packing my new wound. When we returned from our trip, I sent out a very newsy email telling my "groupies" about having the flu, the infections, and my three-night stay in the hospital.

This is a small part of that email and what I felt the Lord was showing me in the experience. I wrote:

> Among the lessons that the Lord showed me through this, one of the things that I saw clearly was **how great a testimony we share by our countenance….Our actions speak a million words.** None of this has been fun. But what good does complaining do?
>
> When I was admitted to my hospital room and I was first visited and "mapped" (for the size of the infection) by the nurse practitioners, I was asked how I was.
>
> I guess they hadn't heard an answer like mine: "I'm SO happy to be here; I'm so grateful to be getting the help I need!" They couldn't hold back their laughter.
>
> I believe more strongly than ever that **the Lord grants "favor" to His children.** I believe the Lord hand-picked Dr. Golshan as my surgeon. …It's a "quietly" known fact that Dr. Golshan is one of the best surgeons at Brigham and Women's Hospital. And I have had

so many unfortunate things happen. The Lord has begun to present opportunities for me to open up and share who I am in Christ to Dr. Golshan...just through my reaction to the hurdles I've had to overcome, things that most cancer patients never have to deal with.

From a comment that Dr. Golshan made when I was lanced a week ago, he knows how great my faith is. Who knows how the Lord might use this....But I pray He will.

I'm still in a pretty weakened condition from being so sick with the infection. My energy level is at 10 percent power, I think. Slowly, I'm getting stronger.

Grady is becoming quite a nurse! We did go away for a few days for our anniversary, and Grady had to "pack" and dress my wounds that are still open and draining and require special wicking to help them to drain. He's doing much better than I ever thought he would. Again, "Praise Jesus!"

One year ago today, April 9, 2007, this all started with a "worrisome" mammogram....Not the year I would have chosen; but I can praise God for the lessons learned, the opportunities the Lord has given to me, and for **"understanding"** and experiencing "the **JOY** of the Lord is my strength"...even (and especially) in "suffering."

Blessings and Love,

Kathy

Just as Tracy suffered pain in her ribcage from the radiation (and still has occasional discomfort), so did I. Radiation had changed my skin and the underlying connective tissue between my ribs. There was no flexibility or elasticity. The entire left side of my rib cage responded as though my skin was a size too small and it was made of leather. It seemed the repercussions from having cancer were never-ending. Often, I found it difficult to keep discouragement at bay as the wound packing continued and the changes and impairment to my side became more obvious.

It was April before I was finally well enough and able to attend our church cell group meetings regularly. It was almost as discouraging and unbelievable to everyone in our group as it was to me that I had a second infection site that was now being packed. It seemed that all hope of regaining my strength and ever being well was like chasing butterflies blindfolded...impossible and pointless!

And then there was a glimmer of hope!

Sent: Friday, April 18, 2008, 12:00:20 PM
Subject: Winning the "Infection" Battle

...Great news! This morning there is a significant difference in the appearance of the area that has been so ugly. The area is much less red. The drainage has also slowed to almost nothing! We will still need to continue "packing" the wound as it heals. But there is an improvement.

Unless the Lord decides to speed up the normal process on this, I'm still looking at a few more weeks of being "packed." Man! I can't wait until this is finished.

My poor skin has been through so much! ...Barely healed from radiation and then being irritated for a month by the bandaging and rebandaging...taping and retaping....

On a MAJOR PRAISE...answered prayer!

Radiation often causes rib pain. It feels much like being VERY bruised. After our small group family prayed over me on Wednesday night, **my ribs stopped hurting**!!!!!!!!!!!!! Praise Jesus!

The incisions to drain the infection need to heal from the inside to the outside. Maybe this is where Jesus has decided to begin in my wound healing: starting with the ribs under the wounds!

Blessings and Love,
Kathy

As my small group family gathered around me, it was Cherie who spoke with spiritual discernment. "Kathy, you have been such a trouper through all of this and a testimony to so many. The devil knows he's a defeated foe and is grasping at straws as he tries to bring discouragement

244

upon you. Just look at the major things you have come through and the encouragement you have brought to others. And now you are being kicked down by not just one infection, but two!

"We are standing around you as your family in Christ and coming against the spirit of discouragement. We are praying for God to release His healing to your body and rid the wounds from infection and to heal and restore your energy."

...Immediately and as Cherie prayed, the pain in my ribs vanished!

"I was not a girly girl." Judging by the age of my little sister, I was almost 6 years old. (That was my rocking horse she's riding.)

My senior high school prom. And yes, that's Grady. June 1967

Look! Grady and I both "found a pony!" October 2001

Kathy and Grady on a visit to Spain while Tracy was living there. January 2002

Kathy and Grady enjoying some pool time while attending a business convention days after her Dad's memorial service, and only weeks before Tracy's diagnosis. May 2005

"Everyone knows that I'm a snorkel-aholic..." The photo was taken days after my first appointment with Dr. Golshan and just before the biopsies that confirmed I had breast cancer. May 2007

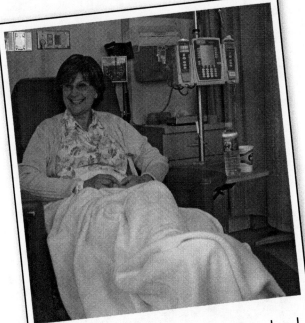

Kathy's last infusion for the research trial and the final step in phase 1 of treatment. September 17, 2007

Kathy enjoying an evening sunset at their favorite little "4 star rustic" Bajan resort weeks before her scheduled surgery. October 2007

"Soon I was carrying my head high and so happy to have hair." Grady's job often demanded travel. I was glad when I was well enough to join him. May 2008

Final infusion of Herceptin. Hurray!!! Sunday afternoon, July 13, 2008

Chapter 29

"Hair" I Am!

The last weeks of April dragged on; the routine of seeing my visiting nurse every morning continued with the exception of the days I was in Boston and seeing Karen.

With a "twenty-minute warning" phone call, I headed for the shower. The one difference and improvement to my schedule, however, was that in the evening and on weekends Grady was in complete charge of my wound care. He actually became so good at wound packing, I preferred to have his help rather than to be at the mercy of the nurse's schedule. (A far cry from the man who was embarrassed and awkward as he helped me dress after shoulder surgery a year earlier.)

After my Herceptin infusion at Dana-Farber, usually I made a quick appearance next door at Brigham and Women's Hospital and the Comprehensive Breast Care Unit to see Karen for an evaluation. It wasn't until the first of May that Karen declared we could cease packing the wounds.

Ever so slowly my energy level began to return. Between all of the infections I had early in the winter and then during the spring, I think I must have been on every antibiotic known to man. As we tried to combat the infections, I showed allergic reactions to whole families of antibiotics.

In mid-May, Grady had arranged to attend a business conference in Huntington Beach, California. Even though I was still in relatively poor condition energy-wise, I wanted to travel with him. At the conference there would be friends that Grady and I had known for years and who had stayed in touch throughout my illness.

The opportunity to break out of the mundane and do something different gave me a goal to work toward and a reason to strive for physical wellness. I continually felt like each time I was improving or feeling better, something happened that would knock me flat on my back again. With something fun on the horizon to work toward, I would struggle to get back up emotionally as well as physically and move forward.

Just as Cherie had said, it seemed the more I encouraged others, the harder the devil worked to bring discouragement upon me. When Cherie verbalized this, it was brought into the "Light," and I had fewer and fewer days of discouragement as I focused on deliberately choosing joy.

One of the crazy little things that continued to be discouraging to me, however, was my hair. It didn't want to grow! Week after week I would look at my friend Denise, who also had chemotherapy, and she was on her second and third haircuts. I was still wearing scarves and my wig. Half joking, half serious, I would tell her, "Denise, I covet your hair." She understood my frustration.

Prior to cancer, my hair was medium brown and straight. As my hair began to grow back, it was growing in a ridiculous pattern. It was chocolate brown (like my dad's) with bits of silver, and wavy. Spots were growing quite nicely, and then other spots were still patchy. On one side of my head the hair was long enough to cover the top of my ear, and on the other side of my head the hair was just barely there. The top was a mix of short and longer hair growing in every direction. If it wasn't so sad looking, it might have been laughable. After chemo, you NEVER know what will grow back. When Tracy's hair grew back, it did have more body and waves initially—typical "chemo hair"—but it grew back exactly the same color it had been.

A friend of Tracy's who went through chemo when she was forty-something had auburn hair. It grew back snow white. One evening as she was dressing for a special event, she had put on a sophisticated, conservative dress and had chosen a string of pearls from her jewelry box. When she glanced at her reflection in the mirror, in shock she shrieked, "OH MY GOODNESS! I'M BARBARA BUSH!"

The very next day she decided to color her hair.

On May 1, and in desperation, I called a hairdresser who had experience cutting and shaping "chemo hair."

"Sandy," I said, "I'm a mess! I don't know if you can do anything with my hair or not. It still may be too short. If I come in, would you take a look and tell me if there is any way to improve this...this mess?"

Sandy gave me some encouragement and invited me to her salon for a début without my wig. If she didn't scream and run from the building when she saw me, I honestly thought Sandy might tell me to let my hair grow for another week or two before coming back. Instead, she gave me the biggest boost to my self-esteem. She snipped here and there, giving style to the hair that previously had looked as though it had been shaped by a visually impaired dropout from a topiary class.

In ten quick minutes and with a little styling gel, Sandy had me unashamed of the hair I had kept covered. She transformed what was there into a perfect "Jamie Lee Curtis" haircut. At first it felt a little funny to be without my wig or my scarves, but soon I was carrying my head high and so proud and happy to have hair!

Sent: Sunday, May 4, 2008, 5:11:15 PM
Subject: "Hair" I am!

Greetings All!

Some of you have emailed to say if you don't hear from me regularly, you get a little concerned; especially after my last round of unexpected setbacks with the infection.

I'm happy to say, "I'm doing well!" Last Monday I was in Boston to have my wounds evaluated, and I was delighted when I was told, "*no more wound packing!*" THAT was the best news I had in a month! I can't begin to tell you how relieved and thankful I was to hear those words.

The smallest victories mean so much. When I was so sick I began to wonder if I would ever feel normal again; and then last Saturday I cooked bacon and eggs for Grady. I could not help but "give thanks." ...I felt well enough to fix a REAL breakfast and eat it! Most of you reading this cannot appreciate these words; these are words **coming from** a **HEALED** cancer patient.

...And hair! ...It's one of the things I missed most. I have a wonderful wig that has served me well as I have gone through chemotherapy.

But I really missed my hair and coveted everyone's hair and wondered if they knew just how lucky they were.

Gentlemen, the Lord has given me a greater compassion for those of you who face what I faced, those of you who are thinning, balding, and remorseful at what lies in the drain catcher after every shower. There is not another woman that you know who feels more compassion for you.

I have referred to Vernon Brewer's book *WHY?* and spoken of the impact his book has had on me and my own battle with cancer. Vernon was a cancer patient who was not given "a prayer" for survival. A five-pound tumor was removed from his lung. And yet, God had *other* plans and this man, indeed, survived.

In his book he shared about the beauty that *can* come out of destruction. I read in his book that something very incredible happened to the landscape in England after WWII. Botanists found that in the countryside that had been bombed, plants and flowers thought to be extinct for decades upon decades now flourished!

I think I can draw a parallel to that picture and what it's been like to go through cancer....But, you know, it isn't true just for cancer. Any trial or hardship can either drive you **INTO or OUT OF the arms of the Lord.**

I hope I've grown through this experience....I hope the Lord has completed a purpose in me. ...I'm not a "finished" work....

But I hope I've completed another round of being "fired" by the Refiner. I hope I shine a little brighter for my Lord....

I've had a few ask, "So you're finished with treatments, right?" I'm finished with the toughest part.

Yes, the cancer is gone, and in a few weeks I'll be having another MRI to confirm that I am cancer free. Both Tracy and I had difficult forms of breast cancer...different types...but both very nasty types of cancer.

Because of the type of cancer I had, I will be on Herceptin a while longer, with treatments every three weeks. And yes, this is a chemo drug that is put into my body through the port that is in my chest.

Praise God, I've done pretty well on this drug. But I am monitored closely for heart damage from the drug, and next week I will have another test for my heart function.

Please pray that the Lord would continue to protect my heart from damage.

I will be monitored for the rest of my life as a cancer patient, with regular trips to Boston for exams. I trust in the Lord for my healing. I am healed. But at the same time I also know the importance of being wise in having regular checkups. I'm so glad my doctors are young!

Blessings and Love,

Kathy

Attached to the email, I sent a photo of my new "Jamie Lee Curtis" haircut. The response was overwhelming as my friends and prayer partners cheered me on.

Chapter 30

I'm His Child (and Acting the Part)

Karen said that until my draining wounds were completely healed, I could not swim. As I packed for our brief trip to Huntington Beach, Karen's words put a small cloud over our escape to a warmer place and my hope of using a pool. I wanted to begin working muscles and stretching tissue affected by radiation.

I set out to purchase a swimsuit on the outside chance that I would be healed and ready for the plunge. If finding the right swimsuit is ordinarily a challenge, a mastectomy takes the dreaded task to a whole new level.

The Friends Place at Dana-Farber had some mastectomy swimsuits, but nothing that I really liked. What I wanted didn't seem to exist. Mary was assisting me as I searched through the inventory on the rack. "Well," she said, "If you don't find a mastectomy swimsuit that you like, buy a regular swimsuit that you do and I will sew a pocket into the bra for your prosthetic."

That sounded like at good idea! In reality, however, regular swimsuits are not cut in a way that the areas requiring covering are covered. All recently radiated skin needed protection from the harmful sun's rays for a full year. And believe me, that meant a lot of skin needed protection! This was a command that did not work well. Most swimsuits are designed to reveal skin rather than cover it.

It didn't take long before I realized mastectomy swimsuits were a specialty item for a good reason. Reluctantly, I swallowed what little pride I did have and made a purchase from an online catalog store. What I bought didn't look much like a swimsuit but was more like a summer jogging set. The top had a floral pattern in shades of rose and was similar to a tank top. The bottom was identical to a pair of black shorts. Not exactly what you might find on the Rivera, but then again, neither was I!

As much as this purchase was not what I had in mind, it was what I needed, and I soon discovered it scored high in versatility. Covered by a long-sleeved cream-colored blouse, and with a wide-brimmed sunhat trimmed with a pink ribbon, sunglasses, and sandals, even I was impressed by how elegant I looked! I was instantly dressed for the outdoor café when it was time for lunch!

Our departing flight from the East Coast was early, and I was looking forward to some time to relax beside the pool and maybe a quick dip before dinner.

The pool at the hotel was beautiful. My wounds were so close to being healed, I was sure it would be fine for me to swim. The second wound appeared to be in the last stages of healing. To my shock, while putting on my swimsuit, I noticed the second incision was oozing and draining. I was horrified! I could not imagine why it was draining again. Away from home with no wound packing supplies, I panicked!

Frantically, I called Karen, hoping she had not left her office yet. She was just finishing her day and picked up the phone as soon as I dialed her extension. I explained to her what was happening. Karen was as calm as ever. She instructed me to "dab on some Neosporin and cover the wound with a Band-Aid" and "stay out of the water."

Her explanation was simple. The wound must have had a small pocket that still had drainage. The altitude while flying and the change in barometric pressure likely caused it to "pop." I was extremely relieved that this was nothing to be excited about, but it did dash my hopes of using the pool.

I think the Lord knew just how disappointed I was to be banned from the pool.

Because I was still weak, I could not participate in most of the activities that were planned for the convention attendees. I felt trapped by cancer even though it was gone from my body. Limitations lingered and dictated my activities.

Just like any loving father watching his child struggle through illness, the Lord placed a kiss on my hurting and frustrated soul. He provided a once-in-a-lifetime experience and a gift of pleasure I could not have imagined and I will never forget!

The hosts for the convention arranged several different group excursions. There was a sign-up for a shopping trip to Laguna Beach, a bus tour along the coastal highway, and then the activity that Grady and I really wanted to do: an afternoon tour of Huntington Beach on a Segway. However, because of my lack of stamina and energy, we settled on a "Wildlife Sea Safari." We both love the ocean, sea life, and boats, but my expectations were not very high for what we might see. I didn't expect much more than to see a few seals or sea lions and to enjoy a nice, relaxing boat ride (which was about the extent of my endurance).

The configuration of the vessel was perfect and provided good visibility of the water from almost any vantage point on board. Wisely, we chose seating where we were semi-shaded from the sun and facing the water. A seasoned marine biologist crewed the ship, and he was the kind of guy who obviously loved his job.

As we were leaving the harbor, the captain of the vessel pointed out sea lions sunning themselves on the rim of the channel marker leading to the open ocean. Expectantly, he told us about the sea life we were likely to find as we headed into the open water, and he invited us to interact with the biologist on board.

My senses were stimulated and I was fully engaged by the experience as the sea sprayed into the wind from the hull cutting through the rolling waves. But being on a boat was not a new experience. Grady and I had spent lots of time around the water and boating—ever since our days of dating when I was only sixteen. We had not, however, ridden a Segway!

Quietly, I was complaining to myself that I should have been well months ago. But I was not—thanks to infections that seemed to last forever. I was still weak and *still* recovering! I was (again) grumbling and murmuring about my "have nots" instead of being thankful for my "haves." Thinking of my "couldn'ts" instead of my "cans"!

We had to choose an ordinary boat ride because of my weakened condition, and I was missing the chance of a lifetime and riding a Segway. Poor me. I was as thankless as thankless could be, as I wanted something "different" even though I liked what I had!

The first dolphins appeared several yards in the distance and off the starboard side; the biologist pointed. And then there were more dolphins, and more and *more!* Within minutes our vessel was in waters that were teeming and churning with Pacific dolphins as far as the eye could see in every direction. It was mating season, and pods of white-sided Pacific dolphins migrated to these waters off the California coast annually.

Pacific dolphins are slightly smaller and have a different shaped head than their bottlenose cousins. They were a variety I had never seen in the wild. I was mesmerized by these incredible athletic animals as they propelled from the water and into the air, diving and again propelling straight up as they turned with acrobatic moves in mid-air and then landed on their side, creating a massive splash. Like most dolphins, they are "bow runners" and love to play in the surf that is displaced by the bow cutting through the water. Soon the six- to eight-foot mammals, with their distinguishing markings of a black-colored back, gray sides, and white underside, were so thick around our ship, I don't know how they kept from colliding with each other or the vessel.

Before I knew it, I was hanging over the shortest part of the gunwales for a closer look as the dolphins swam alongside the ship, breaching the waves and almost close enough to touch. What a thrill! That day will be etched in my mind forever— dolphins as far as the eye could see in every direction, frolicking in the surf, breaching and spouting.

The captain and the biologist had been conducting sea tours for years. When asked about this unbelievable sight, both were flabbergasted. They guessed that the numbers of dolphins that we saw that day easily ranged into in the thousands. Neither man had seen a gathering of so many pods of white-sided Pacific dolphins—ever. The experience was indescribably spectacular!

Although this was not the excursion I would have chosen had I been fully recovered, I would have missed one of the most exciting moments of my life if I had been well and if I had been able to choose differently. I was taken in a direction I did not want to go. That direction had an amazing ending and proved to be so much better than what I *thought* I wanted. How amazing! What a perfect gift from a loving Father.

A few days before our trip to Huntington Beach, I had seen Dr. Lin for my one-year checkup. This was a routine visit, with the exception that extra vials of blood were drawn for the research project. Ordinarily, I think there is a bit of apprehension for a one-year anniversary date for most cancer patients. I'm sure my doctors know much more than I do, but for me, I was thinking, *Of course I'm cancer free! I'm STILL on Herceptin.* I had no concern or apprehension about my one-year checkup. I was at peace.

With so many doctors on my medical team and all of them wanting to see me for follow-up, Dr Lin ordered the MRI and mammogram (for my natural breast) in June, and I would follow up with Dr. Golshan for my radiology report.

Dr. Lin had some exciting news for me. After my infusion of Herceptin that day, there were just three more treatments left! July 13 would be my final round of Herceptin. When Dr. Lin originally calculated my completion date, it was based on starting the extended Herceptin treatments sometime in February. Because my final rounds of H/T/C were tailored to the mastectomy pathology findings, my radiation and Herceptin started the first week in January instead of mid- to late February.

As time distanced me from my last radiation "boost," I became more aware and discontented with the stiff, radiated skin that covered half of my chest—especially as my activity level increased. My reach was severely impaired, and I knew I could not blame the shoulder surgery of March 2007 for the shortfall. My reach was restricted by stiffened tissue and reasons directly related to cancer treatment. It was a problem that I needed Dr. Golshan to help me to solve when I saw him in June: how much improvement could I expect by having reconstruction?

At our appointment, I asked Dr. Golshan about some of the things that were troubling me. Emotionally, I was having difficulty finding the courage to face anything as medically invasive as reconstruction and sacrifice another year in recovery. I wanted to be free. On the other hand, I hated my limitations and the physical restrictions I was left with.

Dr. Golshan understood. "I don't blame you. You have been through a long and difficult time. Your body has been through one assault after another. You can wait; you don't need to make that decision now. But you may want to talk with Dr. Caterson and let her know how you are feeling physically and emotionally."

"I wish I could talk with someone who has been through a DIEP flap procedure. Do you think Dr. Caterson has another patient who would be willing to share her experience about this surgery? I'm so torn."

"I'm sure she does. Call Stephanie's office and ask to be matched to someone."

We talked about the benefits of lymphatic massage and physical therapy to possibly break up surgery-related scar tissue. I was willing to try almost anything that didn't involve a scalpel and might help me to regain upper torso mobility.

Within days, I began physical therapy. One of the first things my physical therapist did was to break up the adhesions that had impaired and shortened my reach. With one session, I improved dramatically.... *Thank you, Lord.*

Prior to my appointment with Dr. Golshan, I prayed. I wanted to do something for him. He had done so much for me. There were countless times he had been sent an emergency page. "Kathy Crews is back...." Or, "'She's' on her way...or in the Emergency Department." Even when I was in Karen's capable hands as lymphatic fluid was aspirated from my chest, he was there. His compassion was incomparable. I wanted to bring him a gift.

Lord, what can I possibly do for this man? How can I say thank you? What act of kindness can I offer?

Absolutely nothing was coming to mind.

Lord, speak to me.

I heard silence.

I started to become impatient, and the Lord remained quiet.

I practically never grocery shop on weekends unless it is necessary. After church on Sunday morning and two days before my appointment with Dr. Golshan, I needed a couple of things at the store, and I spotted some beautiful fresh strawberries. Suddenly, I was fighting the urge to buy the berries; they were not on my grocery list. Nevertheless, the berries found their way into my shopping basket as I argued with myself. *I don't need these; what am I doing with these strawberries when in a few weeks I can pick fresh ones in a local farmer's strawberry field!*

Later that day, Grady and I visited my mom and parked our car directly in front of her rhubarb patch. As I heard the words in my spirit, they came out of my mouth. *"Strawberry-rhubarb pie! Oh, thank you, Lord!"* And then, doubting the Lord, I said, "Lord? Are You sure?"

The next day I meticulously made the pie crust and cut up the rhubarb and the strawberries for the pie. I had grown up in a home and an era when pie crust did not come from a box and pie filling did not come from a can.

When the pie was baked, it could not have looked any more beautiful. Once the pie had cooled, I carefully wrapped and boxed the pie.

Lord, I need some help with the thank-you note. How can I say how great a part You have played in choosing him for my care?

On Dr. Golshan's card, I wrote that I had prayed about my team of doctors and believed that God guided me in selecting him as my surgeon. There were no better hands that my life could have been in as I prayed that he would be guided by the wisdom of the Lord....I could not have had greater appreciation for how well he had cared for me. "May the Lord's hand guide and bless you always."

With the thank-you note written, the pie was ready to be delivered to Dr. Golshan on the morning of my appointment.

Carefully, I set the pie on Dr. Golshan's desk in the exam room, and Grady and I waited.

When Dr. Golshan came in, he was trying to stay focused on our appointment, but his gaze kept drifting toward the wrapped pie. Finally he asked, "Is that for me?"

"Yes," I said. "I made a strawberry-rhubarb pie for you."

"You made me a pie?"

"I did! Dr. Golshan? You do like strawberry-rhubarb pie...don't you?"

His eyes filled with expression. "I *love* strawberry-rhubarb pie!"

Oh, Lord Jesus! You are so cool! ...Strawberry-rhubarb pie—who would have guessed!

I wavered back and forth about reconstruction as the weeks began to turn into months. Once more I was extremely fortunate that after Tracy's diagnosis we had upgraded our medical coverage and we had insurance options. I was leaning very hard toward not having reconstruction, but mostly for the wrong reasons. I simply didn't want to be inconvenienced by more surgery.

Although the skin looked healthy, whatever tissue was left under it was in terrible condition. As hard as my physical therapists tried, there was only so much improvement to be gained. The scar tissue was thick, and I felt as though one side of my chest had been doused with super glue and the tissue was firmly stuck to my ribcage.

While shopping for something to wear to a friend's wedding, my frustration reached a new level. Many dresses were V-necked and revealed some degree of cleavage; my turning point arrived. As good as prosthetics are, there is no way to fake the natural contour and fullness of the slope of the chest, collar bone to breast. I had none! Most of the tissue that once covered the top of my ribs had been removed. My skin was stuck flat against my ribcage with absolutely no extra flesh or tissue to provide shape over my ribs, collar bone to points south!

Every dress I tried on revealed this ugly truth. The left side of all of the dresses looked odd. I couldn't imagine living the rest of my life dreading every event that demanded a shopping trip and buying a dress. I needed to make an appointment with Dr. Caterson to at least talk with her again about the reconstruction.

When I called Dr. Caterson's office, the only thing I was sure about was that I wanted to talk with someone. It's a surgery not to be taken lightly. It's a true time commitment because of the difficulty of the surgery and the length of time required for recovery.

I was given the name and phone number of one of Dr. Caterson's DIEP flap patients. Shirley had experienced the surgery and she knew better than anyone what this was like. She had had a mastectomy, lived with prosthetics, and now she once again had (reconstructed) breasts.

Hello Everyone!

On Sunday, July 13, I had my last dose of Herceptin. My days of chemo are over! My prognosis is excellent.

When I saw my surgeon, Dr. Golshan, for my tests that were done in June, the Lord gave me one more opportunity to share my faith with him in a very simple way: a homemade strawberry-rhubarb pie and a "thank you" note.

With the number of fluke things that I had to deal with after my surgery, I do believe the Lord "hand-picked him as my surgeon," and I told him so in my note.

My tests were all normal, and so he has set me free until I see him again NEXT year! I have been told my heart function has remained stable and should improve now that I am finished with Herceptin.

I still have lingering discomfort in my feet and lower legs from one of the chemo drugs I was on. There are lingering effects from all of this, and I'm told it will be a full year or two before I feel like me.

Everybody LOVES my new hair! Especially me. I'm so happy to have hair again! I have so much to be thankful for. If I had been diagnosed just four short years ago, I might not have had such a good prognosis. The discovery and common use of Herceptin has made all of the difference in the world for women diagnosed with HER2/neu breast cancer. It's part of the reason I decided to be a part of a research protocol. We all learn and (hopefully) all benefit from the findings.

I will still have many years of follow-up where my annual doctor's reports will be used for the research. Dr. Golshan tells me, "This is a lot like a marriage; you can divorce us at anytime... but we would prefer that you don't!"

It seems each time I go to the hospital, the Lord directs my attention to someone. Three weeks ago, when I was at Dana-Farber, I met Vinnie and his thirty-two-year-old daughter, Mandy.

For two years, Vinnie complained to his doctor in Lowell, Massachusetts, about stomach pain. In April, Vinnie had exploratory surgery. He is stage IV with colon cancer.

Vinnie is fifty-eight, tall, striking in appearance, and the picture of health. His prognosis is not hopeful without a miracle, and Vinnie and Mandy know this.

As Grady listened to Vinnie, I tried to speak into Mandy's life the importance of surrounding herself with people who can support and comfort her through her Dad's illness. The Lord provided the opportunity for me to share with her a little bit about my past year and how important all of you have been in my life as you have supported me in so many ways.

God's ways definitely often do not line up with our plans. I'm sure there is much we will never understand this side of heaven; it's hard to remember that when facing death. His knowledge surpasses ours and our view from a human standpoint. Often we hear people say, "Well, *everything works to the good....*"

There are many who are included on my email lists who don't know exactly where *that saying* comes from. It's actually a modification or paraphrase of the Scripture: "All things work together for good for those who *love God and are called according to His purpose.*" And the verse to follow says, **"For those whom He foreknew, He also predestined from the beginning to be *molded into the image of His Son....*"** Romans 8:28-29

If the Lord Jesus, Himself, experienced physical suffering and pain, are we to expect less? It's how we go *through* those trials that evidences to others if we are "being molded into the image of His Son," or if we are gritting our teeth and struggling through in our own power.

Way back in April–May 2007, I first shared with Pastor Peter in an email that there was a strong possibility that I was facing cancer. His response in part was "His 'grace' is sufficient...."

No words ever spoken to me were truer! God's "grace"...His "unmerited favor" is enough.

I began asking the Lord at that time to "show me how His grace *is enough.*" And He did!

This has been the most amazing year of trusting Jesus *for* my life and *with* my life that I ever could have imagined. I only hope I have been "*molded into the image of His Son*" a little more.

I have *experienced* the truth and the promises of God.

"In my weakness...He has been made strong."

"The **JOY** of the Lord (truly) has been my **STRENGTH**."

"The Lord inhabits the *praises* of His people."

"I can do ALL THINGS through Christ Jesus who strengthens me."
…Even battle cancer, thanks to Pastor Peter's reminder to me.

I know where my eternity will be spent. No, I really don't think I'm ready to go there yet; but from the beginning of all of this I knew I would win either way *because* of my trust in the One who holds my life in His hands. The simple fact is I just had to surrender to that truth and *allow* Jesus to carry me through. The Scripture is true. The whole concept of coming as a little child works! …Simple child-like faith.

I pray the Lord's direction for each and every person my path has crossed through this "adventure" in faith.

I pray for each of you who have been so diligent in interceding in prayer before "the throne of Grace" for me.…And I pray for each of you who do not know (yet) just how much the Lord who created heaven and earth loves you and wants YOU to know Him on a deep and personal level…as His child.

Blessings and Love,

Kathy and Grady

Chapter 31

I'll Do It!

The summer of 2008 was especially short in New Hampshire. It was May before the last small patch of snow melted over the flower beds.

Mom stayed in Florida longer than usual because it seemed that summer might never come. It was July before warmer weather truly arrived.

Tracy and Antonio stayed an extra long time in Spain after Tracy finished her responsibilities with the Spanish exchange program and her students.

Everything seemed to be behind schedule that summer except for the one thing that I was looking forward to most: finishing chemotherapy. I had my final round of Herceptin on a Sunday afternoon, July 13. At last! I was truly ready to move on.

My only connection to the hospital would be my regular checkups (which were many) and to have my port cleared with a saline flush every four to six weeks until I decided it would no longer be needed for any reason.

It was over! I had survived cancer, radiation, and infections and it was over. There would be no need for further prayer requests, no more email updates on my progress, and no further need for my church family to bring in meals. It was time to move on and love life and become more involved in the activities that I enjoyed most. It was a new beginning and I was ready to seek the Lord in a new mission field. Like, maybe, something a little less intense than encouraging other cancer patients in Boston?

Although the summer season of 2008 eventually happened, the warm days departed almost as soon as they arrived.

At long last, Tracy flew home from Spain, and immediately she was in the fray of preparing for the new school year and the arrival of her students at Milton Academy. It was also time to collect sponsorship for Making Strides Against Breast Cancer.

As one of a special few, Tracy was invited to meet one of the research doctors at Dana-Farber. That group of breast cancer survivors who had been invited learned what has been discovered in recent years about the disease. The doctor had no idea that one of the young women before her was a triple-negative survivor whose mother had recently finished her final dose of Herceptin in her fight against HER2/neu.

The doctor began to inform and teach: "This is what we know about estrogen receptive breast cancer." And she extended her arms wide apart.

"This is what we know about HER2/neu." She brought her arms in half-again closer.

"This is what we know about triple-negative." And she dropped one of her arms and held up her thumb and first finger on one hand separated by a whisper of air. "But what we do know is this: If triple-negative breast cancer does not return within three years, *it does not return.*"

Tracy gasped in a "whoop" that was about to escape from her lips. She was three years and one month cancer free! Tracy was hearing straight from the lips of a doctor who was doing research on the type of cancer she had just overcome, SHE WAS HEALED!

Some of the women who were there knew Tracy and about "Tracy's mom's battle." The cancer cells that they looked at under the microscope that day were HER2/neu.

Tracy heard something very important, directly from a research doctor, which further confirmed what the Lord had revealed to me while Tracy was still going through radiation. And as Tracy looked through a microscope, she saw the same type of cancer cells that had once invaded my body, and what they looked like.

In support of Tracy's walk to raise money for breast cancer research, I sent an email to my list of friends and prayer supporters. In part this is what I shared.

Sent: Thursday, September 04, 2008, 12:20 PM
Subject: Cancer Research

Greetings Everyone!

Next month is breast cancer awareness month. I can't believe that October 22 is the one-year anniversary of when I had my surgery....WOW! And I can still give you a running account of the events I was going through a year ago this week.

Once you've battled cancer personally or been on your knees in prayer battling this disease for someone you love, you are never the same.

The research doctors at Dana-Farber are fabulous at sharing information with other hospitals and doctors in the field. Again, through an opportunity that the Lord made possible, I know this is true. I had lunch at the hospital with a research doctor from Scotland, who had hand-carried cancer slides to Boston for study and research. (The cafeteria at Dana-Farber is small, and sometimes you dine unexpectedly with the most interesting people!)

I also went through radiation with a research doctor.

...A few interesting nuggets of information I have learned along the way:

The leading cases of cancer are: lung, breast, colon, and prostate cancer.

Since 2003, government funds for cancer research have decreased.

There is 1 cancer death every minute in the U.S.

One-half million Americans will die from cancer this year.

1 in 4 deaths in this country will be cancer related.

1.5 million will be diagnosed with cancer this year.

...Ten million of us have survived the battle!

Become informed on this subject....Someone you know and/or love *will* need your help to make it through their battle against this disease.

I know and have experienced the importance of supporting cancer research.

Blessings and Love,

Kathy

As the support pledges mounted for Tracy's walk, again she surpassed her dollar goal as people who loved our family gave. Even our doctors.

October ushered in a spectacular fall. In all of my life I don't think I had ever seen the trees more vibrant with beautiful colors. For that matter, on Columbus Day weekend, we took my mom and my eighty-eight-year-old aunt out for a drive to admire the foliage, and in all of their days they had never seen a more beautiful display of autumn colors. There really isn't a more gorgeous place on planet Earth in the fall than New Hampshire (although our neighbors in Vermont and Maine might want to dispute that statement). For a short window of time, we are blessed with a season that stands head and shoulders above almost anything I have ever seen anyplace in this country.

After completing treatment for cancer, my appreciation for the simple things in life impacted me differently. I was alive! And I was alive in a way that was new.

As much as I wanted to bask and soak in how I was feeling, enjoying the simple pleasures, I had a sense that the Lord was moving me forward: forward—despite feeling conflicted by the plans for more surgery. There seemed to be a nudging in my spirit that I needed to do this and do it now. I could not resolve in my own mind if this was because the Lord still had lessons for me to learn in the trials ahead—or was this about *others*? Maybe it was both.

With reluctance, I called Dr. Caterson's office and scheduled reconstructive surgery for January 7, 2009, and a consultation on November 20, 2008, to discuss the details for DIEP flap breast reconstruction.

After making my surgery date, I made a second phone call to the patient whose phone number I had been given earlier in the summer. Nothing can take the place of talking with someone who has been on the operating table.

The original contact I had with Shirley was shortly after I had been given her phone number; but now as I faced this surgery, I needed all of the details—A to Z. I needed to hear from another woman what to expect and just how difficult this surgery was. Shirley did not hold back a thing.

As we talked, we learned that we were similar in stature and weight and close in age. The biggest difference between us was Shirley's incredible patience and motivation to have reconstruction.

Shirley was in her twenties when she was diagnosed with breast cancer and had a bilateral mastectomy. Implants (in her case) did not work out, and she had to have them removed. For Shirley it was like having a double mastectomy twice. Devastating!

Unhappily, she used prosthetics for years and kept telling herself that one day there would be a means of reconstruction that would be right for her. She never gave up hope. Shirley continually searched for that method of reconstruction.

She was on her quest for nearly thirty years before DIEP flap reconstruction was a new surgery and available in Boston! Dr. Caterson had just joined the staff at Brigham and Women's Hospital when Shirley found her.

We talked about everything. The day I had my mastectomy, she was released from the hospital after having DIEP flap. We even discovered she was discharged from the same floor I was sent to after Dr. Golshan had finished my surgery!

Shirley's reconstruction had been long and extremely difficult—seventeen hours. Dr. Caterson found a physiological uniqueness that secretly I feared might be true about myself—small blood vessels. It took Dr. Caterson a grueling amount of time to complete the microsurgery on the blood vessels in the tissue that created the new breast mounds formed from Shirley's own abdominal fat. Because of the difficulty that Dr. Caterson encountered, Shirley was one of the reasons that changes and improvements were made. Dr. Caterson began using CT scans to locate and identify the blood sources within the abdominal tissue, and the scans became a standard means of evaluating if a patient may or may not be a good candidate for DIEP flap reconstruction.

"Oh my goodness, Shirley! I told Dr. Caterson when I met her in September 2007 that if I was unable to have my reconstruction at the time of my mastectomy, maybe another year would bring greater knowledge about the surgery. Oh my goodness! And you were the patient that helped bring change and advance this surgery!"

Shirley told me that a few days after her reconstruction, the anesthesiologist who had been in the operating room visited her. Dr. Caterson was so new to the staff, this doctor had never worked with her before.

The anesthesiologist told Shirley she had never experienced a surgery lasting so many hours, and the entire time—the whole seventeen hours—Dr. Caterson never left Shirley's side or took a break from her work. There was another surgeon present, but not once did Dr. Caterson leave Shirley's side. The anesthesiologist declared, "Dr. Caterson is one amazing lady doctor!"

As the most intimate questions about the surgery and recovery were discussed, I could not imagine that there was any question left unanswered. Shirley was preparing me for my surgery in ways that only another sister who had been there could. She candy-coated nothing! This was not going to be any fun.

During my November appointment with Dr. Caterson, the final details for the surgery were discussed. Because my primary motivation for the surgery was more for function rather than cosmetic, my focus had been on the removal of the radiated tissue. My major objective was to regain the full range of motion for my left arm (which remained elusive after twenty-one months of ongoing work).

Dr. Caterson showed me the approximate area of stiff, hard tissue that would be removed. I was given further understanding about what to expect after the surgery, including information about the two follow-up surgeries that would be done to sculpt the transplanted belly fat (by use of liposuction) into the shape of a breast and the process for creating symmetry to my form. Through the art of plastic surgery, Dr. Caterson would change, repair, and shape my body and provide me with an even *better* appearance than before I was diagnosed with breast cancer.

We discussed the amount of usable tissue that I had for creating a new breast. I was thinking about the practical side of the surgery. "You know, Stephanie, you're the expert here. I would not have chosen you as my plastic surgeon if I didn't trust your judgment. I'm not sure I know how to explain my feelings. As you remove the radiated tissue and cover the area with my own abdominal flesh, if that means breast reduction, that's okay. I'm giving you total authority and all I can say is, 'do your best work!' You know my greatest concern. I would like to have as much of the radiated skin removed as possible. Do whatever you need to do. You are the final judge as you use the belly tissue to cover the area that will need repair. I don't understand a thing about recreating breasts; you do and that's what matters."

THAT was one of the smartest things I could have done!

The days flew; my surgery date was near and I sent two different emails to my prayer supports—one to the many men on my list and one to the ladies. I found that as I waged my war against breast cancer, this was a subject that the men in my life (and Grady's life) wanted to understand. Breast cancer can and does strike men.

About one percent of breast cancer is diagnosed in men. That translates to just under 2,000 cases. Approximately 450 of those men will die. I appreciate the former drummer from the rock group Kiss for speaking out about his diagnosis in February 2008. For men, this subject (in many cases) is hidden… "off-limits" and "taboo"; but men truly want to understand, and I did not exclude them as I shared my story. Several of Grady's business associates asked to be included and receive my emails. Most of the men wanted to hear our story because they have ladies in their lives: wives, sisters, mothers, and daughters that they cherish and want to protect and defend. …That's what real men do. They love the women in their lives and they want to know how to comfort and support them. I willingly gave these men a "window" to peer through for the sake of understanding breast cancer should such a diagnosis interrupt their lives.

Subject: Jan. 7, 2009

Hello Gentlemen!

I sent out a more detailed explanation to the ladies concerning the surgery I am scheduled for on January 7. This really is more about quality of life rather than vanity.

The tissue that was radiated has remained hard, thick, and without flexibility or elasticity even after physical therapy. I have lost significant range of motion with my arm because the area that was radiated is pretty much stuck to my chest wall.

This skin will all be cut away during the plastic surgery that Dr. Stephanie Caterson will be doing on Wednesday.

For the men, I'll stick with the headlines for my prayer requests as I go into this:

Please pray not only for my surgeon but for everyone who will be in that operating room.

Pray for God's presence and that HIs hand would guide every "cut" and "stitch" that Dr. Stephanie makes.

This is a near marathon surgery. If all goes well, the surgery will take eight hours.

Please pray that Dr. Stephanie would not grow weary and that she would feel the power of the Lord energizing her through this lengthy operation.

Immediately after surgery, I will be in the ICU for twenty-four hours and monitored every fifteen minutes as I am watched for BLOOD CLOTS and checked for blood flow into the transplanted tissue.

Pray for God's touch on the surgery sites for healing and restoration.

...And lastly, I had a horrid time with my surgery a year ago October with an allergic reaction to something. I was itching so badly I thought I would come out of my skin! We are not sure if it was a medication I was given or if it was the **compression boots.** I CAN'T be allergic to these things!

Please pray that the staff looking after me would have the wisdom of the Lord in monitoring and treating me and that I would not have *any* allergic reactions from any meds I am given or from anything I come in physical contact with.

I will be going into surgery at 9:30 a.m. on Wednesday. I should be finished around 5:30 p.m. After twenty-four hours in ICU I will be transferred to the seventh floor at Brigham and Women's.

The normal and expected hospital stay is for five days, so hopefully I will be coming home sometime on Monday, January 12.

Recovery is a solid six weeks. The biggest concern is allowing all of the internal injury to heal and not tearing what is newly transplanted and mending together.

Grady will be with Tracy during my time in surgery, and she thinks she will be able to take a couple of days off from work to help me at home when I am released.

Grady will send emails while I'm in the hospital to let everyone know "HOW GREAT I'M DOING!!!"

I'm feeling very much at peace and I'm sure all will go very well.

Blessings and Love to all!

Kathy

And to the ladies' email I added this small bonus of information:

I'll be able to "putter" at doing little things after two weeks...but I'll be coming home with drains and tubes still attached, so I may need "a little help from my friends" in the beginning.

There usually is a silver lining to the darkest clouds. In preparing for this surgery, I needed to supply the extra fat for the surgery. It's been great eating dessert almost every night! And the other benefit from this surgery is an "all-expense-paid tummy tuck"! (My consolation prize.)

The tissue used to reconstruct my new breast will come from my tummy...it's a nice little vanity bonus for all of the physical grief and pain I've been through. If you've got to go through something as crummy as cancer, it's nice to have something to smile about at the end of the battle. And even without this, I can say the Lord has given me plenty of blessings along the way as I have come to this point in my recovery.

Thank you ALL for your love and support. I will have Grady use this list and send updates to all of you while I am in the hospital.

Blessings and Love,

Kathy

Chapter 32

Lost in Space

Wednesday, the day of my reconstruction, arrived. I could not have been more prepared. I had done all of my homework ahead of time and I knew exactly what to expect. I was confident. Friends were praying and I was at perfect peace and feeling the Lord's presence and Grady's support.

The curtain that separated me from the other patients was drawn, but I could hear activity all around the cubicle where I waited. There was lots of scurrying as the hospital staff prepared the army of patients to be rolled in the direction of the many surgery suites.

My curtain began to move; and standing there in crisp blue surgical scrubs stood…Dr. Golshan? The expression on my face must have spoken my surprise.

"You didn't think I would let you go into surgery with Stephanie without checking in with you first? I haven't seen you for a few months, but that doesn't mean I don't know what's going on."

I smiled as I reached toward him. "This is a surprise! Thanks for stopping by….I'm so happy that you did."

"After I'm finished with my surgery, I'll check on your progress with Stephanie. If Grady is in the family waiting area, I will fill him in on how your surgery is going."

"Oh, that's great, Dr. Golshan. This is going to be a *very* long day for him. I know Grady and Tracy will be anxious to know what's happening."

As he pulled back the curtain and turned to leave, he said, "At some point during your recovery, I'll stop in during my patient rounds to visit and to have a look at Stephanie's handiwork."

"Okay. I'll be looking for you. I'm sure you will know where to find me."

A blend of respect, trust, and familiarity had found its way into my patient/doctor relationship with Dr. Golshan. In him I had found "the best!" For a cancer patient, nothing could be more comforting.

Within the system at Brigham and Women's Hospital, every step of a surgery can be monitored by hospital staff so that families can remain informed—from the first incision to closing. It's comforting and reassuring for those who are waiting; it provides a sense of looking out for that loved one...almost like being there. I felt better knowing that Dr. Golshan would reassure and inform Grady and Tracy about how things were going.

The next time the curtain rustled, it was Dr. Caterson. "How are you?"

Grady answered for me. "She's as *cool* facing this surgery as I have ever seen."

"That's great. I've brought my marker to do a little art work on your tummy."

Grady excused himself and stepped outside my curtained cubicle.

As Dr. Caterson was drawing lines going in every direction and an outline on my abdomen I said, "Do you know what the best part of getting ready for this surgery has been?"

Dr. Caterson took her eyes off her "drawing" and looked slightly puzzled.

Laughing, I answered, "Eating shamelessly for the sake of giving you a little *extra* material to work with. I loved having dessert every night for the cause."

We both chuckled.

"Okay," she said. "I'm finished. I don't anticipate any surprises, but you need to know that if we get in there and discover the blood vessel we will be using for blood flow for the transplanted tissue is inadequate, we will do a TRAM flap and use only what muscle is necessary. I have a couple of release forms for you to sign. Any questions before I see you in surgery?"

Right then and there I nearly jumped off the gurney and ran! *I did not want TRAM flap reconstruction!* I gasped under my breath as panic attacked my confidence.

"Yeah. I do. How did you decide to become a plastic surgeon?"

Dr. Caterson smiled. "Well, actually, I was on my way to becoming an astronaut and I took a career detour."

I wasn't sure she was serious. I blinked in disbelief. "You're kidding! How did that happen?" Her answer only caused more questions.

"I became so intrigued by the physiological effects of what happens to the body in space, I found myself on a new career path. But originally, I wanted to be an astronaut.

"Time to 'roll' and move you into surgery. See you there, even if you won't remember it."

As Dr. Caterson left the cubicle and as the sedative that was administered began to take effect, I remember thinking, *Wow. This lady has got to border on genius. Her career choices were aerospace and plastic surgery? She's on staff at* **this** *excellent hospital and some of the best doctors in the world? Yup! I'm safe. Thank you, Jesus.*

Before I completely lost consciousness, Grady prayed with me, kissed my cheek, and watched as I was wheeled toward surgery. My foggy thoughts were still on what I had just learned about my doctor. *Wow! ...An astronaut.*

Most of what I remember shortly after the surgery is fragmented, disjointed, and hazy. Both Tracy and Grady have some pretty hysterical stories about "Mom under the influence of a controlled substance."

After surgery, my first memory is being in a dimly lighted area. I thought I was in a dungeon...or was it a *space station?* I saw a strange door that kept opening and closing; each time a person went through the door and then re-emerged, they looked like someone entirely different. Sometimes they went in a woman and came out a *man!*

An oxygen mask covered my nose and mouth. And then I remember the *pain!* Oh! The pain!

Much to my confusion, the pain was in my left arm. I reached in slow motion with my right hand in the direction of my discomfort. My right hand lacked coordination.

"Oo-oo-w! My arm."

Suddenly, Tracy was beside me. (*That's funny; a second ago she wasn't there,* I thought to myself. *Did she come through THE DOOR?*)

"Oh! My arm."

"Your arm hurts?"

I nodded.

"Why does your arm hurt?"

"Because."

"Because 'why,' Mom?"

"Stephanie was leaning on it."

Tracy decided that from the glazed look in my eyes, I was still sedated beyond making sense and I was lost someplace in a different galaxy. She thought it would be fun to take advantage of the moment with her mother in such a vulnerable condition.

Tracy continued to question me to see how far I'd take my story. "Mom, how do you know the doctor leaned on your arm?"

I looked at her like she was the one who was crazy. "Someone told me."

Tracy was chuckling. "Well, is this normal?"

I nodded my head again in the affirmative.

"But why did the doctor lean on your arm?"

Tracy's questions were beginning to perturb me. *She's a smart girl; she should be able to figure these things out.* "Because," I said in tearful sympathy, "Stephanie was tired!"

Tracy and Grady doubled in two, roaring with laughter.

When I looked up again, Tracy and Grady had vanished...into thin air....

In the moments before Tracy vanished, she was tending to my essential needs after the surgery. My mouth felt sticky and awful.

Having helped friends as an advocate after their surgeries, I had coached Tracy on what my needs would be immediately after my own. Tracy had gotten some ice water, mouthwash, and a sponge swab to cleanse the icky feeling from my mouth. The icy, cold, minty water was refreshing as she swabbed my tongue and the inside of my cheeks. I would doze for what (I think) must have only been minutes, and each time I opened my eyes and Tracy was there, I asked her to swab my mouth and moisten my lips with Vaseline.

One of the times that my eyes closed, Tracy and Grady thought I was sedated enough that I might actually sleep. And they vanished, leaving me a little more than confused by what seemed to be their instant disappearance.

Grady sent this email the following morning to the countless numbers of people who were praying. He sent it before I had the opportunity to tell him about the remainder of my bizarre night after he *disappeared*.

Good morning everyone,

It is about 9:30 and I am at the hospital. Kathy came through the surgery just fine. Her surgeon says she is a new woman!!

At the moment she looks like she was on the losing end of a bear wrestle!

Actually, considering she was under anesthesia for about nine hours, she is looking pretty good. The doc said that physiologically she (doctor) could not have asked for a "better set-up."

She will be moved earlier than expected to a regular room sometime after noon today.

Will keep you posted with any more news.

Best regards,
Grady

Although Dr. Caterson's orders and plans were for me to be admitted to the Intensive Care Unit after surgery, that never happened. There was no room. Every bed in the ICU was filled. You cannot imagine the confusion this caused for me as I attempted to wade through what I had expected to happen while coming out of anesthesia.

I was left to wait out my care in an area of the hospital that was strangely like where I was before surgery. Even in my drug-saturated mind I knew I shouldn't be there! Someone had made a very serious mistake!

Dr. Caterson had told me exactly what would happen in the Intensive Care Unit. My mind had locked onto the information she had given me:

there was a nurse who would be assigned to my care. The nurse would monitor me every fifteen minutes to make sure that the blood supply to the newly transplanted tissue was being adequately oxygenated. Someone would be constantly checking my vital signs. None of those things happened. I was not in that place that Dr. Caterson had described.

My bed was *suspiciously* close to *The Door* where people went in, and came out as someone else. Each time The Door opened, a flood of bright light bathed the entrance and spilled out onto the floor of the darkened room. I was being held captive!

I could look directly across the hallway that led to The Door. There was another bed and a "prisoner." It seemed, however, the "prisoner" across from me kept changing, and sometimes they *vanished...just like Grady and Tracy!*

I began to feel very uncertain with my surroundings and the alien nurses who seemed to look different each time they stopped by my bedside. My mind was a confused blend of reality, fantasy, fear, and will to survive. Later I found it to be hilarious how many people I told about the Lord and the miracles He was responsible for as Tracy and I had both had successfully battled cancer. Under the influence of controlled drugs, I became a literal fountain of praise for the Lord.

If my mind was trying to hold fast to Jesus, my body was feeling as though I had just come from Dr. Frankenstein's lab! I grappled with the octopus of tubes that were attached to me, and I could not find the "alien" nurse's call button that was conveniently pinned to the sleeve of my hospital gown and out of reach. Searching for the call button, my hands repeatedly came up with another drainage tube with a bulb on the end of it.

I found the only way to summon help was to wiggle my head and dislodge the position of the oxygen mask on my face, causing the oxygen levels in my blood to drop and an alarm to sound. Desperately, I wanted to be someplace else...anyplace else! Surgery had lasted an entire day, and there were no windows to indicate if it was day or night, adding further to my confusion. Each time someone came to my rescue after I wiggled out of my oxygen mask, my needs and questions were always the same. "I'm thirsty, my lips are dry. And what time is it?"

Each time I was given the time, I asked, "Day? Or night?" And then, "Is that all?" The night was endless. My brain could not absorb any concept of time.

Some of the people who visited my cubicle didn't seem to fit in with everyone else dressed in their uniform of "blue pajamas." I couldn't imagine who these other people in regular clothes were and why they were telling me they were sorry that I had to stay where I was. There were no beds available in Intensive Care. With each new face, I shared how good God was. He would meet my needs (even if there was no room for me in the ICU).

"The night of confusion" outside The Door was repeating itself over and over. I was stuck in time and in this place—somewhere in *space?*

Before I was taken into surgery I had reminded Dr. Caterson about the allergic reaction to the compression boots after my mastectomy. (It was either that or from one of the medications.) As a precaution, she prescribed covering my legs with stockings under the compression boots.

Before dawn, I began to itch, but only from my knees to mid-thigh. The nurse came running when I squirmed out of my oxygen mask and the alarm sounded. I complained to her that my knees itched. My complaint went unresolved as the nurse told me that compression boots had been ordered and she could not remove them.

Dissatisfied with her answer but unable to focus on anything for long, I asked for ice, Vaseline, and what time it was, and repeated, "Day...or night? Is that all?" I wiggled, squirmed, and itched for the remainder of the night.

At last, morning arrived and Dr. Caterson started her day. As strange as the night had been, I was delighted to see a friendly face that I recognized. My first words to Dr. Caterson were, "I itch!"

Dr. Caterson's eyes immediately were drawn to the compression boots covering my legs to mid thigh. The nurse to whom I had complained earlier was standing in my cubicle as Dr. Caterson began to remove the culprit medical boots. As the boots were removed, I saw that compression stockings had been put on my legs. However, they covered the skin just to my knees, explaining the mystery of why only part of my legs felt itchy.

Dr. Caterson's words to the nurse were simple and to the point. "So...if the patient has an order for compression boots, and an order for compression stockings to protect the skin because of an allergy to the boot material, *don't* you use a shorter boot on the leg?"

Yes! You tell her, Stephanie. I'm sedated, and had I known the stockings only covered my lower legs, even I could have figured that out!

The next concern on Dr. Caterson's list was blood flow to the newly transplanted breast mound. Dr. Caterson used a "Doppler": a tiny wand-like device with a cord attached to a miniature amplification box. She moved the wand to several locations on the surface of the perfectly pinked skin that only yesterday had been my belly. Through the amplifier, the sound of my blood could be heard as it flowed through the blood vessels she had painstakingly sewn together hours earlier.

"Ah-h-h," said Dr. Caterson. "That's the sound of music to my ears. You're doing great. I'm going to order some physical therapy for you, and I'll see you later today."

I could not believe what my ears were hearing. *Wait a minute. Physical therapy? What's this? Don't you know I've had a night on Mars? I'm not ready for physical therapy!*

In what seemed to be only minutes, two female physical therapists appeared. My morning lesson was to learn how to roll to my side with my knees bent to protect the surgery sites that had turned my belly into a breast.

Soon, I was guided onto my feet. Bent in two and with help, I took my first steps (that were more like shuffles) to a chair that was positioned a few feet from my bed. Exhausted by the enormous effort involved in accomplishing this amazing feat and only hours after surgery, I sat and, within minutes, dozed off.

When I was awakened to shuffle back to my bed, I asked again, "What time is it? Day or night? ...Is that all?"

Chapter 33

DIEP Flap: Not for Wimps or Sissies

Tracy had morning classes to teach, but after she finished, she joined her father at the hospital. Dr. Caterson (sufficiently pleased with my progress) ordered for me to be taken to a room on the seventh floor, rather than the ICU.

Having been a patient many times at Brigham and Women's Hospital, Tracy knew exactly how excellent the care should be. When she heard about my night "lost in space," she was upset. Tracy is not one to raise her voice or yell; she simply becomes "teacher stern" in her mannerisms and makes her point clearly, and without mincing her words.

Apparently, she knew whom to speak to about her concerns. "Had I known you were going to leave my Mother to herself and without a bed in the ICU, I would have stayed to care for her. You should have better informed me. *She's* my Mother!"

In my groggy-foggy mind, it wasn't that I thought my care was bad, I just had to become creative in order to have one of the alien nurses stop by my curtained cubicle to swab my mouth and tell me if it was day or night. At least no one was expecting the impossible from me…well, at least not before the physical therapist arrived!

Once I was settled in my room, my assigned nurse demanded that I move my left arm in my own strength. My arm (which I was still convinced had been leaned on through the surgery) was extremely painful with lymphedema—a condition that can occur when lymphatic fluid backs up into the arm after lymph nodes have been removed. I looked at the swollen, almost unrecognizable limb at my side and told her I could not move it. Instantly, she began to bark orders at me that were impossible for me to follow. Suddenly, I wanted to return to the dark place I had been rescued from—and the planet that never saw the light of day.

I was becoming more aware of how awful I felt. My arm hurt, my mouth and lips were still miserably dry, and now I felt belly pain where the tissue for my new breast mound had been removed. It sounds like a great idea when you grab that fistful of flab that most of us have around our middle and say, *If I could only get rid of THIS!* In actuality, when you have a "tummy tuck" and get rid of *THAT,* it feels like you have just taken the skin on your lower abdomen and reattached it to your chin!

The tissue that had been joined (minus several inches of flab) felt stretched and shortened as the anesthesia that had helped reduce the awareness of discomfort began to wear off. I knew I had just experienced the most painful surgery I could have ever imagined. As much as I knew about DIEP flap surgery, once again, I did not have a clue! There is nothing like experience to teach the real lessons.

Influenced by the pain I was experiencing, I growled back at the nurse who was making impossible demands. "I am not a wimp. I have already been through more as I have battled cancer than you can **begin** to imagine." (I knew it was true. Dr. Golshan had said so.) "I cannot move the arm because it will not move. It is too heavy for me to move without help. I cannot... You can leave; when my husband arrives, he will take care of me today." *(There!)*

To this day Tracy laughs about the first few days after my surgery. I tried so hard and was determined to understand all that was happening around me as I attempted to take charge of my own care and to figure things out. We also discovered that while exhausted, uncomfortable, and on pain meds...I became bold and I was not to be challenged unduly!

After snapping back at the demanding nurse, I found that each time she attended to me she had a smile on her face and she was kind and pleasant as we attempted to work together.

The next day I was sent a lovely card of apology for my inconvenience and a beautiful flowering plant...from the president of Brigham and Women's Hospital.

On Friday, January 9, 2009, at 1:20 p.m., Grady wrote as he stood guard outside my room:

Well Hello Everyone,

It is around 2:00 p.m. on Friday and I just left Kathy, who is sleeping very peacefully at long last; she had a very busy morning with lots of interruptions.

She wanted to make sure that I shared something that happened early this morning as Dr. Caterson's resident intern was checking in on her: The doctor was doing a "Doppler reading" on the surgery area and was logging in the readings; at the time he commented on the fantastic blood flow to the area, which is tantamount to how they evaluate the whole thing (I guess).

Kathy said to the young doctor, "Do you know how much prayer is supporting me and all the staff attending to me?"

He of course said "no" but that he thought that Kathy's results were significant enough to actually make note of the fact that Kathy was a person of faith and that very active prayer support was truly a part of her care.

Kathy was very excited about this, as you can imagine.

She has had a tiring day but should continue to strengthen, and I feel tomorrow she should show much improvement in her energy. It is not hard to figure out that it's hard to rest in the hospital (too many interruptions).

Our very best to all of you,

Grady

As soon as I began to feel stronger and ever so slightly better, I did the wrong thing; too much!

It was still only a few days beyond my surgery. My plastic surgery team of interns were amazed by how well I was progressing, and I quickly pointed out to them that there were countless numbers of people who were praying for me and that was the reason I was doing so well.

I was still restricted from using the shower, but I desperately wanted a shampoo and sponge bath. Reluctantly, my nurse granted permission. I did what I thought I could do, much to my regret almost immediately. The task was simply more than I could handle after such an extensive surgery. My blood pressure plummeted. It bottomed out at 78 over 40-something and stayed there the entire day, with my oxygen levels bordering 79 percent and "unacceptable."

Anne (not her real name) was my nurse and had only been out of nursing school for a few years. She was soft-spoken, gentle, caring, and so sweet. I didn't understand at that moment what the Lord was doing, but I soon began to see that the Lord was drawing Anne toward Him. The signs were undeniable.

As her night shift began, she realized the danger I was in and began hovering over me as she monitored my vitals. After DIEP flap surgery, it is vital for transplanted tissue to receive adequate oxygenation or there is a chance that the tissue will die.

The plastic surgery team was in and out of my room multiple times as their worries increased and evening approached. While sleeping, my blood pressure would likely drop further. The concerns were significant. I did the only thing I knew I could do...pray! And I needed to ask others to pray with me.

Anne was in my room; I phoned a friend who had been receiving my email updates. Anne overheard my conversation with Cat as I ask her to immediately send out a prayer request. I specifically detailed my needs to Cat. In part, this is the email she sent Sunday evening, January 11, 2009, the night before I was supposed to be released.

Hello prayer warriors!

I'm following up for Kathy, who has hit a "bump in the road" after her surgery. She is asking for prayers because her oxygen levels dropped quite a bit this morning—the belief is that she tried to do a little too much for herself. Apparently oxygenation in the tissue is crucial for successful reconstruction, and her levels dropped from 93% to under 80% today. While the levels are currently hovering around 81–83%, she has asked that we all: Pray specifically that her tissue oxygenation levels recover back up to the 90+ levels, and that the reconstruction healing would resume those initial positive levels.

Kathy was hoping to go home tomorrow, and if her oxygen levels rise again, that may still happen. If those levels remain low, they may elect to keep her longer.

Kathy is experiencing some wonderful opportunities to witness for Christ in her postoperative recovery phase. Let's also pray that God continues to use her witness as a testimonial to His goodness and how He answers our prayers. Our God is SO good!

Thanks for taking the time to read this email from someone who is a stranger to many of you. Thank you, also, for all your prayers for our friend. May God keep you and bless you!

In His name,

Cat

Anne had heard the request for prayer, and then thirty minutes later *saw* my numbers beginning to improve. By 10:20 p.m. my levels were above the "acceptable" range at 94 percent and holding. Anne was constantly monitoring my oxygen levels; there was absolutely no way for her to miss what was happening as prayer was answered!

It was then and there that I felt certain I was to give Anne a book that I had brought to the hospital with me. The unfortunate thing, however, was that the book was in my overnight bag in the closet and I was not well enough to retrieve it.

When morning came it was a new day and a new issue. A wide red line was making its way from the incision site on my abdomen to the top of my leg. All hope of being released from the hospital disappeared when the "Plastics" team made their rounds and assessed my condition. The orders came that I would not be allowed to leave until this new infection was under control.

Early that morning I called Cat with another prayer request to be sent and by 9:00, the word was out.

Good morning, all—

I heard from Kathy a short time ago, and want to update you. Kathy will be staying in the hospital at least another day—but the good news is her oxygen levels went up last night. By 10 p.m., her levels had gone up to 89%, and by 11 p.m., they were at 94%---which is a tremendous improvement. She does have some redness and irritation on her stomach, where they took the new skin for her reconstruction, and the hospital staff believes there's an infection at that site. Her prayer need is that the infection will clear up so that she can return home.

Even better, the improvement in her oxygen levels has given her tremendous effectiveness in her witnessing, especially to one young nurse named Anne who has been caring for her all night. Please keep Anne in your prayers. Let's all pray that as she witnesses these miracles in prayer, that she will desire the incredible power of God in her own life.

Kathy has asked me to convey her thanks to all of you for seeking the Lord on her behalf—you are, indeed, mighty prayer warriors! I am blessed to see the results of our prayers, and to see this testimony to our Lord! WOW!

God bless you all,

Cat

With prayer and antibiotics, I began to respond and the redness receded. Later that evening when Dr. Caterson came to my room on her rounds, I was coherent enough that I wanted to understand the things about my surgery that I did not know.

"Wow, Dr. Caterson, Shirley forgot to tell me just how difficult the first few days after surgery can be."

Dr. Caterson laughed. "Shirley responded differently than you. She doesn't even remember the hospital."

"One of the first things I remember after I was brought to my room is excitement. The interns on the Plastics team were practically jubilant as they were recording their examination findings. Explain why. What did they see that they hadn't seen before that had them reacting the way that they did?"

Dr. Caterson began to explain the uniqueness in what she found at the donor site for the transplanted mound that was now in the first stages of becoming a reconstructed breast.

"Blood supply is critical in this surgery, as I told you earlier. The primary blood vessel that nourishes the tissue for the reconstruction normally extends about halfway across the belly. In your case, that blood vessel was larger and longer than we ordinarily see. Yours extended two-thirds of the way across your abdomen. Such an extraordinary blood supply is uncommon. This not only gave us excellent blood flow, but gave us more usable tissue for the newly created breast mound. You have set the bar a little higher and set a new standard for one of the better results that we have experienced. I was extremely pleased by what I found, and of course, the Plastics team could barely believe their ears as they listened with the Doppler to the blood circulating in the transplanted tissue."

I was interested and curious about plastic surgery for women like Tracy who have had lumpectomies. Dr. Caterson's answer to my question made a lasting impression.

Dr. Caterson said she would prefer to have a clean slate to work with. There are several different choices for reconstruction after a mastectomy. The results cosmetically are infinitely better when starting from scratch, with all options open for reconstruction choices. "When a woman comes to me looking for cosmetic improvement after a lumpectomy, it can be more challenging."

As I thought later about Dr. Caterson's answer, it made so much sense. No woman wants to go through a mastectomy. But on the other hand, I have spoken with women who after having a lumpectomy went back into surgery two or more times as clean margins were elusively chased, leaving a noticeably distorted breast from the multiple surgeries. This is an important subject often overlooked when facing surgery.

When a woman is told "cancer"…"mastectomy"…a horrible image comes to mind. I can say honestly, however, there really is a silver lining to that ominous cloud. When a surgical choice is given and there are options, that decision should not be made hastily. It's important to know as much as possible when deciding: lumpectomy versus mastectomy and reconstruction.

In another conversation with Dr. Caterson many months after reconstruction, I watched her eyes light up as she spoke about being a plastic surgeon specializing in breast reconstruction. She recounted the time when she first saw what it meant for a woman facing breast cancer and scheduled for a mastectomy to waken and have a reconstructed breast mound in place. For me (personally) that was not the best choice, but for so many other women, it is. Every woman facing breast cancer has a unique story that will unfold before her as she walks the walk. Again, guidance from the right doctors at the right facilities makes all the difference for the options presented and the overall outcome.

When Dr. Caterson saw what an incredible difference reconstruction made, not just cosmetically, but emotionally in the lives of women facing breast cancer, she knew this was what she wanted to do with her life. And yes, she really was on her way to becoming an astronaut!

Twenty-four hours after Cat had sent the prayer concern about the infection, the Plastics team was well impressed by my improvement. That seemed especially true for Jason, one of my favorite interns on the Plastics team. His intenseness and interest in doctoring reminded me of a brand new, young and compassionate Dr. Golshan.

Without further medical surprises, I would be allowed to leave the hospital on Wednesday afternoon....A hospital stay of one week.

Because of the infection and the day I lost while my blood pressure was so low, I had make-up work to do for physical therapy. I had yet to walk independently around the floor of the ward. That sounds easy enough, but the challenge of standing upright in spite of a belly wound that ran hipbone to hipbone caused discomfort with every step.

Tuesday morning would be the day to conquer the hall, and after completing my walk, I returned to my room to sit (on my own) in a chair. As I sat, I was very proud of the checklist of successes for the morning. Quite unexpectedly, I heard a knock and the sound of footsteps entering my room.

"Hey! Dr. Golshan! Hi!"

Dr. Golshan smiled as he entered the room. "I told you I'd be keeping an eye on you. How are you? I heard about the little surprises you gave Stephanie with your ups and downs. And another infection (at the donor site)?"

"Yup! It's been another medical adventure, but I'm much better now. I know it's because of all of the prayers." I wasn't afraid to make reference to my faith. After all, Dr. Golshan had been the recipient of much of that prayer since I had become one of his patients. He even had a new title; and a year earlier he had a strange and sudden change of travel plans when I was desperately ill with an infection. At the least, he knew I believed what I believe.

"Can I have a look at what Stephanie has done?"

I had heard that Dr. Golshan questioned if I had adequate abdominal tissue. I think he was surprised by Dr. Caterson's findings of the extensive blood source that had provided extra tissue for the reconstruction. He complimented Dr. Caterson's work and before leaving my room asked, "When is your next appointment with me?"

"In March. Dr. Lin will order my MRI and mammogram, and I will follow-up with you for the findings."

Because the cancerous tumor did not present in a mammogram and because of dense breast tissue, Dr. Golshan felt a breast MRI on my healthy breast should be part of my normal annual screening. Dr. Lin ordered the same care for Tracy.

"I'll see you in March. I'm glad this has turned out so well; you are another step closer to all of this being behind you. You'll do great."

Oh, do I wish his words had been true....

Chapter 34

"Lord? Say It Ain't So!"

We develop memories by our emotional attachment to the moment. One year ago today, I had a fruit salad for lunch as I waited for Grady to arrive at the hospital and at long last take me home after my surgery and subsequent complications. It was sunny, but Boston was bone-chilling cold on Wednesday afternoon, January 14, 2009. Ah, I remember it well!

I didn't see Anne before leaving the hospital. I felt badly that I missed the chance to thank her again for her care and to give her the book that was still in my overnight bag. I was so certain that it *was* the Lord prompting me to give her that book. I felt troubled that I was going back home with the book still in my bag.

As I prepared to leave, I was given a stack of prescription slips, vials to measure the fluid that was draining from the three tubes attached to my body, and most importantly, a pain pill for the ride home.

Grady remembered to bring a down pillow from our bed to protect the front of my body from the seatbelt that would rest against fresh incisions. We were barely outside the city limits when the excitement of leaving the hospital and the effects of the pain medicine induced a sweet feeling of peace, and I fell asleep as the car hummed north on Interstate 93, in the direction of home.

It doesn't matter how messy you left things; home always looks wonderful after a weary week away....And I was home after being weary, weak, and away!

All three of our blue point Siamese kitties and Max, my tabby Persian, came running at the sound of my voice. As soon as Grady helped me to settle into the recliner that once more would become my bed for the next five weeks, there were at least two purring bodies snuggling in the blankets with me.

As promised, my sister-in-law Caron stopped by with a fresh pot of soup. It was so good to be home!

In the days that followed, Grady built a fire in the fireplace and worked from home. It took me some time (and healing) to master getting out of the recliner without help. Belly wounds do not make for an easy recovery. It's a slow and painful process. Muscles in my abdomen were left intact, but still I needed to move carefully. Abdominal tissue had been stitched internally and needed to heal. Getting out of the recliner became a learned technique.

The old routine of having the visiting nurse stop by became the new routine. At least this time, it was only for a few days. Because I had been glued together with surgical glue and not stitched (at least not visibly), there were no bandages except for protective gauze sponges around the three drainage tubes coming out from both hips and from under my arm. It wasn't long before I mastered caring for myself (with Grady's help). I was beginning to feel like an expert on recovery and what warnings are potentially dangerous. I thought once I was home I would begin to improve quickly. But I lagged behind in my recovery; my expectations were much higher for bouncing back than what I was experiencing.

Twelve days after surgery, on Monday, January 19, I made my way to my computer for the first time in weeks to send an update to everyone.

Subject: On My Knees...

Greetings!

...I'm still not exactly "on my feet," so let's say I'm still "on my knees."

As well prepared as I thought I was facing this surgery, nothing could have been farther from the truth. This has been very hard physically....I still think it will be a week or two before I am even thinking about tackling life normally.

I knew going into this that the Lord would give me plenty of opportunities to share my faith....He did. Even as I was out of my mind fresh from surgery, I was praising Jesus! ...I don't remember a thing I said...but it must have made an impression on "some nurse (???)" because she came looking for me when I was moved to a room, to tell me how much she was taken by my testimony of the power of prayer. I looked at her with confusion, knowing she looked familiar, but for the life of me I could not remember where I knew her from.

...I'll share more in a few days....Just wanted you all to know, I'm "crawling along" if not completely on my feet.

My friend, Judy, is coming to stay with us for a few days to help us with chores and meals.

On Thursday, we will be going to Boston to have all of the drainage tubes removed that I have hanging out of my flesh...there are three. ...Not fun...very tough surgery....

Blessings and Love,

Kathy

Judy, my friend from Maine, was with Grady when he came home at the end of his work day on Monday. She had been in California visiting family and had flown into our local airport to spend the week. She was more than happy to take time for a visit and stay while I needed the help to get back on my feet. It was nice to have an old friend pitch in, not only for the help, but for the company. Having her with us the week following my release from the hospital made a substantial contribution to my recovery, and I began to inch toward improvement.

While the three drainage tubes were in place, showering was a ridiculous challenge. The three tubes with their "bubble ends" had to be gathered and pinned together and attached to a cord that hung around my neck as I attempted to shower and work around the aggravating dangling trio.

Eight days after my release from the hospital, two drains were removed. The following Monday, the last tube was removed, and I was good to go and going great! At least for a *few* days....

Only five days after the last tube was removed, I began to decline physically. I wasn't running a temperature; but I was not feeling well. As much as I dreaded making the call, I knew what I needed to do (only too well). I called Brigham and Women's Hospital and asked for a doctor from the plastic surgery team to call.

If there is a hospital that excels for immediate response and returning calls, this is that hospital! Within minutes my phone was ringing and it was Jason, the young intern I liked so much. He was on duty for the evening, and I was so glad he knew me as a patient.

I explained my symptoms, and his instructions were precisely what I did not want to hear. "Come to the hospital."

"Aw, Dr. Jason, can't I wait until morning? I don't want to come in now."

"I think we should have a look tonight."

"Can we make a deal? Will you call Stephanie and ask her for an opinion first? Tell her I'll come first thing in the morning; it's late, Jason. I just don't want to sit around waiting at the hospital. Saturday nights in the Emergency Department are so busy."

Jason agreed to consult Dr. Caterson and called back with her orders. She wanted the surgery site examined that night; the concerns were reasonable and legitimate even if I did not like what I was being told.

I knew that the success rate for DIEP flap surgery was excellent. I also knew from articles I had read that in 2 to 3 percent of the cases, the surgery failed, often from lack of blood flow. Jason brought that reality to mind. "You don't want to take a chance of there being a problem with the new breast mound. Isn't it better that we all have some peace of mind that the transplanted tissue is still completely healthy?"

He promised that he would inform the intake nurses in triage that he was waiting for me. Good to his word, when we arrived at the hospital, almost immediately I was taken to a cubicle in the Emergency Department that was bustling with Saturday night activity.

Jason was the first of the three interns on the Plastics team who flowed in and out of the cubicle. Next came Lisa. And then Ron. Once they gathered the information from their findings, I became so involved listening to the three young doctors brainstorm, debate, and problem solve, it was like living a real-life episode of *Life in the ER!*

Separately, each doctor came in to ask about my symptoms; my response to each was the same: "Have you ever seen *The Incredible Hulk?*"

Puzzled by my question, they all answered the same hesitant way. "Y-y-yes."

"Well, I feel like him. From my collarbone to the newly transplanted breast mound, I feel like I'm going to burst out of my skin!"

"Interesting…any other symptoms?"

"I'm still totally worn out. I know recovery takes time, but shouldn't I feel a little better?"

Jason looked through the mounting information from tests and what the team had collected. He said, "You are only three and a half weeks out from your surgery date. It's a long recovery. Your energy and activity level should be pretty limited, still."

After the three young doctors each took their turns questioning, prodding, and debating, it was suggested that there was still significant swelling associated with the surgery. An ultrasound revealed there was a large pool of standing blood that had developed either during or shortly after surgery. The young doctors reasoned it was a combination of two things going on simultaneously, causing the pulling sensation. They concluded that as soon as the swelling began to subside and my body absorbed the large pool of blood (seen with the ultrasound), I would be fine. It sounded reasonable and logical. At 2:20 a.m. (now Sunday morning), February 1, I was released to return home.

On Thursday, February 5, I had a routine follow-up appointment with Dr. Caterson. It "coincidentally" worked out to be just five days after my trip to the Emergency Department. I had made the appointment weeks earlier, and it could not have been timed any better. Dr. Caterson examined the new surgery site carefully to make sure nothing was overlooked in light of my trip to the Emergency Department. All appeared to be healing just fine.

During the next few days, nothing changed; where I did have feeling, my skin was taut and uncomfortable. Despite how I felt, I was tired of being dominated by recovery, and I made the decision to press on and increase my activity level. Feeling isolated and cut off from friends, I ignored my physical condition and ventured to church on Sunday. It was so good to be out. When asked how I was feeling, my response was more accurate than I knew. "My flesh is tired. I want to move on, but my flesh is holding me back."

Later that day, I wanted some fresh air and some gentle exercise. For early February, it was cold, but mild enough to enjoy a brief walk. It was my first exercise in five weeks, and it felt good. The air was just cool enough, and my pace slow enough, that when I returned to the house I felt chilled. That should have been the first warning.

We ate an early evening meal. Without warning, as I was cleaning the kitchen, I began to feel weak and shaky. The sick feeling had me reaching for the thermometer and heading for the recliner. My temperature was slightly elevated; just barely 100 degrees. Shortly after taking Tylenol, it began to drop, and I settled into the recliner for an early night's sleep. I blamed my sudden illness on the fact that it was still flu season, or maybe I had been exposed to a virus. Or perhaps I had simply been too active and just needed some extra rest.

Through the night my dreams were disjointed and delusional. My sleep was equally fitful and restless.

Early the next morning, I awoke to Grady in the kitchen and the aroma of fresh coffee brewing. It was 6:20; my hand brushed against my pajama top and I felt something wet. Immediately I thought, *My fever broke. That's good.*

I threw back the covers in which I had been cocooned. Still shaky and zapped of energy, I made my way to the bathroom. From the bathroom, Grady heard my panicked shrieks of terror.

"I have a problem! There's a problem! Oh, Lord Jesus! Something terrible has happened to me! What is happening...what is this?"

Frantically, I ripped my pajama top off and pulled up my tank shirt that was soaked! From my newly transplanted breast, serous drainage fluid was leaking from a wound that was angled on the underside of the flap and hidden from my sight.

"Grady! Call the hospital! One side of my breast flap has ripped away from my body and I am oozing serous fluid. I've split a seam! Oh! Grady, I need help!"

Chapter 35

Living the Lessons

As Grady and I sped in the passing lane toward Brigham and Women's Hospital with the rest of the morning commuters on their way into the city, I was singing my heart out. A praise and worship CD was playing. I was shaking, I was scared, and I was singing praises to God. Despite my crisis His praise was on my lips, and loudly.

I watched the minutes on the clock tick by. I knew Wendy would be at home with her young boys, and 8:00 seemed like an acceptable time to call for help.

"Hello, Wendy? It's Kathy. Grady and I are on our way to Boston. Something terrible has happened. The new breast mound has split away from my side. Wendy, please send out an email prayer request right away; I am terrified I'm going to lose the transplanted tissue. I will have Grady call you as soon as we know anything at all. Please pray that I won't be taken back into surgery to have the new breast mound removed. I don't have any idea what to expect."

Immediately, Wendy sent the request and a large group of people began praying. God was being invited to go before me.

If there was ever a time similar to how miraculous it must have appeared to Moses when God parted the Red Sea, I saw the impossible happen when we walked into triage at Brigham and Women's Hospital. There was not one single solitary soul waiting for care! There was not *one* person sitting in the dozens of chairs in the waiting area at this hospital that saw more that 58,000 emergency cases in 2008. The waiting room was empty!

Patients are taken into the exam area and a safe environment for initial questioning is provided. Grady and I both knew that he would not be allowed into the restricted area for nearly an hour. At that moment, I didn't feel safe without him. I desperately wanted him with me. My fears were running rampant and I was consumed by the unknown. Before the surgery I had joked that the worst that could come out of this was a slim and trim belly, and now I feared that just might be the case. I was horrified…a mastectomy all over again? *Oh, Lord Jesus, no!*

I could not have had a better nurse that morning. Each time I had previously been in the Emergency Department at Brigham and Women's Hospital, all of my nurses had been female. This morning, however, Michael was my nurse. He was calm, cool, and a character. Before I knew it, Michael had me laughing. He was likely in his late forties, and he was the perfect nurse to distract me from my runaway thoughts.

As he collected the necessary medical information, he noted that I had a port. He left for a short time and returned to my cubicle with the all-too-familiar "fish hook" shaped needle and saline to flush my port.

"Michael, does this mean that I really will have to stay?"

"Oh, Honey, you don't want to leave me already? …Do you?"

A while later I asked, "Can my husband come in?"

Michael posed with hands on his hips. "You've got a husband? Now why didn't you tell me about him sooner?"

He made a joke out of everything, and I was distracted by his corny humor.

"Who is working today from the Plastics team?"

Michael listed the doctors on duty, and when he mentioned Jason's name I said, "Oh! I love Jason!" Again, Michael pretended to be jealous. He dramatized his reluctance to have Dr. Jason come to my cubicle and bid for the attention that he and I had exchanged one on one, as he left in a huff to summon him.

Hours had passed since I had walked into the Emergency Department, and Jason had results from some tests that had been conducted. There wasn't any question; I had another infection. The mystery was "What kind?" What was its source?

As Jason began his examination, there is no way I could despise his youth. He knew what he was doing, and I felt it through the confident way in which he worked. Jason expanded the size of the tear that separated the newly transplanted tissue from my chest wall. He cleansed the wound and proceeded to... wound pack! I was positioned slightly onto my side and couldn't see much that was happening, but Grady was watching every move and with his nose stuck in the middle of Jason's work.

I could hear Grady's voice from behind me. "That's new. This morning before we left the house, I helped Kathy bandage the tear. Her back was not red, Jason. This infection is really moving."

The gaping hole was large. As I rested on my side, I caught glimpses of what was happening as Jason worked. From my perspective, the length and width of gauze filling the hole looked endless. I saw my similarity to a rag doll who had lost her "stuffin's" and now I was being repaired.

When Jason finished he announced, "We'll see how that looks later tonight. We are going to keep you in a holding pattern and ready for surgery. We'll begin an IV antibiotic upstairs as soon as we can get you into a room."

Wisely, I had not eaten before leaving the house that morning. By 2:30, I was still in the Emergency Department and my stomach was growling.

I had been "ultrasounded" and x-rayed. Fluid samples and blood had been drawn, and I was being treated like a possible surgery candidate. There was no chance that food of any sort would pass my lips.

Earlier that morning, I did two things as I was leaving the house and on my way out the door. I grabbed the soaked clothing I had been wearing, to show the extent of the serous drainage. And I remembered the book that I should have given to the young nurse who cared for me when I was in the hospital for my reconstructive surgery.

At long last, I was released from the Emergency Department and admitted to the seventh floor—the very same Tower floor I had been on for each of my previous stays and exclusively for women recovering from cancer-related surgeries. Amazingly, I was taken to the same section I was released from four and a half weeks earlier!

I began to judge how I was responding to treatment by what I was and was not allowed to eat...nothing! *(I guessed that fasting and prayer was an important part of my recovery.)* Eventually, I stopped asking for food with the expectation I would be given any. I asked for food only to second guess what was happening and to find out if I was still being considered for surgery.

Dr. Caterson came to my room late that night—after 9:00. She looked worried. For the second time in less than a year, I was fighting a serious infection. With my past and unpredictable experience on different antibiotics, it was trial and error, with hope that I would respond.

She was leaving in the morning to attend a conference about DIEP flap surgery, and my care would be in the hands of the Plastics team (Jason, Lisa, and Ron) and under the supervision of the surgeon who had assisted during my reconstruction. Dr. Golshan was notified *(Kathy's back!)*, and of course, I was still his patient.

Before leaving, Dr. Caterson assured me I would be well cared for and she would be calling in and monitoring my progress. Of course I wanted her here instead of there at a time like this; but I had every confidence in the doctors caring for me. Knowing Dr. Golshan's concern for his patients, I knew there was little reason for worry.

Teaching hospitals are so different from non-teaching hospitals. There is a level of enthusiasm about care that is, well, enthusiastic! I could not help but laugh out loud at the parade of my former nurses who wanted to see my reconstruction one month post-op. Several said, "Oh...I'm so sorry you're back in the hospital, but honestly, I am so happy to see you. We see patients immediately after this surgery, but we NEVER see how the surgery heals and how it looks at this stage of recovery. Do you mind if I have a look?"

I was glad that my malady was of some value for teaching, and the reception I was given by the doctors and nurses was both warm and respectful...even if I did feel slightly like a Barnum and Bailey's Circus sideshow.

The reaction was always the same as Dr. Caterson's handiwork was inspected; an elongated, expressive "W-o-w."

Although I was quite ill, I walked the halls of the ward. My attention was drawn to the "white boards" outside each room where each patient's name was written in black marker. Under her name, her doctor's name was written. I began wondering about these ladies on the ward. We were all different—but we all had one thing in common. All of us were admitted to "Tower 7" because of cancer. Whether it was for reconstruction (or problems related to infection), a mastectomy, or ovarian cancer, our point in common was cancer. At each room I read the names written and I prayed for them; quietly I hummed or sang to the Lord as I passed by, for He inhabits praise...

I had no idea if I would see Anne during my stay, but I was hoping that I would.

This is a portion of an email sharing what happened.

Greetings Everyone...

God **ALWAYS** gives us a chance to get things right...and a month after reconstructive surgery, I was back in the hospital with another infection, and guess what nurse was assigned to me all four nights? Anne! Between the hours of midnight and 1 a.m., I'm really not at my sharpest or most coherent; but each night Anne attended her other patients first, and then came and spent a little extra time with me and to hear the stories of how faithful God has been to our family.

Here's what happened: I was admitted into the hospital on Monday, February 9, with the possibility that I might have to go back to surgery. I had another infection that spread pretty fast and for my first twenty-four hours, I did not respond to the high-powered IV antibiotics.

Tuesday morning, there was a slight improvement; Tuesday night the Plastics team was contemplating surgery for me again.

At 4:00 in the morning on Wednesday, Anne came to check the boundaries of the infection that had been outlined with a marker. The line extended across my chest and around my back to my shoulder blade. No improvement...still very red. And she left to update my records.

A nurse's aide entered my room to take my blood pressure and temperature as Anne departed. In all my many nights on Tower 7, this woman had only attended to me once before. She asked how I was, and I shared my concerns about the possibility of being sent back to surgery when the Plastics team came in for the morning rounds. She began to talk about faith, and instantly we knew we were both sisters in Christ!

She shared with me about being raised by her grandmother on a little island off the coast of Honduras. And told me that years after she was grown and raising a young family of her own, her grandmother was diagnosed with breast cancer. There was no money or medical means for surgery; the only *possible* answer for her grandmother was a miracle healing from the Lord.

Month after month, each Thursday night the two women fasted and prayed ALL NIGHT LONG.

Two years into their obedience to pray and trust God for healing, God was faithful! She shared in great detail exactly what happened as God rid this woman's breast of cancer.

Her grandmother lived twenty-eight years after being healed by the Lord!

As this wonderful lady turned to leave my room she stopped, closed my door, and ordered, "**Sing with me!**" She began to sing with AUTHORITY, the most powerful words of healing that I have ever heard put to a tune. I raised my hands and just invited the words of her song to be my own.

Two hours later, Anne came to my room with the Plastics team. **In the two hours…from the time she had last examined the skin color of the infected area, I had gone from red to a lighter shade of pink and the infection had shrunk!!!!!**

I was released from the hospital on February 13…with a huge bag of packing materials to pack my open wound (just like last year when I had the infection). The interesting thing this time is this: it's March 10, **and the wound is completely closed and healed**! Four weeks!!! Wow!

When I was first packed, I was sure Dr. Jason was packing at least six pairs of socks in the wound, it was so big!

I saw Dr. Caterson last week and she could not believe how quickly I have healed. …There is only one answer…The Lord.

Blessings and Love,

Kathy

As soon I was physically able, I retrieved the novel from my overnight bag and placed it on the table beside my bed. One morning when Anne came to my room before her shift ended, I said to her, "While I was recovering from my reconstruction, I had a sense that I should have given you that book there on my table. God always allows us second chances to get things right, and sometimes that happens in the strangest ways. I believe the Lord allowed me to be readmitted into the hospital so that I would see you again.

"If you would like the book that is on my table, it's yours. It is a Christian novel. The bottom line of the story is 'God loves us unconditionally. He meets **each** of us exactly where we are.' I have a sense in my heart that the Lord wants you to understand that truth about Him, Anne. God loves you and He wants you to know Him as a Father who loves you, His child, deeply."

For a moment Anne stood silent. "How will I get the book back to you?"

"It's a gift; just like God's grace. You simply have to reach out to accept and receive the gift. It's yours."

Anne reached to pick up the book. She stood quietly looking at its illustrated cover. Softly she thanked me and leaned toward me to offer a gentle hug before she left.

In the months that followed and during the summer and the fall of 2009, there were three more surgeries on my calendar.

In order to complete that which was started in my reconstruction process, in May 2009, the port that had been installed on July 2, 2007, was removed. When reconstruction is done on one side, the reconstruction needs to match the natural breast that is healthy and remains. Ultimately, surgery for both breasts is required. I had a pie in the sky idea that everything could be matched, adjusted, and shaped in one surgery. Wrong! Multiple surgeries are involved, none as difficult as what I had already been through. The entire DIEP flap reconstruction process took about a year. A great deal of time is required between the surgical procedures. Tissue that has been cut and shaped needs time to heal and time for all swelling to subside before the next surgical step can be taken.

Removing the radiated skin that inhibited my range of motion provided the results I had hoped for. I regained significant functionality with my left arm upon completing a few additional months of physical therapy that centered on breaking up scar tissue associated with the breast surgeries.

To this day I am thankful for the misery my left arm caused. If not for the slow improvements of my stubborn left arm, I may have chosen conventional chemotherapy, which very well might have produced a different ending. Instead, for the sake of buying time before the mastectomy, I chose the research protocol. God used the experience not only to further medical knowledge about HER2/neu breast cancer and its treatment, but also as a witness of my faith to my doctors and others, and to save my life. Praise God!

My final reconstructive procedure was completed on December 30, 2009. Very candidly I will say that the results were worth the time I invested in searching for and in finding Dr. Stephanie Caterson...my "out of this world" plastic surgeon!

Chapter 36

So...What Is Faith?

Prior to my reconstructive surgery in January 2009, Grady and I made reservations at our favorite little Bajan vacation resort. We had booked a week early in November 2008, before the winter breezes intensified, producing stronger currents along the shoreline.

A month before our travel date, I received a phone call. There had been a fire and the resort was closed and would remain closed until December 1, 2008. We would be relocated to one of the sister resorts on the island for our November vacation.

This was not an acceptable alternative, since I booked where I booked because that's where the snorkeling is. I bargained to change our arrival date to December 6. I felt apprehensive about the later dates, but staying at one of the sister resorts defeated our main purpose for going. I reasoned that I was uneasy because the weather would be less predictable. Snorkeling would only be "fair" at best.

When we arrived, our favorite "4 star rustic" resort was a construction site mess. Buildings were still being renovated; saws were buzzing, hammers pounding, workmen shouting orders. It was far from peaceful, but still it was nice to be on vacation, albeit amidst construction chaos. The TV satellite was still down. Ordinarily, CNN News was the only connection to the outside world. We were on a tiny island and very much cut off from world news and events.

The Saturday morning that our vacation was over and we were leaving, we learned there had been a devastating ice storm in New England. Homes throughout our area were without power. Trees laden with ice snapped like toothpicks, taking down power lines all over the Northeast and making roadways impassable.

Our flight back to the States cleared international customs in Charlotte, North Carolina, and we had a lengthy layover. Despite the long wait, we meandered to our boarding area. There was only one other passenger waiting for the Boston-bound flight when we arrived. She was talking on her cell phone, and when I overheard her say "Kittery," my interest was engaged.

Once she had ended her call, I politely excused myself and apologized for asking but, "Did I overhear you asking what it is like in Maine?" Again I apologized if I was being rude. "We have been out of the country and only heard this morning that there was a terrible ice storm and hundreds of thousands have been without power in New England for days. Do you know about the conditions in Boston and points north?"

The lady turned to me and began to tell me what she had just learned from those at home in Kittery, Maine. We both wondered what we might find upon landing in Boston; she hoped she would not have difficulty retrieving her car from the hospital parking lot.

"Oh…. Do you work at one of the Boston hospitals?"

"Yes," she said. She had been at a conference in Texas and had left straight from the hospital a day or so before the storm paralyzed most of northern New England.

"Which hospital?" I inquired.

"Dana-Farber."

Imagine my joy! (Suddenly the storm lost its importance.) We had a point in common! (Meeting this lady never would have happened if there had not been a fire at our favorite little resort, causing us to change our travel dates.)

I told her about the shock of Tracy's diagnosis and then my own twenty-three months later. It was an amazing experience to be in a clinical research trial. My doctors were ecstatic when the pathology report came in—I had a 100 percent response to the chemo. It was just the coolest thing imaginable as countless numbers of people prayed and we saw those prayers answered, for Tracy's healing in 2005, and then for mine. "As a family we absolutely love and appreciate Dr. Nancy Lin; she was Tracy's doctor first, and then when I…"

Suddenly this lady looked at me like she couldn't believe what she was hearing. "I'm returning home from San Antonio, where Dr. Lin and I attended a conference together! I'm an oncologist on Dana 9 also."

(Well, can you just imagine that!) I couldn't help but chuckle to myself and wondered what it was that God was up to with this "chance" encounter.

We talked for nearly an hour as we waited to board our flight to Boston. As much as I talked, I listened to the things she shared with me. Among the multiple cancer-related subjects we spoke about, this doctor said something very interesting.

"Overall, people of *faith* have better results when fighting cancer than those who are not."

I had heard this from others, and read this…but this was the first time I had actually heard the statement straight from an oncologist working in the trenches at a cancer research hospital with some of the toughest cases and most seriously ill cancer patients. Faith makes a difference.

I looked up the definition of the word *faith* in Webster's New World Dictionary. It lists four definitions for the word. 1: unquestioning belief specific to God, religion, etc. 2: a particular religion. 3: complete trust or confidence. 4: loyalty.

The Bible (in part) defines faith this way: "Now faith is the evidence of things hoped for, the conviction of things not seen." (Hebrews 11:1)

It further says: "And without faith it is impossible to please God, for whoever would draw near to God must believe that he exists and that he rewards those who seek him." (Hebrews 11:6)

When I was a child, occasionally my Dad would say to us as a family, "Come on. Let's go for a ride." Ordinarily, I acted like an excited bouncing puppy and I asked, "Where are we going? Where are we going?"

Dad would usually respond with, "Oh, I don't know. Let's just get into the car and we'll see where it goes."

My faith was evident. I didn't know what was ahead, but I was willing to go. I knew Dad loved me and the plans he had for me were good.

Without my willingness to put my faith into action, it was impossible for me to be a part of what my father had planned. I believed in my Dad's desire not for harm but for something good. The first step was to agree to join with my father in order to receive the rewards *in* the adventure. I needed to embrace his idea, even if I did not know what that idea was, and even if it proved to be long or much too complicated for me to understand as a child.

Like any kid, I would ask that classic question, "Dad, are we almost there?" In my impatience, never did I say to him (even when the adventure seemed too long), "I've gone far enough. Let me out!"

There may have been times in my exuberance or impatience to arrive that he might have thought about dropping me off someplace along the way, but somehow as I settled on obeying my dad, we always made it down the longest roads. We stuck it out together. How the journey went depended upon me… my attitude…my willingness to cooperate, to trust Dad…to listen and obey. My behavior and mood were factors and had their effects on others. Sometimes in a positive way, but often not! The journey in the car was a discipline I had to learn, and I usually only wanted to get to where the road ended.

Occasionally in the fall, Dad would simply take us on a long ride. We traveled over unpaved and rough back roads often. It was before the days of seatbelts, and I can remember bracing myself as Dad attempted to avoid and protect us from the worst ruts along the way while taking the more "scenic route." One of those back roads ended at Frost's Orchards, where we would buy apples. Frequently, the apples became fresh home-baked pies made by Mom and my grandmother.

While Mom and Dad visited with the Frosts, the destination was perfect for a game of tag or hide-and-seek in the orchard with the Frost children.

It was so very long ago, but to this day smelling the sweet, fresh aroma of an orchard or seeing the bright red fruit hanging in abundance from the limbs of apple trees reminds me of Frost's Orchards and childhood adventures with Dad.

Sometimes, I knew the road that Dad had chosen and I was excited as I recognized the landmarks while we traveled southeast toward the ocean for a day of sun, swimming, and sandcastles.

After our day at the beach, we would pack up the towels, pails, and shovels and shake the sand from the beach blankets, and we would stop on our way home at a picnic area.

Upon arriving at the park, we would romp and play. The park was ideally located on an ocean inlet. I loved the end of that road; the salty breeze, watching the older kids skimming stones across the water, and tidal pools at low tide; there was a gigantic swing set…and so much to explore! When the sun showed the first signs of sinking low in the summer sky, Mom would set up the picnic table with the remaining soggy sandwiches. The last of the fruit punch in the gigantic Thermos was warm from the sun and diluted with the melted ice cubes. It was AWFUL…but somehow, delicious! …I still remember.

Each journey brought new excitement as I wondered where it might lead. …In innocence and absolute trust I had "faith" in Dad's goodness to me. The reward in accepting my father's plan and *arriving* at the end of the road was always pleasant and good. But as I began to grow a little older, it was always the adventure of the journey with Dad and the *interaction and closeness* of being together that meant the most, giving even greater reward and satisfaction to arriving at his chosen destination for me.

In hindsight, my faith in God as Tracy battled cancer was a stepping stone for what was ahead and my own diagnosis. Through Tracy's illness I found myself having a difficult time as her mom remembering that God loves Tracy even more than I do. I was confronted with new levels of faith put into action for an unknown journey. Speaking as a mother, it was extremely difficult and conflicting for me, as I desired to protect Tracy *and* have the faith to release her into her Heavenly Father's hands.

I watched my own mother wrestle some of the same feelings I had gone through as she helplessly watched me battle the disease. Just as I had done, my mom questioned why God, a loving Father, would allow this to happen to "my" child…*His child.* It seemed unimaginable.

"Consider it wholly joyful, my brethren, when you are enveloped in or encounter trials of any sort or fall into various temptations. Be assured and understand that the trial and proving of your faith brings out endurance, steadfastness and patience." (Amplified Bible, James 1: 2–3)

As I surrendered *into* my faith as I fought cancer, an interesting thing happened. I felt a supernatural separation between the physical aspects of what my body endured and the spiritual person of who I am in my relationship with my Heavenly Father. The spiritual *rewards of seeking the Lord* as I walked by faith became my focus. Cancer and physical pain became secondary to the importance of what God was teaching me. As I drew close to the Lord in prayer, I understood better than at any other time in my life what it means that "He rewards those who seek Him." His rewards were everywhere: in His presence, the people my life touched, those who were praying for me, my doctors, the miracles....I was *so* blessed!

A very funny thing happened as *His joy* became *my strength*. Each time my doctors spoke about how much I had been through, intellectually I knew it was true. But in my spirit I heard, *That's funny; it hasn't been that bad....Has it?* While going through much of the battle, I was captured by a Holy Spirit amnesia, similar to what a mother experiences in childbirth! ...He is "The Helper, The Comforter...." (John 14:26)

Many cancer survivors that I have spoken with have said the very same thing. Fighting cancer was the most spiritually rewarding time in their lives. The exception to that statement has come from those who struggled through in their own strength, who became angry, rejected God, and turned their backs as they refused to "draw near to God, believing (trusting) that He exists," hence foregoing the "reward" *faith* produces.

Would I want to go through cancer again? No, thank you! But I can tell you this: "the good" (on a spiritual level) definitely outweighed "the bad" (physically). Experiencing my Heavenly Father's presence so acutely for so many months as I clung to Him in prayer...I would not have traded for anything!

Yes. It was worth the long, rough road to recovery. My faith grew and my trust in His goodness grew, as I made the conscious choice to focus on the Lord in praise, worship, and prayer. Relying upon my faith, I walked through the experience...a long and difficult experience. The trials and adversity gave me a taste of understanding what it means for faith to "produce endurance, steadfastness and patience."

I praise God with each breath I take, and for the gift of living. I will forever thank Him for leading me beyond my own daughter's journey through cancer and the phone call that completely shook, reshaped, and strengthened my faith and my spiritual core: "Mom...it's cancer."

Afterword

Greetings Everyone!

I wanted to end with a personal note. Although there were several points I wanted to make as I wrote *Mom…It's Cancer,* one of the most important goals I had was to share what it was like dealing with the initial shock of a diagnosis of cancer. I hope I was able to do that as you read Tracy's story and then mine. Having so recently gone through cancer with Tracy, there really was less of a shock value after my own "worrisome" mammogram.

When Dr. Golshan called with the awful news, "The biopsies reveal cancer…" it surely wasn't what I wanted to hear, but it was my *new* reality and I was better prepared for the journey before me because of Tracy's diagnosis and what I had learned from her.

As I began writing, I frequently found myself in social settings and telling not just women but also men about breast cancer…on airplanes, at Christmas parties, church events, in a field picking strawberries, even out on my three-mile walk! With the amount of interest and curiosity about breast cancer, I felt driven! *I've got to finish my book and get it into the hands of those who are facing breast cancer…men **and** women. I want to help others to make the right life-saving decisions as they are facing cancer…or better yet, **before** facing this disease!*

I'd like to ask a favor: if you have learned anything of value as you read *Mom...It's Cancer,* share that information with someone. Share what you have learned by loaning them this book, buying them a copy as a gift, recommending it—but please, please help me to help others! Although the intent of this book is not to provide medical information, I have given to you what I think I learned and understand about breast cancer.

It's sort of a wacky thing to say about a book entitled *Mom...It's Cancer,* but I really hope as you read about this very serious topic, you were entertained and were able to laugh. Hey! I was the one going through it and I sure found reasons to laugh. God is good! ...And pretty humorous sometimes.

Oh, and one more thing I forgot to tell you. When I was nearly finished writing this book, the Lord brought to mind a long-forgotten dream: when I was a teenager, I wanted to write! It was a deep, secret longing that was buried and forgotten until the Lord reminded me. Huh! It only took forty-odd years and cancer for me to have something worthwhile to say, I guess!

As we are getting ready to go to print, I have been in discussions about media links. Presently I can be found on Facebook.

I sincerely hope you enjoyed reading this book. I wish you peace and good health. And as with all of my friends, I will end with:

Blessings and Love,
Kathy

www.momitscancer.com

LaVergne, TN USA
19 January 2011
213122LV00003B/2/P